HUNTING THE DESERT WHALE

D0310420

This edition, issued in 1964, is for
members of The Companion Book
Club, Borough Green, Sevenoaks,
Kent, from which address particu-
lars of membership may be obtained.
The book is issued by arrange-
ment with the original publishers,
Jarrolds Publishers (London) Ltd.

"A blessed companion is a book"—JERROLD

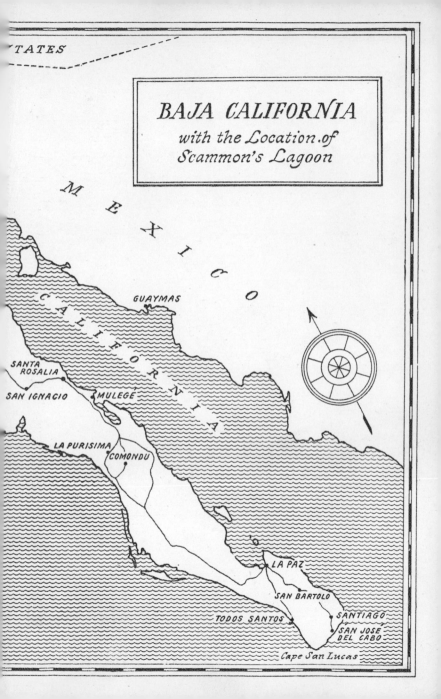

BAJA CALIFORNIA
with the Location of
Scammon's Lagoon

Epworth Mechanics' Institute Library

	Date first available for issue	24 MAY 1968

This Book must be returned to the Librarians within
SEVEN DAYS from the date marked below.

24 MAY 1968			
3 - AUG 1968			
2 DEC 1968			
21 FEB			
30 JAN			
11 AUG			
10 AUG			
20 MAR			
7 JUN 1984			
10 JAN 1985			
11 APR 1985			
06 DEC 1985			

Part I, *Hunting the Desert Whale*, © Erle Stanley Gardner 1960
Part II, *Hovering Over Baja*, © Erle Stanley Gardner 1961

Made and printed in Great Britain
for The Companion Book Club (Odhams Books Ltd.)
by Odhams (Watford) Limited
Watford, Herts
S.464.UB

CONTENTS

Part One: *Hunting the Desert Whale*

Part Two: *Hovering Over Baja*

CONTENTS

ILLUSTRATIONS

MAP

PART ONE

Hunting the Desert Whale

ANTICIPATION AND TEMPTATION

MY FRIEND, Murl Emery, is a devastating influence.

To begin with, Emery won't fall in step with the world. He won't buckle down to business in the orthodox sense, and he insists upon living a life of variety and adventure. When he finds himself confronted with the need for money he packs his bed-roll and a few provisions into his four-wheel drive pick-up, puts in fifty gallons of petrol and a like amount of drinking water, drives out into the desert and finds a mine.

Ordinarily, one would say that was a better way to spend money than to make money. But it doesn't work that way with Murl. He finds the mines. He gets his money out of the ground. Sometimes it takes longer than it does at other times but he invariably gets what he goes after.

Nothing works according to logic or the laws of averages with Murl. The guy has an encyclopaedic knowledge of minerals, a rough-and-ready knowledge of geology, he knows the desert from one end to the other, and he has a supreme contempt for civilization.

For many years now Murl has made his living in this un-orthodox fashion. He probably spends more time in camp than he does at home. He is completely self-reliant and thoroughly original, both in thinking and behaviour.

Murl Emery was raised on the Colorado River. His father spent his life on the Colorado and Murl's son, Pat, has, for nearly all the thirty years of his life, been on the Colorado. In Murl's earlier days the Colorado River was very different from what it is now. Living on it was a career in itself. The Colorado was a big, untamed, roaring, dangerous body of water swirling its way through narrow canyons, expanding to a placid stream for a mile or two, then boiling into new rapids. From the time it left the Grand Canyon it flowed through a bleak desert where a man had to know a lot about nature just to survive. Every year the river took its grim toll of human life. Murl Emery knew the river when it was rough and rugged and he in turn became rough and rugged like the river.

Then civilization entered the picture. The Hoover Dam was constructed and following that other dams "tamed" the river until it became a succession of lakes. Where formerly only the hard-bitten prospector or expert boatman dared make his way, keen-eyed and wary, now there are paved roads and sportsmen by the thousand come flocking to the new recreation area, carrying boats on trailers, driving cars well stocked with fishing equipment. The silence of the desert is shattered by the snarl of outboard motors as boats plane along at twenty-five to thirty-five miles an hour or idle along at a leisurely trolling speed. The development of plastics, of fibreglass, outboard motors, and the construction of dams has changed Murl Emery's environment so that it is difficult to recognize—and Murl doesn't like it. But modern inventions can't change Murl Emery. Environment may change but the man is the same.

What has happened on the Colorado River is only in a small measure what has been happening all over the country. If you question this statement just look at a map today and try to find some reasonably nearby place where there is still adventure; where one must be self-reliant in order to survive. Strangely enough, however, there is such a place within a few hundred miles of the sprawling population congregated in the congested district of Southern California. South of San Diego is Tijuana. South of Tijuana is Ensenada. South of Ensenada is adventure unlimited.

Over on the desert side, Calexico is the border city of the Imperial Valley. Through Calexico runs the high fence of the international boundary. South of that fence is Mexicali. A hundred and twenty miles south of Mexicali is the little fishing port of San Felipe. The road is hard-surfaced all the way. South of San Felipe there are fifty-three miles of dirt road to the little fishing village of Puertecitos. The trip to Puertecitos can be made by a good driver in an ordinary well-constructed automobile—although it is surprising the number of motorists one will find in trouble on that fifty-three-mile stretch. South of Puertecitos civilization comes to an abrupt halt. You don't go below Puertecitos unless you have a four-wheel drive automobile, ample stores of petrol and drinking water, and know what you're doing —that is, you *may* go but you may not come back.

So it was as natural for Murl Emery's attention to gravitate towards Baja California as it was for an iron filing to gravitate towards a magnet. As it happened, I had first felt the appeal of Baja California some thirteen years ago, and in 1947 I had engaged in what was in those days a rather spectacular feat: I had driven all the way from California down the 1,200 miles of "road" to Cabo San Lucas, the end of the peninsula. Then, in 1948, I had repeated the trip.

I had written a book about the 1947 trip, *The Land of Shorter Shadows*—a book which attracted some considerable attention over the years, although it is now out of print. When Murl Emery became interested in Baja California he had read about everything he could find on the subject. He had therefore read my book and given it a great deal of thought.

Murl's thinking is a combination of three equal parts of desert, water and adventure. It was therefore only natural that he should start thinking about the rivers and lagoons in Baja California, and since there aren't any rivers worth mentioning, he naturally started concentrating on the lagoons. And whenever one starts thinking about lagoons in Baja California Scammon's Lagoon stands out head and shoulders above all the rest. Every year the grey whales leave the Bering Sea during the winter and start a long, slow journey round the Aleutian Islands, down through the trackless waste of waters, until they reach the coast of California. Then they move along the California Coast, down Baja California, and about the first part of January begin to show up in numbers in Scammon's Lagoon.

Because of our mutual interest in Baja California it was inevitable that Emery and I should get together. And it was only natural that Emery should start talking Scammon's Lagoon to me.

And when he started talking Scammon's Lagoon it was only natural that I should listen and that my life should be disrupted.

In vain I pointed out to Emery that in the last thirteen years my life had undergone a great change. I had speaking commitments all over the country. I was interested in a television show which was on for an hour every week and frequently created big problems.

13

On my 1948 trip down the peninsula I had been accompanied by Harry Steeger and his wife. Harry Steeger is the owner of *Argosy Magazine,* and around the camp fires we had discussed the problem of innocent men who have wrongfully been convicted of crime. We discussed the better administration of justice; better law enforcement; and from those conversations came the Court of Last Resort. At that time neither Steeger nor I had any idea of the magnitude of the task we were undertaking; of how this idea of the Court of Last Resort would capture the imagination of the reading public; or the amount of time we were going to be called on to give to carrying on the work.

In those days my headquarters at Temecula were isolated. I didn't have a telephone on the place and didn't want one. Now I have telephones all over the ranch. My long-distance bill is astronomical. My work for the Court of Last Resort and my speaking engagements keep me zigzagging about the country by aeroplane and motor-car. The very idea of breaking away from all this in order to adventure into Baja California was fantastic. I explained all this to Emery.

Emery's only answer was to spread out a map of Baja California and, with the stubby nail of his right index finger, gently tap Scammon's Lagoon.

Finally, despairing of pulling me away from my work schedule, Emery and his son, Pat, accompanied by a couple of other adventurers, fitted out a caravan and after some weeks of varied adventure managed to get to the waters of Scammon's Lagoon. They had one boat, which at times they had to drag through sand a foot or two at a time, using two motor-cars in tandem—a four-wheel drive pick-up and a jeep. They spent so much time getting down there that they didn't do more than survey the most interesting spots when they got there. They had only one boat and one rubber raft. While they were there they did, however, learn of the beach between Scammon's Lagoon and Guerrero Negro. This beach is the Sargasso Sea of the Pacific, only it is on dry land. That statement needs a little explaining.

South of Scammon's Lagoon, a range of mountains projects some forty or fifty miles into the ocean, forming a huge crescent-shaped sickle, and somehow manages to turn one branch of the south-bound ocean current in the Pacific into a huge eddy.

Driftage from all over the Pacific Ocean is siphoned into this current, swept round in a huge circle and brought down into this collecting basin. During periods of storm or high wind it is washed ashore. The peculiar thing is that since this shoreline is building up at the rate of half a mile every few hundred years, the wreckage, once caught, is trapped in low, drifting sand hills which can completely cover it within a relatively short time, but, conversely, they can, in turn, be blown away by vagaries of the wind, until almost every week sees some new wreckage covered up, some old wreckage uncovered.

According to Emery, no human being had set foot on this stretch of beach within modern times. On the ocean side it is pounded by a terrific surf. On the land side it stretches back in mile after mile of soft sand: hills of sand blown into odd-shaped dunes and at times swept by winds which drive the blowing particles of sand against the skin in a stinging spray. It is in fact a huge triangular-shaped island of sand. On the north is Guerrero Negro, the "Black Warrior" Lagoon. On the south is Scammon's Lagoon. Landings can be made on the north and south ends of this island but only with a small boat, and the physical problem of transporting supplies across these intervening miles of barren sand is insurmountable.

Scientists from the Scripps Institution of Oceanography, who have been studying the ocean currents, are intrigued by this vast catch basin lying between Scammon's Lagoon and Guerrero Negro. Surveys from the air and the plotting of ocean currents on paper convinced them that here was a beach which held some of the most fascinating wreckage in the world. Moreover, the British Government recently began to take an official interest in the problem because records indicated that a British ship, carrying several million dollars in gold, had been wrecked on a nearby bar and in all probability the wreckage had been washed ashore on this stretch of beach. It was reported that the British Government had started to fit out an expedition to try to salvage this wreckage but had given it up after studying various legal and international complications, plus the problem of how to get men and supplies on the triangular-shaped island.

While my schedule keeps me pretty well chained down, I like to adventure, and I make brief trips into the desert in search of semi-precious gem stones and unusual photographs. I have a couple of very fine boats equipped with powerful outboard motors. I have a whole fleet of four-wheel drive vehicles with which, on occasion, we make brief safaris into the inaccessible desert. But these hurried trips are all short sprints into the wild and back. Years have elapsed since I last went on an adventure.

Murl Emery pointed out that by combining our equipment we could make a real trip to Scammon's Lagoon. Instead of taking weeks to get down to the waters of the lagoon as he had done on that exploratory trip, we could do it in a relatively short time. He had the benefit of all the experience he had acquired on his initial pioneering trip, and in addition to that he had bought a newly invented device which was going to revolutionize beachcombing. This was the "Tote Gote".

It's rather difficult to describe a Tote Gote. To the uninitiated —and I am one—it seems to be nothing but a glorified scooter, powered by a light petrol motor. But there is something about it, an automatic clutch and a few other refinements, which differentiate it from the ordinary scooter and make it possible to take one of these contraptions just about anywhere a man can go on horseback—or at least that was the story as Emery put it to me.[1]

The Tote Gote, Emery said, was made for sportsmen. It was made to go over mountain trails. It was made to go just about anywhere, and Emery had satisfied himself that it would go through deep, soft sand such as one would encounter on the island beach; bearing in mind that during periods of low tide there would be relatively hard-packed stretches of wet sand on which one could even drive a car, if one had a car there. However, when the tide changed one would have to return to base camp through deep sand, and the real beachcombing was farther back, in the soft sand of the drifting dunes.

Looking back on it I don't know at just what stage of the game Emery got my initial interest changed to enthusiasm, or my enthusiasm changed to determination. However, he did it.

[1] Since this was written, several similar devices have come on the market, one of which, the Pak-Jak manufactured in Paradise, California, has such rugged construction and versatility that I have acquired several of these and planned another expedition into Baja California to explore places which had previously been completely inaccessible.

2

WE DECIDE TO HUNT WHALES

DECEMBER of 1959 had found me fighting to complete two book-length manuscripts which had to be in New York before the first of the year. In addition, I was working far ahead on Perry Mason television scripts so that I could have ten days' or two weeks' freedom from the chains of Hollywood. All the Christmas and New Year's activities were crowded into a kaleidoscope of action which left me somewhat dazed on the morning of Sunday, January 2, 1960. Not only did I have numerous guests at the ranch but people were dropping in, in droves, to extend holiday greetings and best wishes for the New Year.

I had told everyone I was going to take the bit in my teeth and break away from routine in 1960. I had said this on New Years 1950–1951–1952 and so on, every year, until the people who heard me simply smiled indulgently and asked me how I intended to get away from my business. I would invariably remark, "To hell with business. I'm going to get out and adventure, camp, and have interesting experiences."

My friends would nod acquiescence, exchange surreptitious winks, and, sure enough, every year I'd start postponing my trip until I had "caught up with the urgent matters". Whereupon more urgent matters would come piling in and I'd repeat the same routine the next year.

Sunday, January 2, 1960, was a surprise to everyone, including me. I sat up nearly all night putting the finishing touches on the manuscripts. I left all my Christmas correspondence, all my Christmas presents, unacknowledged and piled up in the middle of my study. I threw cameras, films and kit-bags in my jeep and I included what was to prove to be one of the most valuable of all the camping possessions I ever acquired—a new Audograph dictating machine powered by transistor and batteries, hardly larger than a camera yet which functioned perfectly through wind storms, sand storms, pelting rains and the flour-fine dust which inevitably follows cars that venture over the dirt roads of Baja California.

I still remember the looks of incredulous surprise on the faces of my guests as I waved a hurried good-bye and, without even stopping to shake hands for fear the inevitable telephone ring would drag me back, took off in my jeep for Calexico.

The next morning the rest of the expedition arrived and we made rendezvous about noon, picked up last minute supplies, made a few minor mechanical repairs and crossed the border shortly before dark.

I was accompanied by two of my secretaries, Jean Bethell, who had been with me on both of my prior trips to Baja California; Peggy Downs, her sister; both of them veteran campers, accustomed to setting up portable typewriters on a fallen log or an up-ended suitcase and batting out notes; and, what was more important on a trip of this sort, acting as my eyes and ears, picking up all available information and cramming it into shorthand books so that the data would be available when needed.

Murl was accompanied by his son, Pat, who has inherited from his father all the love of the Colorado River and adventuring in the out-of-the-way places, but who is somehow more bound to civilization than his father. Both Murl and Pat are rough-and-ready mechanics who can repair just about anything with almost nothing. They have a wonderful father-and-son relationship, understand each other perfectly, and through years of camping in the desert have learned to co-ordinate with the smoothness of perfection.

Our motor transport equipment consisted of two International one-ton pick-ups equipped with four-wheel drive; a jeep station wagon; another covered jeep with a steel cab and extension body. This jeep was also equipped with a power winch. Both pick-ups were towing nineteen-foot Smithcraft, each powered with twin motors and mounted on two-wheel trailers. We also carried an assorted collection of jacks, shovels, tow-ropes, cables, logging chains and similar equipment.

Sam Hicks, my ranch manager, assistant investigator for the Court of Last Resort, assistant photographer and general right hand, who had been with me on the 1948 trip all the way down the peninsula, was in charge of one of the pick-ups and trailers. And we had the company of my "campanero", Joe Gandara, who has accompanied me on many a Mexican adventure, notably the trips into the Barranca del Cobre, the Barranca Urique and through the Tarahumare country. (Some of these adventures were described in my book, *Neighbourhood Frontiers*.)

Joe Gandara knows of my respect for the cultural background of Mexico. Intensely patriotic and loyal to Mexico, he nevertheless realizes the importance of promoting international friendship and he has spent much time with me at my ranch in Temecula, discussing plans for improving international relations between the two countries. He also is eager to promote conditions which will give the American tourist more of an insight into Mexico. Well educated, bilingual, a man who is at home either in the best drawing room or the most primitive camp life, Joe Gandara is a great asset to any outdoor expedition. And he is invaluable in Mexico where he has innumerable official contacts, a thorough knowledge of the people, the customs and the laws, and a natural diplomacy.

Some twenty-odd years ago, when I first discovered Baja California in company with a group of yachtsmen, Anita Haskell Jones was one of the parties making the trip. She is a woman who loves adventure, outdoor life and camping and she has accompanied me on many of my later trips, including the expeditions to the barranca country. Ever since that first yachting trip we have remained warm friends. So Anita was included in this expedition.

This was rather a large party for the type of expedition we had in mind, but at the last minute it was augmented by still another member who was a complete tenderfoot so far as Baja California was concerned.

Some time in December, the editors of *Newsweek* advised me that they wanted to carry a feature article on me, starting early in January, but the magazine wanted a little different approach from that of some of the other biographical articles which had been published. The editors telephoned, stating that they wanted to send a reporter down to interview me early in January. I explained this would be impossible because I was going on an expedition to Scammon's Lagoon in Baja California at that time. The editors immediately became enthusiastic. This was just the new approach they were looking for. They wanted to send this reporter along with us for the first leg of the journey.

I finally consented, upon two conditions: First, that I would talk with the man before we decided. Second, that it would be all right with my companions. So Joe Laitin came down to the ranch and we had some extensive conversations, following which I somewhat diffidently put through a telephone call to Murl Emery, who was at the time working one of his mines in the wild spaces of Nevada. I left a message for him to call at the station where he gets petrol and supplies, and it was a couple of days later that the phone rang and Emery was on the other end of the line.

"What do you want?" he asked, coming to the point at once, in true Emery fashion.

I explained the situation.

"All right, what do you want?"

"I want to know if you have any objections to this guy going along."

"What sort of a fellow is he?"

"Well," I said, somewhat dubiously, "he impresses me as being a nice guy but he looks pretty young."

"That part's all right," Murl said. "We can put another five years on him awful fast."

"Then it's okay with you?" I asked.

"It's okay with me if it is with you," he said, and hung up.

So I relayed word to Joe Laitin that he could come along for the first leg of the trip. I didn't tell him that Murl Emery had said we'd put another five years on him awful fast.

3

DO WHALES TALK?

SINCE a lot of this story is going to concern itself with the Pacific Grey Whale we had better take a look at the mammal we're going after. But I don't want to set myself up as an authority on whales. There are altogether too many authorities on whales and they have too many different and completely contradictory ideas.

The full-grown grey whale runs from thirty-five to perhaps forty-five feet in length. He is big and powerful and once the early whalers started hunting him he became one of the most vicious and agile of adversaries. As will be seen a little later, whalers who had hunted all other kinds of whales and taken the dangers in their stride became so panic-stricken when first introduced to the grey whale in the shallow waters of Scammon's Lagoon that the first whaler into the lagoon had to give up hunting whales, despite the fact that the lagoon was swarming with them, until a brand new technique of killing whales could be invented. Yet today the turtle fishermen, who sometimes venture into the lagoon, will scoff at the idea of the grey whale being dangerous. They say he never attacks a turtle boat.

Now this brings us to the intelligence of the grey whale and to the question of whether or not whales can communicate.

The answer is they are intelligent and they probably can, and do, communicate. Experience has proved this: if you go to Scammon's Lagoon to hunt turtles and confine your activities to turtle hunting, the grey whales you will encounter there will in all probability be neighbourly and give you no trouble. If, on the other hand, you go there for the purpose of hunting whales— whether it be with harpoon or camera—after you have been there a couple of days and "word gets round" among the whales what you are up to, you had better watch out.

Now don't laugh at this idea of word getting about among the whales. I don't know how these animals communicate but they certainly have some way of exchanging basic ideas. It is now pretty well established that the porpoise (which is first cousin to the grey whale) has a fairly complete language. Underwater sounds have been tape-recorded which show that the porpoise is a remarkably intelligent animal, with a means of communication and methods of orientation completely mystifying to human observers and far in advance of anything man has devised, even with all his progress in the field of electronics.

In short, the porpoise, blindfolded and placed in a tank of water, surrounded by movable obstacles, can in some way find a three-inch button no matter where it is placed in the tank and, at a command, will swim to it and press that button.

Donald Douglas, the famous aircraft manufacturer, went down to Scammon's Lagoon two or three years ago with Dr Paul Dudley White. Their idea was to get the heartbeat of a whale and record it on a cardiograph. When they first arrived the whales were placid and docile. Donald Douglas, standing in the bow of the boat, moved up on a whale which was basking on the surface and jabbed him with an oar. The whale gave a convulsive shudder and submerged so abruptly that the occupants of the boat were splashed with water.

"Nothing to it!" Douglas gleefully assured Dr White. "We'll just take little darts with wires fastened to them and put them in the whales by hand."

They didn't get that close to any more whales. On the other hand, the whales got close to them. After they had been in the lagoon long enough for the word to get round that they were hunting whales, the whales decided to turn the tables. A whale came charging up to the boat, smashed the rudder, knocked off the propeller and bent the drive-shaft to a forty-five degree angle —all with one blow of his tail. Then he swam away a little distance, turned round, looked at what he had done, took a deep breath and charged, smashing in the side of the boat.

If it hadn't been for executive ability of a high order and a perfectly co-ordinated effort, those men would have been plunged into shark-infested waters. But as it was they worked with speed and efficiency. They stripped off life preservers, stuffed them into the hole, took a piece of canvas, wrapped it round the outside of the boat, signalled for help and, by frantic bailing, were able

22

to keep afloat until a rescue boat, which had been standing by in case there should be any trouble, was able to come and tow them into shallow water.

Back in 1949 Lewis Wayne Walker, writing in the magazine *Natural History*, told of a trip to lagoons where the turtle fishermen, on being advised of printed reports from the old-time whalers that the grey whale was a vicious killer, ridiculed the idea. These turtle fishermen said they had spent their lives on the water and daily saw many whales, and the whales were not at all dangerous.

A few days later, however, after the expedition had started hunting whales with cameras, the "word got round" among the whales and the situation changed abruptly. These same turtle hunters, who had scoffed at the idea that whales could ever become hostile, came paddling to shore in a panic with a whale in hot pursuit. The whale had charged them, had actually rammed their boat, but because it was a small, light boat, high out of the water, and because it hit the stern, he hadn't smashed it but had only given it a terrific shove with his nose. Fortunately the turtlemen were close enough to shore to make it in time, but the angry whale was making passes at them and was only deterred when they reached shallow water.

However, I didn't know all these things when we started out for Scammon's Lagoon. I learned them afterwards, and the hard way. We now know that while some of the grey whales stay in southern waters, most of them spend the summers up in the Bering Sea. Then they start to migrate in winter and swim some six thousand miles at an estimated speed of four knots an hour until they arrive at Scammon's Lagoon. There the cow whales have their young every second year; there the males gather and the breeding activity takes place.

The whales are there in numbers shortly after the first of the year, and stay until March. A few of them remain until the middle of April, and there apparently are some who remain there the year round. But for the most part the whale activities in Scammon's Lagoon are between the first of the year and the latter part of March.

The whales, when born, are fifteen to seventeen feet in length and they are nursed until they reach a length of approximately twenty-five feet, when they are weaned. And, contrary to general understanding, the whale is a most intelligent mammal, perhaps one of the most intelligent of all the mammals.

My friend, Willard Keith, who is interested in the "Marineland of the Pacific", has told me the story of how they decided to capture a whale and see if it would be possible to train it to do tricks.

It took a lot of ingenuity but they did eventually capture a whale and got it safely installed in Marineland. There, to their surprise, they found that the whale was a thinking animal that speedily learned a whole series of tricks and could put on a performance which would hold an audience completely spellbound. Anyone who has seen the performance at Marineland will recognize that the whale can be trained just as an intelligent dog can be trained and can and will do just about anything human ingenuity can think of in the way of tricks.

Among other things, we wanted to find out if the whales in Scammon's Lagoon did any feeding while they were there, and we wanted, if possible, to find out why they selected Scammon's Lagoon as the goal of their migration. Why not some other lagoon?

Many of the authorities think that all the whale food is in the Bering Sea, that once the whales leave there they go on a virtual fast and live entirely on their blubber until they return north once more. On the other hand, since at least a few of the whales remain in southern waters, it would certainly appear that they do feed, despite the assertion of many authorities to the contrary. But could we *prove* they fed? Could we get a photograph of a whale feeding?

The whale, an enormous creature many tons in weight, lives on some of the smallest bits of sea life. His method of feeding is simplicity itself. He gulps in huge quantities of water, then, closing his mouth, expels the water through sieve-like "teeth", getting rid of all the water but leaving all the small marine animals trapped in the interior of his mouth.

There is no question that the whales put on a lot of blubber in the Arctic Ocean. By the time they reach Scammon's Lagoon, stay there for a few weeks and start the journey back north, they are not as full of fat as when they arrived. But it would hardly seem that evidence such as that would indicate that a whale could swim some 6,000 miles, bear young and nurse the young, or engage in mating activities and then swim some 6,000 miles back —at the rate of four knots an hour—all without feeding. After all, many animals put on a lot of fat just prior to the rutting season and then emerge again considerably emaciated to take up the routine tenor of life.

If, of course, there should turn out to be some particular type of toothsome whale-food in Scammon's Lagoon, the migration might be at least partially explained.

Also, in Scammon's Lagoon there is a peculiar formation of shoals which enables the mother whale to lie in relatively shallow water and give birth to the young. The infant can then raise itself enough to get air.

The whale, of course, is not a fish. Being a mammal it lives under water by first sucking in deep breaths of air, then diving down into the water and remaining until it feels the necessity of coming to the surface for more oxygen. At that time the whale exhales the moist breath from his lungs, and as that moisture strikes the air it congeals and gives us the familiar "blow" which is indescribably beautiful when seen on a still morning against surrounding hills. At such times the early sunlight will catch the plume of moisture and illuminate it as though it were a fountain rising spontaneously from the sea.

My friend, Dr Carl Hubbs, who *is* an expert on whales, has been quoted as saying that he has repeatedly watched groups of whales, separated by a distance of as much as a quarter of a mile, performing manoeuvres with a timing which seems to him most unlikely to be coincidental. He is well aware of the possibility that whales do have some method of communication. He thinks it is quite possible. In fact, just about everyone who has spent any time with the whales feels certain that somehow or other they can exchange ideas.

As mentioned above, we were blissfully ignorant of all this as we started our expedition down Baja California to photograph the whales in Scammon's Lagoon and to explore many miles of "virgin" beach. We did, however, feel certain there would be adventures in store for us. There are always adventures in Baja California and, after all, we were looking for adventure. If we hadn't wanted to find it we'd have stayed at home. So we crossed the border, filled with high spirits, and despite the fact we were intending to take *two* huge nineteen-foot metal boats over the country on two-wheeled trailers, we had a happy-go-lucky "Scammon's Lagoon or bust" attitude; and more or less secretly each one of us hoped that things wouldn't go too smoothly. We wanted an opportunity to cope with the unexpected.

4

A QUICK LOOK AT BAJA CALIFORNIA

AT this point it might be well to take a quick look at the physical geography of Baja California. It is a long, narrow peninsula, about 100 miles at its widest point and not much more than fifty miles wide at its narrowest point. It stretches many hundreds of miles south of the border, down below the Tropic of Cancer, by air a distance of perhaps 800 miles and by road a distance of about 1,200 miles, if one can call it a road.

Tijuana is a border port of entry. It has many of the characteristics of a rough border town. We are prone to hear altogether too much about the vice of Tijuana and attach the blame to Mexico, little realizing that Mexico furnishes the territory but the United States furnishes the vice. That is, it furnishes the customers without which vice cannot flourish.

People should not think of Baja California in terms of Tijuana. Tijuana is isolated. Its tentacles attach to the United States to the north and it is supported by tourists who take the brief half-hour excursion from San Diego which gets them into Mexican territory, geographically speaking, and by those other individuals who go to Tijuana for the bull fights, races and other things.

Ensenada lies some seventy miles of well-paved road to the south of Tijuana. Here one begins to encounter the real charm of Mexico and its distinctive atmosphere. The American who reaches Ensenada is in search of fishing, of relaxation, of boating in sun-swept waters, of enjoying the beauty of incomparable marine scenery along an ocean drive, of meeting charming, soft-spoken, courteous people, and beginning to get the feel, the atmosphere of old Mexico.

A hundred-odd miles to the east Mexicali is another border city which is just across the line from Calexico. Mexicali is entirely different from Tijuana. It is the capital of the northern

27

state of Baja California. It is a city of homes and factories.

There was a time when Mexicali also was a city of vice, but those days have long passed. The Mexicans, with a stern iron hand, have cleaned up the place. As the resorts of vice were torn down, beautiful houses sprang up, industry began to move in. The surprised Mexicans found legitimate business was vastly more profitable than vice had ever been.

Somehow the erroneous impression that the Mexican is lazy has permeated the United States. The Mexican peon is a creature of infinite patience. If there is work to be done, he does it methodically, unhurriedly and steadily. And he gets it done. If there is no work to be done, he waits. He waits as he works— patiently.

The high-class Mexican is a creature of dynamic energy and of iron nerves. I have seen public officials in their Mexican offices subjected to strain that would wreck the nerves of any American business man I know. I have watched these officials dispose of a steady stream of people, reaching almost instantaneous decisions, giving orders, making suggestions; firm, courteous, just, sending people away with the feeling they have been treated fairly. Frankly, I don't know how they do it. I am supposed to be a human dynamo, but I couldn't do it.

I have some friends in Mexicali who are always branching out into new businesses, are always successful. While some people like to hold up the United States as a bugaboo to Mexico, referring to it as the "Colossus of the North", I have been kidding my friends in Mexico recently by expressing fear of the "Colossus of the South".

South of Mexicali there is a large area of fertile farming land. A well-paved fast road runs through this farming land 120-odd miles to the south, to the little fishing port of San Felipe. San Felipe is on the Gulf. Ensenada is on the Pacific Ocean. They are separated by a high range of mountains. A dirt road winds through these mountains connecting the two cities.

To the south of Ensenada there is a stretch of agricultural land and some improved highway. To the south of San Felipe there is a road which can be traversed by the ordinary car in good condition, to a little place on the Gulf bearing the name of Puertecitos. This country is unbearably hot in summer but attractive in winter. It is on the Gulf side, with blue waters, alive with fish, to the east, and barren, desolate mountains of sun-baked rock all but devoid of vegetation, to the west.

Beyond Puertecitos adventure starts. The man who goes more than a few miles to the south of Puertecitos in a car had better have a four-wheel drive, or at least a pick-up with a four-speed transmission. He must have some knowledge of rough-road driving and he must have a certain amount of courage. He will also need drinking water, provisions and plenty of reserves of petrol.

For a distance of twenty miles or so the road goes up and down in short pitches. These grades are not over a few hundred feet in height, but they *are* steep. And these steep pitches are very, very rough in places. The fact that this road can be dangerous is attested to by the remains of battered vehicles with snapped axles or those whose brakes failed, throwing them out of control. Occasionally, one will see the ruins of a loaded truck down at the bottom of the canyon to the side of one of these grades and a wooden cross indicating that the road had taken its grim toll. On such occasions salvage operations will be performed with a rescue truck. Everything that can possibly be removed will be taken and, in the end, there will be nothing left except bits of splintered wreckage and the wooden cross.

Yet the man who is experienced in driving over rough roads, who has a sturdy four-wheel drive vehicle in good condition, can take this trip without giving it a second thought. There is one warning. A man should not be in a hurry on the roads in Baja California. If he is in a hurry he won't get there at all.

In some ways the land has not changed much in recent years. In other ways it has. Since my first trip in 1947 many changes have been made in the road. Much of it has been improved, although the less rugged portions remain as they were.

There is one place which has been altered considerably. And that was at the most dangerous point on the road, a place referred to in an earlier book as "The Point of the Picture of Death". This was where the road made an abrupt turn round a rocky promontory shortly before entering Coyote Bay to the south of Mulegé. Mexican travellers had painted a skull and crossbones on a projecting rock just before the road came to this point. It was a grim warning. The road was narrow. It made a sharp turn with a straight drop to the sea on one side and an overhanging rocky wall on the other. The road had literally been blasted out of the rock and was in the nature of a half-tunnel. That is, the wall of rock directly above the road made a jagged overhang. This overhang was so low that when I first encountered it in 1947 there was some doubt whether the top of the cab on the Dodge power wagon I was driving would clear it.

One of our party was seriously injured at this point, despite our precautions. Within a few months the territorial government started work on The Point of the Picture of Death. Much of the overhanging rock was blasted away, the turn was made less sharp and the road was widened. The picture of the skull and cross-bones remained. Thereafter, from time to time, the road has again been widened and improved.

I have derived a certain amount of amusement from reading the accounts of writers who subsequently made the trip over this road, and who somewhat patronizingly referred to my alarm at The Point of the Picture of Death. No person who made that trip prior to 1947 (and there were very, very few) ever referred lightly to The Point of the Picture of Death. Nowadays, writers who are traversing Baja California are legion. One meets them quite frequently in the northern part of the peninsula, headed south with optimism and various types of equipment. Asking them where they are going, one almost invariably receives the breezy reply that they are going to La Paz. Three hundred miles farther south one encounters few of these caravans. Most of the optimistic La Paz travellers have turned back.

Even today very few adventurers drive the long road to La Paz, despite the fact that it has, for the most part, been greatly improved.

5

WE FIGHT OUR WAY TO GUERRERO NEGRO

IT is a long, tedious drive for the 120-odd miles from Mexicali to San Felipe but the road is paved and, except for a ten-mile stretch which is a little rough, is in good condition. Tired and cold (there was no heater in my jeep), we stumbled into the modern hotel which had been erected there and went into the dining room lighted by electricity and were given menus which included everything from steaks, through all the standard Mexican dishes, to fish which had been freshly caught and tastefully prepared. We had a delicious meal, then slept until well after daylight the next morning, secure in the realization that at last we had escaped the tentacles of the telephone.

Then we went out and bought Mexican rolls. I don't know what secret recipe the Mexicans use in making their rolls. All I know is that they have a wonderful flavour and the bakery at San Felipe makes some of the best rolls I have ever tasted. Whenever I have been there I have made it a point to lay in a supply of these rolls, and this time we put in bag after bag, fitting them somehow into the load. Then we were off for Puertecitos.

Because we were taking along two nineteen-foot boats on trailers, there had been an irresistible temptation to load up the boats with various and sundry articles until we had somewhere around 1,000 pounds in each boat. In addition to that we had two pick-ups loaded to capacity with petrol, drinking water, food, tents, sleeping bags, portable typewriters and cameras.

We made the fifty-three miles to Puertecitos uneventfully. Then we went a few miles on beyond Puertecitos and made camp by the ocean.

The next day we had our first taste of bad roads and of the adventure which seems always to lie in wait along the bad stretches of road in Baja California. We came to a steep grade, where we found a car blocking the road about half-way up the grade.

These grades take just a little more explaining. When I say they are steep, I mean that they are steep. They *can* be negotiated, as I have mentioned, with cars that have only two-wheel drive but usually it takes at least a pick-up with a four-speed transmission to make it; and only a four-wheel-drive car gives one a proper sense of security in tackling those grades.

However, because so many pick-ups with two-wheel drive have made passes at these grades and have got stuck up near the top and have spun their wheels, thereby digging holes, the really steep parts of the road are almost unbelievably rough. A driver with a four-wheel-drive car can crawl up them satisfactorily. Any other car must make a run for it and then start accelerating. The result is that riding the steep parts of these roads in two-wheel-drive cars is very much like riding a bucking bronco.

This particular car that was blocking the road was a jeep station wagon but it wasn't equipped with a four-wheel drive. The Mexican driver had made repeated passes at the steep grade, had failed every time he tried, and each time had been forced to back down the grade for a new attempt. Finally he gave up. The man's wife and two children were with him, and he had quite a few supplies in the car. Right at the start he had lightened the car by carrying all his supplies to the top of the hill. He neatly spread a blanket on the ground for his wife and children and they sat there waiting for help. The driver was careful to park his car in the middle of the grade in such a way that no other car could get round it. Then he sat there waiting. There was nothing else to do. He might wait a few hours, he might wait all day, all night and all the next day. He might have to wait for two days. These things are common in Baja California.

Then, unexpectedly, our caravan came along. Since our pick-ups were towing the trailers it was decided that my jeep would be the one to act as tow car, and so we got the other car to a place where I could inch round it, and tackle the job.

Trying to tow a car up these rough, steep roads can be quite dangerous. If the man in the car behind loses his head or does the wrong thing, if he lets slack accumulate in the tow ropes so that there is a jerk, all sorts of problems can result. The grades are too steep to drag a car up that is only dead weight, and if the other driver has his power on, there are places in the road where

Among the cardones

Ocean scenery south of Puertecitos

Murl Emery

Pat Emery

Sam Hicks

he might go a shade faster than the car ahead and so present the dangerous problem of slack in the tow rope.

Much to my relief my Mexican driver was very skilful and a good tow. I got him over the bad places in the road and up to the top without incident. My jeep didn't even take a long breath, it just buckled down to work and pulled him along.

At the top we came to a stop. The family of the Mexican were all but delirious with joy. The driver jumped out of the car, unhooked the tow rope, then ran to embrace his wife and his children. Everybody was laughing and crying at once.

I drove my jeep on for about 100 feet and then, moved by some premonition, drove it off the road to the edge of a steep canyon, put it in compound low gear, put on the brakes, shut off the ignition, got out and put rocks at the front wheels. I was just adjusting the second rock when there was a bang that made the jeep shudder as though it had been hit by a cannon ball. I was knocked to one side and looked up to see the headlights and radiator of the jeep we had just rescued looming directly above me. Fortunately it had come to a dead stop.

It seemed that in the delirious excitement of the moment after all their fears of being marooned on the road for several days had subsided, the Mexican had forgotten to leave the car in gear or to put on the brakes. While the family were embracing and laughing and crying with sheer joy and relief, their car had started to move.

The rest of my party, arriving at that moment, had dashed after the moving car but it had gained momentum and was headed for the deep canyon. There was only one way to stop it and that was to run it into my jeep, hoping that my brakes would hold. Laitin made a desperate grab through the open window of the car, caught the steering wheel and held on long enough to give it the twist that would head the runaway car in the general direction of my parked jeep.

My brakes, the compression of the motor, and the rocks under the wheel held beautifully. The jeep station wagon hit it a terrific blow and stopped. My tail light was smashed into a mass of crumpled metal and broken glass, and one fender on the jeep station wagon proceeded to give up the ghost; otherwise no harm was done.

Tears and smiles of jubilation changed again to near hysteria

33

so far as the woman and children were concerned, but the Mexican, when faced with misfortune, became as calmly competent as a veteran sea captain in a storm. He immediately got busy separating the cars, trying to salvage the fender, pulling it up so that it didn't rub against the front tyre, and this time blocked all four wheels securely with rocks.

All I wanted was to get away from there before something else ran out of control and into me from behind.

We helped get them loaded and then started them on ahead of us so that if they should have any more trouble we'd be coming along behind where we could give them a lift—and so that he'd be up in front where he'd be a problem rather than a risk. As it turned out, that was the only grade the husky little station wagon couldn't negotiate. It got by all the others under its own power.

It seems simply incredible that Mexicans can transport merchandise over these roads by truck. Yet they do it. However, there is quite a percentage of mortality among the trucks. For instance, the next time we came along this particular stretch of road a truck had just gone out of control and plunged over the bank. We looked down on a mass of petrol drums, beer, soda water, provisions, flour and canned goods; all the luxuries of civilization which must be freighted were scattered about in a manner which makes one realize the tragedy of the loss.

The Mexicans who operate these trucks are, for the most part, working on a shoe-string. They load the trucks to capacity. The roads are so narrow they can't have dual treads but they do get the most expensive durable tyres that money can buy. For the rest, they keep the truck running with ingenious home-made repairs, baling wire and hope. On the tyres, however, there is no question of economy.

Here and there people grow the staple foods. They keep goats and sometimes chickens. But all the luxuries must be brought in over roads that only a Mexican truck driver has the skill and the will to negotiate. When a truck is lost, which is a not infrequent occurrence, it represents dire economic tragedy to the owner and usually death to the driver. Yet they carry on.

Some forty-odd miles below Puertecitos the road turns abruptly and starts up through a long sandy wash towards a level plain at the edge of the granite country. This is a long, steady

34

pull, the soil is fertile but dry and sandy, and yet, except for the fact that it is an uphill grade on a sandy pull, the road is fairly good. Here the country was literally carpeted with wild flowers.

The season of 1959-60 was one of the wettest winters Baja California has ever known—and we were destined to feel the impact of the weather. Down at Scammon's Lagoon where we were headed there is a normal annual rainfall of about half an inch. Now there had been seven inches in the last two months—with more to come, only we didn't know it. So we crept up the sandy road carpeted with wild flowers until we came to the granite country.

It is impossible to describe this granite country in words and it is exceedingly difficult to get photographs that tell the story of this vast expanse of weatherworn granite, lying silent in the sunlight; a country of mountains, deep canyons, native palm trees, elephant and cirio trees. Both the elephant and the cirio trees are found in Baja California. I think there is no other place in the world where the cirio tree grows. The elephant tree has crept north into the extreme southern desert section of California, but these trees are indigenous to Baja California.

The cirio tree looks like a huge parsnip when it grows up straight. It has a cone-shaped trunk with branches that normally are only a few inches in length and are covered with green leaves. However, the cirio tree does all sorts of weird things. At times it blossoms out into a star at the top. Frequently this star turns into half a dozen long branches growing straight up like a huge Roman candle. At times the cirio puts out limbs that twist and turn, and then again the whole tree itself for no known reason will bend until it is like some huge, grotesque elephant's trunk.

The elephant tree is a stubby tree with light-coloured bark, reminding one somewhat of an elephant's skin, and regardless of the height it attains, it always leaves the impression of stubby strength. It seems to get close to the ground so as to brace itself. The arid region in which it grows has most of its water in the form of brief torrential showers, followed by drought. The elephant tree greedily stores water until it seems to be suffering from dropsy. The bark is pale and wrinkled, the trunk is swollen and stubby, yet the overall effect is one of rugged strength and great beauty.

Up in the granite country winds laden with drifting sands from the lower levels have carved the huge granite boulders near the summit into grotesque shapes; sometimes creating wind caves in them, sometimes making holes and arches completely through the rocks. Lower down in the wind-protected areas the granite has weathered until there are times when it seems some giant hand has baked a loaf of granite bread, weighing several thousand tons, and then has sliced it into five or six pieces. This country is fertile, despite the granite ledges. Ocotillo, cirio, elephant trees, the bisnaga cactus, and much of the smaller desert foliage grow in profusion. The granite casts weird shadows and the dazzling sunlight is so intense in the dry air that these shadows seem jet black by contrast. It is the home of the famous Baja California big-horn sheep, of deer, of rattlesnakes, and occasionally springs of poison water. It is a country which lies quiet in the sunlight, yet there is a strange power about it.

After the road leaves the flower-covered desert it winds for several miles along the edge of the granite country, then comes to a flat mesa where recently a venturesome individual started making adobe bricks, apparently for no other reason than that there was a deep well with plenty of sweet water and lots of suitable soil. The bricks were to be sold at Gonzaga Bay.

There are mines up here and there is a lot of gold in the country. Near the deep well one can usually find a hard-bitten miner making his headquarters and mining gold from some secret source, extracting the gold from the rich ore by the most primitive of methods and so making enough to live on but not much more. We make it a point to carry a few luxuries for gifts to people such as these: cigarettes, perhaps a few oranges or tomatoes, bread and matches. These are luxuries beyond price in an isolated country. These men are deserving. They are glad to receive such gifts as tourists can bring, but they are not spongers. Nor are they beggars. They are men who are eager to find some way of earning a living.

The Mexican who has a little corner of ground can grow corn, keep goats and manage an existence. The Mexican who hasn't these things must have a job if he is going to support himself, and in parts of the country jobs are very hard to find. So the ingenious labourer who wants to work but can find no employment devises various schemes by which he can eke out an existence. Here and there one will find volunteer road labourers; men who walk out into the places where the road is the most dangerous, make a camp of sorts and voluntarily go to work on the road, trying to keep it in some sort of repair. Grateful drivers will from time to time leave them cigarettes, perhaps a loaf of bread or a handful of frijoles. These labourers gratefully accept whatever is offered and continue their work on the road, living in a primitive manner which is almost unbelievable.

We came on one of these camps where the shelter had been formed simply by taking the hood of a wrecked truck, propping it up on end with stones, to give shelter on the windward side, and then putting cloth on the other side, weighting the cloth down with stones and so furnishing a partial shelter in which two men could find a little protection from the weather. This camp was as neat as a pin; well kept, and the men were alert and intelligent. They were twelve miles from the nearest place where supplies could be obtained. After receiving a few pesos from grateful truck drivers, they would cheerfully walk the twelve miles to exchange their pesos for a few of the bare necessities of life, then walk back; covering the twenty-four miles in a day, carrying their meagre supplies in a small sack. The next day at daylight they would be out working on the road.

And yet, somehow, there is a feeling in the United States that the Mexican is lazy.

Here were men who had created their own jobs; who worked hard; who lived under the most primitive conditions; who never had quite enough to eat; yet who kept themselves clean and presentable; who maintained a spotless camp and were eager to be of service. Working only with somewhat battered shovels and a pick, without even the aid of a wheelbarrow, these men were limited as to overall efficiency. Yet they did the best they could and the truck drivers, themselves working on a slender margin and beset by financial troubles, nevertheless recognizing the spirit of the volunteer road workers gave them a peso now and then or bits of food which the truck drivers themselves could ill spare.

It is that spirit of friendly co-operation, of courteous recognition of a person's intentions, the desire to live and let live, which is so characteristic of Baja California.

37

Leaving the flat mesa we descended once more into the granite canyons and made camp that night at the site of an old mine. The next morning we were on our way past Lake Chapala, which was now filled with water, and turned south on the road to Punta Prieta where lies some of the most photogenic country in the world. There are miles and miles of mountains and valleys. Drifting cloud shadows soften the scenery. There are veritable forests of agave, yucca, cirio, elephant trees, the huge cardon, the various varieties of cholla cacti and other desert plants. And over it all is the cloak of complete silence.

Here one has turned one's back on the clock. There is unhurried peace and silence. During the night there will be the hoot of an occasional owl, the weird cacophony of the coyotes; but during the daytime one encounters only brooding silence. It is impossible to account for the charm of this country or its fascination, but those who are familiar with the land of Baja California are either afraid of it or they love it, and if they love it they are brought back by an irresistible fascination time and again.

That night we camped south of Punta Prieta. It was Thursday night and we were still a day and a half from the salt works where there had recently been installed a ship-to-shore telephone service which could be used in emergencies for long-distance calls. The representative of *Newsweek* had been instructed to get in touch with the office by telephone, at least by Saturday morning. When he tried to point out that that might be difficult, they had told him, nonsense, there were always telephones available, to go and make the trip but to be sure to report by telephone Saturday morning.

We couldn't possibly get to the salt works at Guerrero Negro before Saturday afternoon, but Murl Emery pointed out that Pat could take my four-wheel drive station wagon, drive all night, and get there sometime on Friday. Pat Emery was willing, so he, Joe Laitin and Joe Gandara threw some sleeping bags into the jeep station wagon and took off. We made camp and had a good night's sleep.

On rising we found that a smoked turkey we had taken along was beginning to show signs of mildew, so we re-smoked it in a home-made smoking tent, had breakfast, checked the cars and went on.

We had one more night's camp and then arrived at the salt works shortly after noon on Saturday. We found that Joe Laitin had made his telephone contact with the magazine. The only question they had asked him was the model of the Oldsmobile I was driving at home.

Charles J. McClaughry, the manager of the salt works, is a remarkable executive. He has managed to instil in all his employees an innate dignified courtesy which permeates the place and gives one the impression that here is no soulless corporation exploiting the native labourer, on the one hand, and the resources of the country on the other, but a dignified, cohesive body of men all co-operating to the utmost to attain several objectives: profits for the owners, high wages for the men who work there, better working conditions, and, above all, an awareness of human dignity and the rights of the individual.

Truck drivers wave to each other in passing, working men gravely lift their hats to each other as well as to visitors and smile a greeting. Throughout the place is an air of friendliness, co-operation and efficiency.

I know nothing whatever about gathering salt or the complicated mechanics of maintaining water at the exact temperatures where the different chemicals are precipitated, but I do know something about human nature in the aggregate, and I have been in enough factories, company communities and other gatherings to get the feeling of tension where it exists.

I have never encountered any place where there was more feeling of cohesive co-operation and an underlying appreciation of human dignity and human rights than here at this salt works, and I feel certain from what I have learned that the mainspring of all this—the inspiration—is Charles J. McClaughry. And his wife has been indispensable in creating a social life in the place. I suppose this sounds like extravagant praise, but anyone who has been privileged to see the way life goes on at the salt works, and who has been in enough company-owned mining towns or lumbering villages, will know how easy it is for these little communities to become hotbeds of petty jealousies on the one hand and sullen routine on the other.

Of course, McClaughry must have had good basic raw material to work with. You can't make a silk purse out of a sow's ear, but

39

all human beings have a desire to bring out the best that is in them and McClaughry has implanted this as an ambition in his various employees there at the salt works. To me it was an inspiration to see a one-company settlement maintained in this manner.

We were given permission to use the company road across the salt pans and down to the gauging station on Scammon's Lagoon. This is the only road by which vehicles can reach Scammon's Lagoon. The road traverses some eighteen miles of sand and salt.

We found the salt pans flooded. This flooding was not the result of design but was due to the fact that enough rainfall to cover an average for some fourteen years had fallen in the last two months, raising problems in connection with production which were becoming increasingly serious. When a salt pan has been flooded for just the right period it suddenly starts dissolving and turns to mush with startling rapidity. At such times a vehicle striking a soft spot can sink out of sight very quickly if immediate help is not available.

We found that the salt pans we must cross had been flooded for some time and there was a question whether we might be trapped if we had to cross them many times.

When we first crossed these salt beds the water was only a few inches deep but it had been fresh water that had been standing there for some time. In the circumstances there was a natural tendency to hurry across so that we could get safely to the other side—and hurrying is just the wrong thing to do.

Not only is it a mistake to hurry across the submerged salt pans, but it is a mistake to try to hurry anywhere in Baja California. A speed of six or seven miles an hour across the salt pans will get you where you want to go; but it is a great temptation to increase speed to twelve or fifteen miles an hour. Then the churned-up salt brine is splashed over the undercarriage of the car, over the springs and spring shackles and some of the drops may get caught by the fan and thrown against the distributor. Heaven help you if this salt brine ever gets in the ignition!

After you are across the salt pan the water dries and leaves an encrustation of salt all over the car. Later on, whenever you encounter moist air, particularly on a dewy night, the salt will attract the moisture and if the salt has got to the ignition system, the resulting condensation will cause conditions that will prevent the car from starting.

I made the mistake of going a little too fast, not across the salt pan itself but through one of the puddles in the road which, as it turned out, was encrusted with salt. Water got into the ignition of the jeep, and since it was only a hundred yards from camp I walked away and left the car. I returned after a couple of hours when the water had dried off and it started without trouble.

After that, however, whenever there was a heavy dew at night, my jeep simply wouldn't start in the morning until it had been dried out by hand and then towed along behind another car.

As it happened, we crossed the salt pans this first time in good shape, fought our way through the sandhills beyond and came to the gauging station at the end of the road where we were going to make our first camp.

Ahead of us lay the waters of Scammon's Lagoon and we made camp right on the brink of the lagoon.

6

THE STORY OF SCAMMON'S LAGOON

THE story of Scammon's Lagoon is fascinating, just as the story of Charles M. Scammon, the man after whom the lagoon was named, is a fascinating story of Yankee ingenuity, of the early days of whaling and of the shameful destruction of natural resources.

There is some conflict among the authorities as to just how Charles Scammon discovered his private hunting ground. In fact, when it comes to whales and whale hunting, the authorities seem to be pretty generally in conflict. One authority has it that Scammon befriended a Chinese sailor in Honolulu, that this Chinaman had been exploring the coasts of the United States and Mexico in a Chinese junk and offered to guide Scammon to a veritable hunting paradise in return for Scammon's kindness.

The other account is that Scammon, using the remarkable powers of observation which he undoubtedly had, obtained clues pointing to the fact that somewhere along the west coast of Baja California there was a place where whales congregated. However, so cunningly is the entrance to Scammon's Lagoon concealed that, despite the fact he was searching for such an entrance, he sailed by it without seeing it.

An alert look-out, however, at the top of the mast, taking his attention from the ocean and observing the long, low sandhills, was surprised to see the spouts of several whales coming apparently from a rolling, sandy desert.

Quite obviously whales do not spout on dry land. Despite the fact that the look-out thought he was looking over miles of arid desert and low, rolling sandhills behind an unbroken line of surf, the unmistakable fact was that once attention was directed towards dry land there were plainly visible the spouts of numerous whales appearing over the low sandhills—proof positive that there must be a lagoon.

Scammon had a large vessel and a smaller vessel. He anchored the larger vessel, lowered two whale boats, and sent the whale boats and the smaller vessel looking for a channel into the lagoon. It took them two days and two nights before the whale boats were able to return and report that a channel had been located and the cutter was already in the lagoon.

One marvels at the fortitude of these men who took to the oars and spent two days and two nights in open boats exploring an unknown, dangerous coast line. And after one has realized how tricky the channel to Scammon's Lagoon really is, how necessary it is to get inside the surf line and then come back inside a dangerous bar parallel with the surf-washed shore of an island, one wonders that the men were able to find this channel at all. But the men did find it, and after some manoeuvring Scammon got his big boat into the lagoon and they were ready to start whaling.

As mentioned previously, they took two whales without incident but the next day when they went whaling it was a different situation. The whales seemed to know exactly what was wanted and avoided the boats whenever possible but, when crowded, promptly turned and attacked. And the whales were so agile, so vicious and so powerful that they were christened "the devil fish".

The terminology of whaling is simple, direct, and to the point. For instance, the "Right" whale was so christened simply because the whalers felt he was the right whale to harpoon when there was any choice in the matter. And now the grey whale became known as the devil fish.

After the first few encounters, most of Scammon's men simply refused to man the boats; and when Scammon did get a volunteer crew, the first whale that came towards the boat found every one of the men jumping overboard and leaving the boat unmanned.

The word had got about and the whales were fighting back.

For two days Scammon's crew did no whaling at all, simply trying to ascertain how they could work out a new technique by which these whales could be captured. They were in a veritable whaler's paradise, with whales blowing all round them, but almost half the crew was injured, their boats had been stove in and the whales, seeming to know exactly what the foe was there

43

for, were ready to attack a boat whenever it showed up within range, so to speak.

The carpenters worked long hours getting the broken boats repaired so that they would be seaworthy.

At length a new scheme was proposed: the boats would anchor in shallow water by the edge of a channel. The whales could not get at them in the shallow water but, as whales came drifting past in the deep channel, one of the guns would fire a "bomb-lance" into a whale, hoping to reach a vital point. The seasoned whalers did not think this would work but they couldn't think of anything else that would, so they tried it.

The day they put the plan into execution they fired bomb-lances into three whales. The bomb-lances were ingenious devices, intended to explode after they had penetrated the whale's vitals. Three whales were killed; two of them sank to the bottom but the crew managed to get a line on the third whale and towed him to the boat. Later that day the other two bombed whales came to the surface and were found drifting with the tide. Lines were promptly attached to them, they were towed to the ship, and Scammon was in business.

Within record time Scammon filled his boat and exhausted his supply of bomb-lances. Getting the loaded boat out of the bar, however, was a problem. It was more than twelve days before they found conditions of wind and tide which enabled them to take a chance with the heavily loaded boats; and even then they left a trail of sand behind them as they dragged their keels across the bar.

One of the authorities has it that the Scammon boats were part of the whaling fleet out of New Bedford and that they returned to New Bedford. But, judging from the writings of Scammon himself, it would seem that he was working out of San Francisco. In any event, when the Scammon boats came in loaded to capacity with whale oil and whalebone, there was a lot of speculation.

Scammon had agreed to keep his crew working on shares, and swore each one to secrecy. So there was no word of Scammon's Lagoon or the new whaling discovery. The feeling was that Scammon had simply been lucky.

In those days the whalers went out and stayed out until they filled their boats. Many of the expeditions lasted for four or five years, with the boats cruising from the Arctic to the Antarctic. So naturally the fact that Scammon was back with a full boat within a matter of weeks was cause for speculation.

Scammon apparently made another trip to his lagoon without arousing any comment. But when he again returned within a few weeks with his boats loaded to capacity the competitive whalers became suspicious, and when Scammon started on his next trip a whole fleet of whalers followed, determined to find Scammon's secret whale-hunting grounds.

Scammon would keep in sight of the fleet during the daylight hours, then at night he would double and twist and turn and be out of sight by daylight. But the fleet would scatter and inevitably some of the look-outs would pick up Scammon's sail and again the chase would be on. Eventually, however, Scammon dodged the fleet and once more entered his secret lagoon and started operations.

The baffled hunters cruised everywhere trying to find where Scammon had disappeared, and in the end it was the wind which betrayed Scammon's location. A look-out on one of the whaling ships which had been cruising off Cedros Island noticed the tell-tale taint of whale blubber drying out, and reported to the captain, who promptly turned the ship into the wind and started following the scent which of course kept growing stronger until, to his amazement, the captain beheld the spars of Scammon's ship apparently moored in the middle of a sandy desert; and surrounded by the spouts of whales.

The low sandhills completely masked the lagoon but the spouts of whales some ten or fifteen feet high (and even reaching to twenty feet under proper atmospheric conditions) which had disclosed the lagoon to Scammon, plus the telltale spars of Scammon's ship, betrayed the location to the captain of the other vessel.

But locating Scammon's Lagoon and locating the channel were two different things. Scammon himself has written that on his next trip while there were some forty vessels standing by outside the surf, only eight of them managed to get into the lagoon.

However, the secret was no longer a secret and these hardy seafaring men soon learned the channel, and the whaling fleet

45

moved into Scammon's Lagoon. They began such a massacre of whales as baffles description.

Reading the accounts of the hardened whalers of those days it seems that they themselves were indescribably shocked by the slaughter, carried on amidst scenes of confusion and violence, with the desperate whales attacking the whalers, with harpoons and bomb-lances flying, and boats so thick that at times lines were crossed and boats being towed by frenzied harpooned whales crashed into each other. For a few years this slaughter continued and then suddenly the grey whales vanished. It was thought they were all extinct.

Actually, however, the whales had used their intelligence and, apparently as the result of deliberate strategy, had changed their annual migration from California to Korea. It seems incredible that the whales could have acted in concert in a matter of this sort, yet there is some evidence to support such a theory.

Unfortunately there are not enough accurate records available to be able to tell exactly what did happen, but apparently all at once the whales simply quit returning to the coast of California and to Scammon's Lagoon. The whalers thought the grey whale had become extinct. However, and at about that same time, the grey whale turned up off the coast of Korea, headed for lagoons and warm water.

By this time the grey whale had developed a nasty disposition. After the whales had pursued this new route long enough to be recognized, the contemporary writers state that grey whales encountered on the Korean migration were exceedingly belligerent, and this was doubly true of the males, who would attack a boat on sight.

Nor should one doubt the intelligence of the grey whale. They soon began to associate the long row boat, known in seafaring terminology as the "whale boat", with their hunters. Whalers who worked on the ocean found that as soon as a whale boat was launched the grey whales would vanish but the same was not true when the smaller fishing boats were in the water. And so, for a while, an attempt was made to take grey whales with a very small, light boat, capable of transporting only two people; one person who would scull, and the harpooner, who would wait in the bow.

Within a short time, however, the whales detected this

subterfuge and again the word got about. Soon the greys would veer off from the small boats as they did from the larger boats.

Living under present-day conditions makes it difficult for us to imagine the hardships faced by these rugged whalers who followed the sea. Now we have auxiliary motors and compact petrol or diesel engines. In those days there was no auxiliary power. A sailing ship depended upon the wind, its sails and the skill of its handling. We have now come to accept electric refrigeration as almost a necessity of life. In those days there was no refrigeration available for sailors who had to live day after day, month after month, and sometimes year after year on the whalers. They would stop from time to time at ports and pick up drinking water and a few fresh supplies but after a short time these supplies would be exhausted. Meat, in particular, could only be kept "pickled" in brine. There was no cooling system for the drinking water, which quite frequently became foul. When the wind died down a ship was becalmed. It might well be becalmed for a day, two days, or a week. During those periods the sun beat down upon the deck with fierce intensity. The crew lived on "salt horse" and "hard tack".

Then the whaling ship would follow the whales up into the Arctic, sometimes being caught in the winter ice and either crushed or held a drifting prisoner until the spring thaw. Men who could face the hardships of diet and climate must have been very rugged, very tough and very tenacious.

Reading the early accounts of whalers one is impressed with the risks these men took. Having "darted" an iron into a whale, having let out perhaps a mile of line when the whale "sounded", they would find themselves towed many miles by the anguished creature—towed until they were entirely out of sight of the mother ship which would then have to try to find them. These men were out in a trackless ocean; the mother ship perhaps miles away and getting farther behind all the time. Night would be coming on. The men had to pull the line in by sheer strength, and when one considers the resistance of the water, the slap of the waves and the speed at which the whale was towing them, this must have been quite an operation. Then, having worked in close enough to the whale to reach him with the lance, they tried to pierce the whale's "life". These thrusts with the lance sometimes

47

missed the whale's "life" and so infuriated him that he turned on the boat, smashing it to splinters and leaving crippled men to drown in the ocean. Such battles required strength, co-ordinated effort, a rare degree of skill and an iron nerve.

Darkness would frequently ensue before the battle was over and sometimes a fog or a storm would complicate the situation so that the mother boat might well lose all track of the crew manning the whaling boat. Yet men did these things and did them year after year.

Perhaps one of the most impressive things about the history of Scammon's Lagoon is that, after the grey whale had been hunted enough to become aggressive, he was able to inspire terror in men who had nerves of steel and who had followed the whaling business all of their lives.

It is now very difficult to get access to a copy of the book Charles M. Scammon wrote in 1875, entitled *The American Whale Fishery*, but anyone who is able to find the book and read it will acquire quite a knowledge of whales and will be filled with admiration for the two-fisted, iron-nerved men of the whaling industry.

The slaughter of whales had been so great that when they disappeared scientific writers claimed the grey whale to be all but extinct and within a few years would go the way of the buffalo. However, as so frequently happens, the prophets failed to take into consideration certain other factors which were destined to exert a great influence. The development of the petroleum industry, the strides of science in connection with refining lubricants, soon put the whaling industry on the greased skids, and it was the whaler who became all but extinct. Now the activities of the remaining whalers are so regulated by international agreements that the whales stand better than an even chance of replenishing their numbers.

Following the slaughter of the grey whales in Scammon's Lagoon and the withdrawal of the whalers themselves under economic pressure, the lagoon lay for many years, a virtually unknown body of water, slumbering peacefully in uninterrupted solitude.

After scientists became interested in the ocean and ocean currents, the Scripps Institution of Oceanography, studying the mysteries of the ocean, soon learned that the grey whales were coming back down the coast and returning in numbers to Scammon's Lagoon.

My friend, Dr Carl Hubbs, started making aerial surveys to take an annual census of the whales in the lagoon. And, as reports were made, the Press picked up the information and it soon became known that the whales were returning in numbers to their old breeding grounds.

It is to be remembered that the whale is a mammal and is, therefore, in a way, related to man. Man has recently been bothered with a great deal of heart trouble. The heart of man is a very small organ, but the heart of a whale is a huge pumping device weighing up to 250 pounds. It was felt that if studies could be made of the heart of the whale and its circulatory system, information might be gained which would be of value to the human race.

Dr Paul Dudley White, the famous heart specialist, was anxious to secure electrocardiographs of the heart action of a living whale. He enlisted the aid of Donald Douglas and the Douglas Aircraft Company and soon their research boat, the *Dorado*, bearing Donald Douglas and Dr White, was headed for Scammon's Lagoon, with the results I have previously mentioned.

The problem of getting an electrocardiograph of a living whale is not a simple one. It is necessary to place two electrodes in the whale; one as near the neck as possible, and the other as near the tail as possible.

Having become interested in the problems of the whale's heartbeat, Donald Douglas really went to work. And the following year he and Dr White were once more on their way to Scammon's Lagoon. This time, however, the situation was far different from what it had been the year before. They had been offered the co-operation of the Mexican Government, of the United States Army, and again had the co-operation of the National Geographic Society.

For some months Donald Douglas had been working on the idea of placing electrodes in the whales from a helicopter, and an ingenious power gun had been worked out which would fire twin harpoons simultaneously, spread at just the right angle to penetrate the skin of the whale at head and tail, and designed to furnish maximum electrical contact. The harpoons were so fashioned that they would not go deep enough to hurt the whale, and would, in the course of a brief space of time, be dislodged by its muscular actions. Wires from the harpoons went to a small boat which was strapped to the bottom of the helicopter. This compact boat was packed with batteries and wiring and was so designed that when it hit the water an aerial automatically came up and the electric impulses were sent by wireless from the small boat to a receiving station on the Douglas research yacht, the *Dorado*.

On that expedition they were able to get both the electrodes in whales and, while the results were not all they had hoped for, they did obtain much valuable information.

Scammon's Lagoon, which had lain dormant, so to speak, for so many years was now back in the news, and the attention of people throughout the civilized world was fastened upon it.

The salt works at Guerrero Negro are not a mining operation, as one might at first think. The huge salt pans which have been formed over a period of millions of years by the evaporation of sea water are used merely as a level foundation on which to impound new sea water and harvest this new salt. Strange as it may seem, the activities of this company result in increasing the deposits on the salt pans, rather than decreasing it. Yet, by the use of scientific equipment and modern machinery, they annually harvest thousands of tons of new salt recovered from the ocean.

As the enterprise prospered it grew in magnitude until now there is quite a settlement at the salt works in Guerrero Negro. A road was constructed across the dry salt pans to the head of Scammon's Lagoon where there is a tide-gauging station. This road is just about the only way by which wheeled vehicles can get to the borders of the lagoon. It was our intention to launch our boats from the trailers directly into the waters of the lagoon; then to transport our equipment to an island in the middle of the lagoon and there make camp, hauling our drinking water and our petrol in cans from the mainland to camp.

It is thus seen that the shores of Scammon's Lagoon, dotted here and there with the wrecks of whaling vessels which came to grief, have been through several periods of transition and within the last few years have even heard the whirring of the blades of a helicopter.

And it is now becoming apparent that "word has got round" among the whales that they are once more an object of interest. This makes the whales nervous. They can't understand this sudden renewed interest on the part of man, or the peculiar machines which hover high in the air.

Some of the whales will remain relatively calm in the presence of a helicopter. Some will "sound" at the first intimation an object in the air is taking an interest in them. In fact, I have even seen whales sound, apparently in fright, when flying over them in an aircraft at an elevation of at least 5,000 feet.

So far as we knew, no other person had ever invaded the waters of the lagoon with two strong metal boats, each equipped with twin outboard motors capable of making great speed.

This method of whale hunting had advantages, although it also had very great disadvantages. But it offered adventure and the thrill of the unknown; and, very frankly, we wanted to find out just what would happen.

7

WE ESTABLISH CAMP AT SCAMMON'S LAGOON

It was low tide when we first arrived on the banks of Scammon's Lagoon. We couldn't launch our boats until the tide had come in. So we unloaded the pick-ups, made our camp, put the trailers in a position to launch the boats early in the morning when the tide was up, and then spent an hour or two looking the country over.

There was a turtle camp nearby, and a keen-eyed, leathery-faced Mexican who had spent many years making a living from the sea, came out to greet us. This man, Justo, was quite a character. His right hand was gone. Fishing with dynamite, he had been a little late in tossing the explosive and had lost his hand. We heard afterwards that he had made a tourniquet and walked interminable miles to a place where he could get medical help, accepting the misfortune philosophically.[1]

Justo had worked and worked hard. He made his one hand do the work of two. He had built up quite a turtle business, and at the moment had a large stock of turtles awaiting shipment. His method of shipping was to load the turtles in an open boat equipped with an outboard motor and a small standby motor, then take off across the open sea to Cedros Island some thirty miles away. There he could sell his turtles to the cannery.

That afternoon Justo had secured a turtle which he was waiting to take over to his camp. The turtle had been neatly turned on its back, in which position it was completely helpless, and was lying there on the beach. These turtles make delicious food and, after all, it is the scheme of nature that life must support life; but this was our first close-up meeting with an unfortunate turtle. Once they are turned on their backs on dry land they can't right themselves. They make futile efforts, then finally give up, settle back and close their eyes, apparently sleeping.

[1] Justo had his final misfortune on Good Friday of 1960 when he was drowned in the treacherous waters of Scammon's Lagoon.

Perhaps it was our imaginations but I am willing to swear that this turtle who was lying on his back asleep, and which awakened when I approached, had a second or so during which he was orienting himself and then suddenly his eyes widened and I had the feeling there was an expression of terror in them. I tried to stroke his throat and reassure him but the only result was to start him struggling helplessly. This time I thought his eyes were pleading for help. Anyhow, with three women in the party the result was a foregone conclusion.

We hunted up Justo, who owned the turtle, and told him we wanted some turtle meat. He had a turtle right there at the camp and how much would he take for him? We didn't fool Justo for a minute. He sold us the turtle at wholesale price and because it soon became apparent that we hadn't fooled him we confided to him that what we wanted was to turn Mr Turtle loose and we didn't want him caught again. He was our turtle and as such immune from being netted.

Justo quickly understood. There was a twinkle in his eyes as he waded out into the low-tide muck and slime with his rubber boots, turning the turtle over, moistening its back with sea water, for apparently a turtle becomes even more helpless once his shell dries out. I acquired the greatest regard for Justo then and there. The man might make his living by snaring turtles and selling them on the market but he had a big heart and a lot of warm, human sympathy. He spent almost as much time getting the turtle out into the water, getting him properly wet through, and steered on a course to deep water, as he had spent in catching him in the first place. Nor did he look at us afterwards with the expression one reserves for rich *Yanqui turistas* who are crazy. He smiled understandingly. One gathered that he would like to turn all his catch loose if it weren't for the fact that he had to catch turtles in order to live.

We only intended to stay at this camp long enough to get the boats launched, so we hurriedly unloaded the cars, piling everything helter-skelter on the sandy hills above the high water line, and then went out in search of wood.

Firewood in this place was at a premium. I didn't give the matter any thought at the time. All I knew was that we needed firewood and we had to go some distance to gather it. It never

53

occurred to me in my selfishness to wonder what Justo and his companion at the turtle camp did for their firewood. Afterwards I found out that getting enough firewood to cook a meal involved much walking and much searching.

A few shrubs grew to a height of six or eight inches above the soil and occasionally some of these died and the wood became dry enough to burn. Justo and his companion would start out in the afternoon with a length of light rope about two and a half feet long. They would be gone for perhaps an hour or an hour and a half and come back with a little bundle of sticks tied up in the rope. This was their firewood. The fire was hardly bigger than the light of a candle, carefully fed and nursed with the precious wood so that every bit of flame did its share in cooking a meal.

Murl Emery knew of a place up on a bluff some six or seven miles away where there were larger bushes growing and we took the empty pick-ups and went up to this place, returning with a couple of pick-up loads of firewood. We cooked our supper, spread out our sleeping bags, inflated the air mattresses and built a roaring camp fire.

I have often wondered how Justo and his companion must have felt as they sat by their little candle-sized flame and looked across a couple of hundred yards to where the "rich tourists" had a roaring camp fire some six or eight feet in diameter, sitting round it toasting their bodies and wasting the precious natural resources of the country.

Eventually we let the fire die down but still left plenty of wood for a big breakfast fire in the morning. It was cloudy but we felt certain it *couldn't* rain. The country was soaked! It had more than enough rain to last for years. According to the law of averages the rains must be over. This was only a high fog. We drifted blissfully off to sleep.

I wakened about midnight with the first gentle drops falling on my face. I sighed, thought about getting up to distribute my bed canvas more evenly, but drowsily pulled it up over my head and trusted to luck that it was all right. I went back to sleep and was awakened by pelting rain, pouring down, hitting my bed canvas and running off into the sand.

I was warm, the canvas was keeping me dry. I had nothing to

worry about, so once more I didn't take the trouble to get up and see that the folds of the upper canvas were spread out over the lower canvas so that water wouldn't run into my sleeping bag. After all, I reasoned drowsily, this couldn't be any more than a shower.

Rain came down in curtains, in sheets, in torrents. I later found out that the lower canvas had spread out so that it was catching the drop from the upper canvas and my sleeping bag was lying in a pool of water. By that time it was too late to do anything about it and I felt certain that the next day would be sunny and warm and I could spread things out and let them dry; so again I drifted off to slumber.

Daylight came; a cold, wet, dismal dawn with rain still pelting down. I stayed in my sleeping bag as long as possible and then finally faced the bitter chore of crawling out of a warm sleeping bag and dressing in the midst of a cold rain.

I squirmed my way out of the sleeping bag and rubbed my eyes in surprise. During the night Sam Hicks and Pat Emery had dressed and put up the big tent in the dark. They had put in a stove, built a fire in the stove, and not only was the tent warm and dry but the water which fell on the top of the tent was turning to steam and evaporating, simply from the warmth of the fire in the stove.

Naturally I gathered my clothes and made a run for the tent, only to find that the others had done likewise, and soon we were all dressed, waiting for it to let up.

The rain didn't let up. Everything that had been out in the open was soaking wet. So we had the job of launching the boats in the rain, trying to protect our films and cameras as best we could with what waterproofing we had, and fighting our way out across Scammon's Lagoon to the island where we intended to make our camp—all in a downpour.

The reason I mention all this is that the stove didn't use nearly as much wood as the open camp fire. By the time we had had breakfast, had launched the boats, had squeezed as much water as we could out of the things from which water could be squeezed, and had loaded the boats to make the first trip to the island, we still had a lot of firewood left in the pile.

Personally I didn't give the firewood very much thought. I felt that it would come in handy for Justo and his companion, camped over there on the point, but at the moment my main concern was to try to get to where we could establish a more permanent camp, put up all our tents and try if possible to get dried out before nightfall.

Rain was the one thing we hadn't counted on. We had, of course, brought tents just in case, but we had expected to use these mainly as shelters against the winds and the heavy dews which are customary at night along the ocean.

Our first boatloads took only the absolute necessities for our new camp: a tent, a stove, some provisions, and some of the photographic material. The rest we covered with canvas and left for a second load.

Therefore it happened that my first experience with the whales in Scammon's Lagoon was during a period of rain, of wind-driven moisture and a cold wind from the ocean.

The island where we were going to make our camp was some fifteen or twenty miles down the lagoon but, even heavily loaded, our boats could make a good twenty miles per hour.

At the moment we were not interested in whales. We were mainly interested in dry clothes and a warm fire. I remember looking at the pile of wood we had built up and wondering vaguely if there would be wood we could burn on the island, but it would have been out of the question to have tried to add wood to our burden on the loaded boats, so we put just as much of a load in the boats as we felt they would carry for that first trip and shoved off.

The point is that the abandoned wood pile stayed there for some ten days or two weeks. The frugal Justo and his companion came over and cleaned up everything we had left behind which they felt certain we had intended to throw away; an old canteen which had sprung a leak, the empty tin cans which we had buried and which the coyotes had promptly dug up; everything that we had discarded as of no further use to us which Justo and his companion could use they had picked up and carried away.

But the wood pile? When we came back at the end of ten days that wood pile was intact, waiting for us.

That rain turned out to be the forerunner of a three-and-a-half-day storm. Justo and his companion must have been cold, wet and miserable. They needed firewood badly. They couldn't go out to get it and there was a pile of abandoned firewood of sufficient magnitude to last them for two or three weeks with their frugal way of living; but the thought of touching it never entered their minds. We hadn't told them they could have it, therefore they reasoned we would probably want it on our return. The fact that we would touch a match to it and burn up a three weeks' supply of firewood in an hour or two didn't have anything to do with it. This was our wood. We had gathered it. They wouldn't think of touching it.

I mention this in order to show something of the inherent honesty of the Mexicans of Baja California. I have encountered this time and time again. I remember once that we made a camp and carefully buried all our empty tin cans. Then we started on and for some reason didn't go far before making another camp. A Mexican passed us going down the road, came to our old camp, found the place where we had buried our empty cans, and then turned round and came all the way back riding his burro over several weary miles to ask if we intended to use those cans again or if we had thrown them away, because if we had thrown them away he wanted them very much to use as cooking utensils.

These people lead simple lives. Their wants are few but such wants as they do have are vital. Firewood and cooking utensils are wealth, yet their honesty is such that they would freeze or starve rather than touch something that belonged to someone else.

8

WE MEET OUR FIRST WHALES

THE weather lightened a little after we got under way. I held one of my cameras under a rainproof poncho, despite the fact that my clothes were wet, and stood in the bow of the boat waiting for the first whale adventure.

It wasn't long before we had it. A whale unexpectedly came to the surface a short distance in front of our boat, shot out a great cloud of steamy breath and then plunged down to the bottom thoroughly alarmed by the boats and sending up great disturbances in the water every time his powerful tail propelled him forward.

At the time I didn't know enough about whales to realize that he was getting away as best he could. All I knew was that the water was churning about the boat and I began to wonder vaguely if we could count on these whales being safe.

A few miles farther on we came on several whales drifting along on the surface of the water. They promptly submerged when Emery's boat, which was in the lead, came within a few feet of them. One of the whales, however, didn't go deep. He remained just under the surface, whirled round past Emery's boat, then, as we could see under the surface of the water, made directly for our boat.

I watched for a moment and didn't like the look of him. There was something purposeful about his progress, and he was moving at speed. He was making no attempt to submerge but remained just a few feet under the water, headed directly for us.

"Sam," I said, "I don't know enough about these whales to depend on Emery's judgment. Let's get out of here!"

We had lots of horsepower in that boat so Sam shoved the throttle forward and we moved away, just a few feet ahead of the approaching whale.

At the time I thought the whale was charging but I didn't venture the opinion because I didn't know anything about whales and I was the only one who seemed alarmed. Later on, after I got home and started reading about whales I knew darn well he was charging. It was that day I began to realize something of what we were up against in photographing whales.

A whale is an enormous mammal. He is dark in colour except where there are patches of white on his skin and where barnacles cling to his hide. He comes up out of the blue water, spouts, and goes down. While he is spouting, only a few inches of his huge body are above the water. Sometimes I doubt if he protrudes more than six inches above the surface. When you try to take his picture there is little contrast between the whale and the water. If one is standing in a boat so that the camera is five or six feet above the water-line there is no way of showing a silhouette of the whale's back that is out of the water.

Moreover, an ordinary focal-length lens will make a whale only a few feet away appear to be quite distant. The long focal-length lens will blur the image on the film because a telefoto lens requires a firm, steady foundation and you can't get a firm, steady foundation in a bouncing small boat.

In fact, as we were to learn later, photographing whales in their native habitat is just about the most difficult photographing assignment one could wish for.

We saw quite a few whales on our trip to the island, but I signalled Emery that I didn't want to deviate an inch from our course in order to take whale pictures. We were racing against the tide because once the tide went down we would have to wade across muddy tide flats in order to transport stuff to and from the boats. We had equipment that weighed hundreds of pounds, and the fact that much of our camp equipment was soaking wet didn't simplify matters. A dry tent which weighs a hundred pounds is quite a problem, but let that tent once get wet, getting it transported and put up becomes an engineering feat.

We reached the island and Sam Hicks and Pat Emery worked like Trojans, rushing stuff ashore, putting up a shelter tent and connecting a stove. Then they dashed off in the boats to pick up the rest of the camp and we started trying to gather firewood.

It immediately became apparent that getting firewood was going to be quite a problem. On the island there was a variety of bush which grew several feet off the ground and here and there were some bits of dead brush. But others had camped on the island before us and there was but little firewood, and what little there was, was soaking wet.

After we got the things which we had taken in the boats on that first trip under cover, I suggested that the only way to keep warm and at the same time conserve firewood was to go for a walk and keep walking. That way at least we could keep the blood circulating. I had tried it before on rainy days in wet camps. It worked. So we started walking in the rain, exploring the island, which by this time was becoming soggy with water. The soil, a mixture of sand and dirt, was turning to cold mush.

Fortunately the rain let up soon and while there was a cold wind blowing with the easing off of the actual downpour we had an opportunity to explore the island, perhaps a mile or more in length and at its widest point a little over a quarter of a mile in width.

There was a period of two or three hours while we waited anxiously for the boats, then we heard the motors approaching and shortly afterwards we all participated in the job of moving things into camp.

That was one of the most disagreeable afternoons I have experienced for some time. I carried things back and forth across the muddy soil until I was thoroughly exhausted. I knew that I shouldn't be lifting and carrying those loads. I knew that Murl Emery shouldn't be lifting them. I knew that the girls shouldn't be lifting them. But the stuff was there and we had to get it under cover before dark and it had started to rain again.

With the new load we had additional tents and in our walks we had collected a little firewood so we got a fire going in the stove. Sam and Pat put up a sleeping tent for the girls and a couple of wigwam tents with floors. Everything was wet and the odour of damp canvas permeated the camp.

We brought out a jug of rum, got some hot water, and had hot buttered rums, then broke out some tinned goods and cooked dinner.

Our sleeping bags were wet but, fortunately, not wet through, although they emitted a damp, soggy odour. That night we slept with the sound of rain pelting against the canvas, wind blowing and flapping the tents until it threatened to pull them up by the roots, and always that smell of wet canvas and soggy, down-filled sleeping bags in our nostrils. I would like to report that, being a nervous individual, I was unable to sleep. Unfortunately, however, the truth of the matter is that I instantly sank into deep slumber and from time to time was only drowsily aware of the pelting rain, the blowing wind, the crashing of surf and the soggy smell.

The next day the storm had temporarily abated and along towards noon the sun came out. We hurriedly dragged wet canvases out and spread them on the ground. We dried out sleeping bags as best we could, moved chairs out into the sunlight and congratulated ourselves that the storm was over.

That night it rained again.

Gradually, however, we managed to get things dried out.

After a person has camped enough in pelting rain there is nothing quite as satisfactory as snuggling into a warm sleeping bag inside a good tent and listening to the rain beat against the canvas. It gives one a feeling of dry security.

However, all this wasn't doing our photographic equipment any good. The tents had been pitched on moist ground. The floors of the tents were wet, and no matter what happened we couldn't keep a certain amount of rain from blowing in the openings. Our focal-plane shutters began to stick, the leaves of the between-the-lens shutters started swelling.

Added to this was the effect of hundreds of miles of washboard roads. I know of nothing that will work the devastation to equipment that can be accomplished by a washboarded road unless it is a trotting pack horse in the mountains.

We'd take our tripods and tighten the screws to the last notch. By the time we had gone over a few miles of washboard roads the screws would have been loosened, the tripods would have come to pieces and nuts and bolts would be scattered about the floor of the car. Toothpaste in a bag would jiggle round and the top would come off. Then the pounding of obstacles on the kitbag would squeeze out the toothpaste all over the clean clothes. So by the time we got ready to take whale pictures our equipment had already lived through plenty of rough treatment.

Whale hunting proved to be not as easy as we had expected. It was necessary to wait until tidal conditions were right and preferably we needed relatively calm waters. When the wind is blowing riffles there is not much distinction between the appearances of a wind-blown wave twelve inches high and the back of a whale protruding out of water. Also, the light has to be right, and whales somehow have a disconcerting habit of coming up directly between the camera and the sun. When the sun is low on the water this prevents any worth-while picture.

Moreover, there was the irresistible desire to explore some of the surrounding country. So we decided to postpone whale hunting until we had explored the terrain and could count on calm, tranquil waters. But the waters wouldn't get calm. It became apparent that our rain was just a part of a persistent storm, bits of lashing rain and violent squalls interspersed with periods of fitful sunlight.

One day, when the wind was heavy enough to cause something of a turmoil in the water, we went to the mainland directly across from our island camp just for the sake of taking a walk, getting some exercise and exploring.

This was well within the lagoon itself and there were not supposed to be any really worth-while objects to be found by beachcombing. But we soon found that in the course of time there had been quite a deposit of miscellaneous objects: electric light bulbs which had been discarded from various ships, bits of interesting driftwood and a couple of the glass balls used as floats on fishing nets in the Orient. Then we turned our attention inland and found several nearly perfect obsidian arrowheads.

It was interesting to note that the coyotes had followed a trail just at the back of the seashore and had made a distinct path. I presume the coyotes in this area have learned to feed very largely on marine life. Otherwise it is difficult to account for the large number of coyotes around Scammon's Lagoon. We could hear them every night, and quite frequently during the day we caught sight of them, virtually fearless, maintaining a discreet distance of perhaps a hundred yards or so, but filled with curiosity and pausing from time to time to look back over their shoulders as they trotted away, quite frequently turning to stand broadside on as they looked us over.

I also suspect that prowling round at night the coyotes get quite a bit of water fowl. Vast flocks of duck and geese would come winging in towards evening and settle down in great gatherings within a relatively short distance of the shore. During the period of maximum activity, when new flocks were coming in, the air would be filled with quackings and honkings, then as darkness approached the birds would huddle together and finally become silent, their heads tucked under their wings, sleeping quietly.

At low tide the waters of the lagoon are very shallow, stretching out in places for perhaps a mile with water only a few inches deep.

Once in the middle of the night when we were camped near a huge raft of geese, we heard the sudden whirr of wings and then thousands of birds were flying in panic in the darkness overhead. Their flight was so low and close and their wings beating the air so fast that it sounded something like a jet plane taking off from an airport. Next morning we found a big pile of feathers and evidences that one or more coyotes had enjoyed a sumptuous repast. I have an idea that these coyotes have learned to move silently in the shallow water until they can pounce upon some sleeping bird.

After this experience we started looking along the shoreline in the salt water grass and found many a pile of feathers. The coyotes were well fed—so were we.

One afternoon when we encountered a day that was unfit for whale hunting and we had been exploring the neighbouring country, Emery suggested that it might be a good plan to have some fresh fish for supper.

We took the boat and travelled on one motor only, reducing it to trolling speed, circling the island where we were camped. Emery was piloting the boat and Gandara and I were doing the fishing.

We had gone only a few yards when I had a strike and pulled in a nice fish. Gandara dropped his line into the water and within a few seconds had another strike which had his reel buzzing and sent the line hissing through the water. He was using a plug which Emery valued very highly and when, after a few minutes, the fish made off with the plug, I pointed out to Gandara that he hadn't given the fish enough line, that a good fisherman never lost a plug, etc., etc.

After that we both landed several fish, Emery having donated another one of his highly prized bass plugs to the good of the cause.

Then I hooked on to a fish that at first felt like a snag, but it suddenly exploded into action and took off for China. I gave it lots of line and exclaimed that I had hooked a whale.

Then the line went slack. I reeled in and reeled in and reeled in and felt sure I had lost the fish. Then as I was retrieving the last of the slack I found that my line was apparently fouled on something almost directly beneath the boat. I pulled and tugged, putting all the pressure I dared on the line, and nothing happened. I told Emery that I was snagged and he'd have to manipulate the boat so that I could recover the plug. Emery started to do this and I was giving a series of gentle jerks on the line when all of a sudden my fish exploded into activity once more and the reel started smoking. As it slowed down and I was groping for the handle with my thumb and finger to retrieve a little line, and just as I was getting the handle of the reel in my grasp, the fish took off again with such suddenness that he jerked the handle out of my grip, caught my index finger afoul of the reel and for a moment I thought my finger was going to break before I could extricate it.

That gave Mr Fish all the opportunity he needed. He lunged against the line and snapped it clean in two.

I have seldom seen anyone as pleased as Joe Gandara or as annoyed as Murl Emery.

Gandara pointed out to me from time to time on the way back to our mooring that good fishermen might lose a fish but they seldom lost a plug, etc., etc.

We had some very choice specimens of fish, just a nice pan size of about eighteen to twenty-two inches. Pat expertly extracted fillets from the sides of the fish and that night we had one of the most delicious suppers I have ever tasted.

Mexican corbina caught and cooked all within ninety minutes make a dish that makes my mouth water just thinking back on it.

Picturesque scenery typical of Baja California

Drifting sand in the barren desert north of San Felipe

Speed is forgotten on these roads . . .

. . . and lorries quite frequently fall by the wayside

9

WE CONTACT THE WHALES

WHILE we were waiting for the sort of weather which would enable us to get good whale pictures we were steadily using up our supplies. Our supply of fresh water was exceedingly limited. We had to haul it from the mainland and by the time we had our first clear day, in place of hunting whales we had to dash back to the mainland and go to the salt works to replenish our supplies of petrol and drinking water. There I found frantic messages awaiting me. I must get in touch with Hollywood at once.

Peggy became the sacrificial sheep, or, I should say, the goat. We found there was a cargo plane of lobsters which had been forced to make a temporary landing because Ensenada was blocked in. It was sitting there with motors running, the pilots on the radio, waiting for word that Ensenada was clear enough for a landing.

While we were there the pilots got the word all was clear. We negotiated with them to take Peggy, and piled her aboard with the sacks of lobsters to make a rough, dangerous trip to Ensenada where she hired a taxi to take her to Tijuana, another taxi to take her to San Diego, and then telephoned the ranch to have someone come and meet her. She got on the phone to Hollywood and explained to them that she was in there making arrangements for a chartered aeroplane and that I would be along "at the earliest possible moment".

That gave us a few days to hunt whales, and they were really exciting days.

It soon became apparent that the sound of our powerful motors disturbed the whales and caused them to dive. It *might* have caused them to attack the boats if it weren't for the fact that we were going too fast for the whales to catch up with us, but for the most part the whales simply became frightened.

By this time we had learned enough about whales to know

that when a whale submerged and the water became agitated in a series of whirlpools, the whale was getting away fast and diving deep at the same time.

These animals are so powerful that when their huge tails are called on to furnish motive power for a fast dive the water on the surface is churned into eddies and small whirlpools.

We decided to slow down and try sneaking up on the whales but soon found that didn't work.

So then we decided to go out and anchor the boats, shut off the motors and wait for the whales to come drifting along with the tide.

At the time we didn't realize how risky that could be. We knew there were certain things that could happen. A whale could get tangled up with the anchor line; or a whale could come to the surface, see us sitting there, decide we were hostile and give us a casual slap with his tail which would put the boat at the bottom and its passengers in the hospital or in a shark's belly.

However, we were still labouring under the delusion that the whales were peaceful so we went out early in the morning and anchored the boats. The tide changed and soon the whales came drifting along.

The boats were about seventy-five feet apart and sometimes whales would come by one boat, sometimes by another. We felt that coloured film would give us a better idea of where the whales began and the water left off, although we knew that for purposes of book publication we would have to limit the pictures to black and white. So we had cameras with coloured film, cameras with black and white film, and cine-cameras grinding away on coloured film.

I was leaving it to Sam to take pictures in black and white; I worked a colour film camera with a fairly long focal-length lens.

Over in the other boat Murl and Pat Emery were also grinding away with colour cine-cameras and Joe Gandara was doing the same. I was the only one who really wanted pictures for publication and I felt that Sam, who is a pretty expert photographer, could be trusted to get good black and white pictures of anything that came along.

Then without previous warning came a moment of terrific excitement. A whale was approaching and unless he changed his course it looked very much as though he were going to pass right between the two boats.

What would he do?

If he came up close to one of the boats, would he ignore it or would he give it a slap with his tail? It was too late to haul up the anchors and start the motors. We had to sit this one out.

It was amusing to see everyone start putting on lifebelts as though someone had given the signal for a boat drill. I know that I was excited and scared, and from the way grown men began to whisper and giggle I gathered the others were sharing at least some of my feelings.

The whale came ploughing majestically on. He passed directly between the boats, not more than fifteen or twenty feet from us.

I know he was so close that my lens had a problem of parallax with the finder, which I didn't correct, and it wasn't until two-thirds of the whale's length had gone by that I realized what was happening to my pictures. So I elevated the camera in time to get some good pictures of the west end of a whale headed east. Prior to that time my lens was taking some wonderful pictures of the rippling waves thrown up by a huge whale, bigger than a locomotive, ploughing his majestic way through a tranquil sea.

Afterwards it turned out that Sam's camera had given way under the damp air, the rigors of the trip and years of use.

We didn't realize any of this at the time, but were elated at our "close-ups". After this whale passed without paying the slightest attention to us we felt certain we had solved the whale problem and at the same time had a collection of pictures that would be knockouts.

We had embarked upon this adventure early in the morning before breakfast, and before the girls had crawled out of their sleeping bags. So now we upped anchors, and went back to camp. We had a hurried breakfast, picked up the girls, and started out once more and had another adventure—this time with a "baby" whale, which probably had only recently been born. He had been injured in some way and the poor thing was looking for his mother. He thought our boats might be Mother, and he started hanging around our boats, swimming in circles and on one occasion actually going under the boat and coming up underneath it so that the boat slipped off his back.

We got some hurried pictures but the question arose, where was Mother?

In Mother's eyes this was a poor little destitute offspring in need of attention and protection. To us he was a seventeen-foot whale still capable of smashing a boat with his tail or upsetting us in the shark-infested waters.

A little of that stuff goes a long way.

We got some photographs which fortunately turned out well and then I suggested to Sam once more that we moved off.

Then we ran slap-bang into the middle of a whale circus. I have heard these whale circuses described but no one seems to know exactly what they are. As nearly as we could determine from this one, one bull whale was making passes at two cows who had young calves with them and who didn't want any more romance. The bull whale was swimming in circles, trying to herd the cows into a watery corral. The frightened calves were riding on Mother's backs wherever possible, then jumping completely over Mother and down on the other side. The whales were so preoccupied with what they were doing that they were oblivious to our circling boats.

Here again, however, we had a problem. If we got close enough to get pictures that would be worth anything we were in such dangerous proximity that if one of the whales came up out of the water and rolled over he could roll directly on to one of the boats. If we stayed far enough away with our motors running so that we were out of danger our pictures wouldn't be good.

We started to play it safe, but within a short time were circling the churning waters, trying to get pictures.

Once more after a few brief passes we broke off the engagement, convinced that we had pictures that would "knock your eye out". I still think I did have, but that particular magazine of cine film was unaccountably lost somewhere in transit. Sam's black-and-white camera, as it subsequently turned out, was going through the motions of taking pictures without doing any good, and that was that.

However, Joe Gandara got some very good coloured cine films and fortunately Pat Emery, who is in my opinion one of the best outdoor photographers I have ever encountered, who has made a careful study of photography, who is cool as a cucumber in an emergency, who manages to think of exposure, film speed and all the rest of it at the time when it counts, got some of the most wonderful motion pictures of a whale circus I have ever seen.

Also, as it turned out, Jean, who has become a recent shutter-bug convert, secured some very good colour shots. Sam's camera unfortunately was the black-and-white mainstay of the expedition at that point.

10

COMBING A VIRGIN BEACH

WHILE we had been eager to hunt whales with cameras, we were all equally eager to get down to Emery's "virgin" beach. We made one attempt on a rather windy morning, but soon the wind blew up such a sea that I refused to go all the way and we detoured to shore and then shortly afterwards went back to camp. The wind was blowing hard and the lagoon was a mass of whitecaps. Our boats were heavily loaded with personnel and the Tote Gote and its trailer. We were out there all alone in turbulent waters and I saw no reason to take chances.

The next day the wind had gone down and we loaded the boats and started across. It turned out to be a delightful day and we were able to make a rather uneventful run to the south end of the island where we pulled one of the boats up above the high-tide line just in case the weather should change. We anchored the other boat, Emery set up the Tote Gote and trailer and we started combing the beach.

Murl could put two people in the trailer and transport them, so he started out with people in pairs, dropping one off after about a mile, then dropping the other off, then returning for two more. Gandara elected to stay on the beach photographing whales.

The trouble with this somewhat complicated method of transportation was that it became apparent Emery couldn't possibly explore more than the first three or four miles of the beach and then get everyone back to the boats in time to return to camp before dark.

At the time this didn't seem to be too serious. As always happens on trips of this sort, we were looking forward to future days and were making plans as though we had all the time in the world.

I have seldom enjoyed anything as much as combing the

section of beach that had been assigned to me. I found glass balls from the Oriental fish nets; I found driftage of all sorts, wood which had evidently come from China or Japan which still had Oriental characters burnt into the wood. I found an old mooring which had evidently floated round for many years before coming to a final resting place. I found all sorts of bottles, an Oriental shoe which probably hadn't drifted all the way from Japan, although it was of a type not used in this country. It might have gone overboard from a Japanese fishing boat.

There were all sorts of burned out electric-light bulbs of different descriptions, including many discarded radio valves. There was a broken life ring of the type carried on the decks of steamers to be used in the event of sudden emergencies. And to cap the climax there was even an old toilet seat deposited on one of the sandhills.

Emery himself had little time for beachcombing. He was running a Tote Gote taxi. But he was tremendously pleased with the performance of the Tote Gote and trailer, and we were planning to come back, make an overnight camp and Emery was going to explore the length and breadth of the beach.

So we went back to our camp on the island filled with many plans and lots of good intentions. However, the next day the weather turned bad again and we decided to go up the lagoon on the sheltered side and explore one of the other islands.

All in all it was a period of wonderful activity. The excitement of hunting whales, of exploring new territory and the thrill of anticipation, looking forward to each new day as ushering in a new adventure. There is nothing that can quite take the place of an experience such as this; a congenial group taking each new adventure as it came.

It soon became apparent, however, that we were pretty much chained down simply by the problem of supplies. We needed to replenish our drinking-water cans every two or three days and we couldn't carry enough petrol in our boats to keep us supplied for more than a couple of days at a time since the distances in the lagoon were so great and since the boats were fed from portable pressure tanks and we only had so many of these tanks.

So whether we wanted to or not, it became necessary to make rather frequent trips over the twenty-odd miles of lagoon to the place where we had left our cars, then drive over the submerged salt pans to the salt works where we could get petrol and drinking water. Suddenly, and before we realized it, time was creeping up on us and we still had many things to do. But I knew that I simply had to get in touch with my office by telephone and find out just how much time I had left.

I was hoping I could have another four or five days, but it was essential to find out what was going on. So after we went back to camp we decided to get supplies the next day and I could check up by using the ship-to-shore telephone at the salt works.

Murl Emery is, at heart, an explorer. Someone had told him that if a person was careful in picking channels it was quite possible to take a small boat from Scammon's Lagoon through to Guerrero Negro, by an inside channel that was supposed to connect the two lagoons at high tide. Emery wanted to try it.

In the meantime Peggy was back at the ranch collecting scripts, trying to stall off persons who had to see me "right away" and, I knew, trying to cope with all the emergencies, urgencies and crises which always come up from day to day.

I had told her to line up the different charter aircraft companies so that when I telephoned, if it should appear I was needed, she could have a plane on its way within a matter of minutes.

Emery came up with quite an idea. He would take Jean, Anita, Sam and myself to the mainland with our sleeping bags and all the camp goods that could be crowded into the two boats, then he would return to the island and pack up the rest of the camp. He could pilot one boat; Pat could pilot the other. They could take Joe Gandara with them and start out in time to find the channel between Scammon's Lagoon and the Black Warrior Lagoon.

We could go into the salt works, I could telephone the office, and, if necessary, charter a plane and fly in that afternoon and be back the next morning. Murl, Joe and Pat would cross over into the Black Warrior and the next morning around eleven o'clock would be at a designated spot on Black Warrior Lagoon. We could set up a camp there which would be closer to our base of supplies, to drinking water and petrol, and we could make headquarters there for a day or two. By that time he would have fully charted the channel between the two lagoons and we could go back and forth at will.

By moving camp while I was flying back and forth, we wouldn't lose any time from whale hunting and all I would lose would be a night's sleep. It sounded a good idea.

Murl thought he *might* get through to the other lagoon in one day, but he didn't want to take any chances on the tide. He wanted to ride one tide in an unhurried exploration and feel free to camp that night and await the corresponding high tide the next day.

So early in the morning we started breaking camp, and Jean, Anita, Sam and I were put ashore on schedule; which, it must be remembered, was a distance of some twenty or twenty-five miles which we negotiated in heavily laden boats. Then we hurriedly unloaded the stuff and threw it into the cars. Murl and Pat Emery, each at the helm of a boat and fighting to catch the tide, accelerated full throttle and went hightailing out of there filled with enthusiasm and with a great waving of hats.

The four of us drove across the submerged salt pans, feeling our way carefully, trying to avoid any possible soft spots, and arrived at the salt works.

We got a call through to Peggy at the ranch without much difficulty and, sure enough, scripts had piled up, the telephone was ringing, Peggy was stalling everyone as best she could, telling them that I was "expected momentarily". She told me I would simply have to come in to go over some of the television scripts and proofs and handle some of the more urgent matters that had arisen during my absence.

She had a list of all the available charter planes and would have one on its way within a matter of minutes. It would only be necessary for me to call her again to get a confirmation.

So we waited half an hour and called her, only to learn that one of the pilots was down with Asian flu, another plane which should have been available was in the shop, a third one had been chartered, a fourth which had been leased had been taken on a priority by the owner, and she hadn't found any plane that could make the trip. In the meantime she had phoned Hollywood that I would be going over scripts that night and had made several commitments.

So then, from the salt works at Guerrero Negro, I started calling airlines and so the afternoon wore on.

It had been decided that Sam would accompany me to San Diego while Jean and Anita would stay at the salt works. Peggy had arranged to bring a part of the secretarial staff at the ranch and Sam's wife down to San Diego. They were to leave that afternoon, get suites at the hotel, have typewriters all set up in readiness to start work the minute we arrived.

One of the aviation companies told me it had finally located a Mexican flyer in Tijuana who was available and was on his way. He had in fact left half an hour earlier. I was advised that I could expect him to arrive at about two-thirty. So we went out and waited.

By three o'clock I began to feel nervous. By three-fifteen I was consulting my watch every few minutes. By three-thirty I was desperate. By three-forty-five I had given him up and was wondering what to do next. Then at four o'clock there was the roar of a motor and a plane swept over the salt works, made a steep bank and circled into the landing field.

Jean, Anita, Sam and I were out there in a matter of minutes and we met Francisco Munoz, a veteran Mexican pilot with whom we were destined to become much better acquainted in the weeks that followed.

Since it got dark a little after five o'clock I felt certain that Munoz would insist on waiting overnight, so I asked him hopelessly, and simply as a matter of routine, if he could get us to Tijuana that night.

Munoz is a short, stocky, volatile individual packed with energy and optimism.

"Oh, seguro! Sure, sure, sure! Most certainly. Get in, get in!"

So Sam and I crawled into the plane.

Jean insisted I should take an overcoat. The radio had said there was an intensely cold spell gripping Southern California. I vetoed the suggestion. The plane would be warm and after we landed at Tijuana it would be only a short ride to San Diego.

There wasn't time for any protracted argument. Munoz literally hurled the plane down the runway and up into the air and we were off.

After we had become fairly well settled I looked at my watch, did some hasty mental arithmetic and said, "How are you going to get to Tijuana by dark?"

"Oh, not by dark," he said. "But tonight, sure."

"How long?" I asked.

"Two hours and seventeen minutes from now," he said optimistically.

I glanced at my watch and did mental arithmetic again. That was going to get us in at about six-thirty-five. It would have been dark for at least an hour and we would have been flying in a single-motored plane over rugged terrain where emergency landing fields are virtually nil.

However, we were in the air and there was nothing to do but settle back, make myself comfortable and enjoy the flight.

Munoz had the plane in a steep climb and it wasn't long before we were skimming along at about 10,000 feet. At that elevation the chill was penetrating.

I asked him about the heater.

Munoz took both hands off the wheel to make a characteristic gesture.

"Is broken," he said.

So I settled back to a teeth-chattering journey through the late afternoon sunlight, early dusk and then Stygian darkness, cussing myself for not having taken the overcoat.

I don't know yet why the tail assembly of that plane didn't crystallize and drop off. I was shivering so much the entire back of the plane must have been shaking.

We finally saw the lights of Ensenada and, shortly after that, Tijuana. A little before eight-thirty Sam and I came walking into the U. S. Grand Hotel in San Diego, probably two of the most disreputable-looking characters who had ever entered the place; clad in clothes which had been splashed with salt spray, soaked with rain water, spotted with oil and, I am ashamed to confess, probably with syrup from pancakes and an occasional drip of bacon grease.

We hadn't shaved since we had left the ranch. I had needed a haircut when I left but hadn't had time to get one during the holiday season, and it is safe to say that I was even more in need of a haircut by the time I pushed my way up to the desk and encountered the steely eyes of the clerk.

However, the girls had already arranged for suites of rooms, had set up their typewriters and were ready for work, and as soon as the hotel employees identified us they were cordiality itself.

I took the elevator to the room the girls had fixed up as an office and was dismayed to see the size of the pile of stuff that was stacked up.

I didn't dare leave the room. I couldn't take time to shave or even clean up. There was a pile of scripts to be gone over. I sent the rest of the party out to dinner, had a thick steak sent up to the room and sat there pouring words into my faithful dictating machine between bites of steak. My secretaries came back after dinner, took the records into another suite and started typing.

That night was something of a nightmare. Files of urgent correspondence were stacked up, scripts were piled one on top of the other. It was about three o'clock in the morning when I finally got into a hot bath and got the whiskers off my face.

I was up by daylight and the girls drove us down to the border where we were to meet Munoz. There had been no time for a haircut. I kept dictating all the way in the car.

Munoz met us right on schedule. We crossed the border, adjusted the seat belts in his plane and by noon we were approaching Guerrero Negro.

One of the reasons we had been in such a hurry was to time things so that by the time the Emerys and Joe Gandara arrived at the new camp site we would be there to meet them.

The afternoon before, while we had been waiting for the plane, we had driven one of the jeeps to the new camp site and left it there with the key in the ignition and a note telling them we were taking a plane and suggesting that if they arrived before we did they could drive up to the salt works.

So we suggested to Munoz as we approached Guerrero Negro that he swing round by the new camp site and we could see whether the boats were there and the car was gone, or whether the boats were there and the new camp had been set up.

As we circled the place it became apparent that the car was just where we had left it the afternoon before, the boats were not there, and there was no sign of the boats in Guerrero Negro Lagoon.

So we asked Munoz to circle the lagoon, then fly over the

connecting channels between Scammon's Lagoon and Guerrero Negro and then, just to give us a good view of things, we could fly over the island beach and give it a good once-over.

We soon located the boats. They were out in the vast series of sandy mud flats separating the two lagoons. From the air these sandy mud flats seemed to be quite extensive.

We could only surmise that there had been a dispute over the location of the channel because Pat had gone to one side of an island and was hard aground, and Emery had gone to the other side and was hard aground. They were both out of the boats and wading in an attempt to find a channel.

From the air it seemed absurdly easy to differentiate between the channels which wound among the flats of sand and mud, but we knew that from down on the water where the boats were located it was a virtual impossibility to tell where the channels were.

One thing was certain: the boats were never going to get to the Guerrero Negro Lagoon early that afternoon, and from my observations I felt they couldn't make it at all.

However, we dipped low over the boats and wagged our wings reassuringly, waved encouragement, and then flew out over Scammon's Lagoon to look at the whales and then over the virgin beach.

A whale seen from the air presents a very remarkable spectacle. It looks like a submarine lying just below the surface of the water, or coming up to spout a cloud of white vapour. Mother whales lay just below the surface of the water while the baby whales reposed just above them or perhaps just a little to one side.

As we flew over the lagoon great flocks of geese arose below us and we were looking at the whales through white clouds of wild fowl. Then we made a swing over the virgin beach and I am ashamed to say that I missed it entirely. I became very much disappointed in what I saw. As it turned out, I was looking far too close to the shoreline and wasn't looking back far enough in the low sandhills where the wreckage had been deposited during periods of storm and high tide. On later air trips I corrected this mistake, but at the time I derived an erroneous impression. All I can say by way of explanation is that it takes quite a bit of practice to appraise a beach from a speeding aeroplane.

If the aircraft is too high, the objects one wishes to observe are flattened out to nothing. If one flies too low, the skimming sand whizzes by faster than the eye can appraise it.

Anyhow, I muffed it. I came to the conclusion that while this beach was fascinating, the rest of the unexplored sandy stretch wasn't greatly different from the four miles we had already explored. In the light of subsequent developments my face was destined to become very red indeed.

On the way back we made one more survey of the channels and even allowing for the fact that the tide was a long way from full, I still felt that the boats couldn't make it.

Munoz said that on his way back to Tijuana he could drop a message which the boatmen would receive. So we landed at the salt works, transported ourselves to a building which the management had very generously placed at our disposal, and I wrote a note to the boats telling them to go back to the first camp on Scammon's Lagoon.

Gandara had one favourite story which he told from time to time about the stranger asking the native how to get to the post office. The man had said, "Well, let's see. You go two blocks straight ahead, then turn to the left three blocks . . . no, that road's torn up. I tell you what you'd better do. You'd better go to the left for four blocks, then turn to the right for two blocks . . . no, that road hasn't been cut through." The man paused and thought for a moment, then slowly shook his head. "I'm sorry," he said. "You can't get to the post office from here."

So I wrote a note in which I referred to the Emerys as "land-lubbers" which I knew would raise their blood pressure sufficiently to make up for any lack of hot coffee, told them they couldn't get to the post office from there, and to come home. Sam took the note to Munoz to deliver, but while he was waiting for Munoz to take off, found one of the local residents who scoffed at the idea that the Emerys couldn't get through. They simply had blundered on to the wrong channel. There was, he explained, one of the men at the salt works who knew every foot of the lagoon and could get them through on the evening tide without the slightest question of doubt. He would arrange to have that man leave at once in a boat, hunt up the stranded

78

boatmen, show them the right channel, and they would be in shortly after dark.

So Sam, prompted by optimism, tore up my note and hurriedly scribbled another note reading, "Stay where you are. A professional pilot is on his way to guide you landlubbers to safety. Wait for him."

Munoz took off with a roar of the engine and with rare skill managed to drop the note almost exactly into Emery's upthrust hands; quite a feat when one considers wind and velocity.

Emery waved his acknowledgment, Munoz dipped his wings and headed back for Tijuana.

The pilot duly went out and found that the high tide was unusually low, that the channel he had expected to use couldn't be navigated, and so turned back.

We waited all night for the Emerys to join us, rolling into our sleeping bags when it became apparent they had missed the afternoon high tide and couldn't possibly arrive until the next day.

The next day we talked with the man who had taken the boat down in an attempt to reach the channel and he thought that it was impossible for the boats to make the grade with tides such as we were having at the moment. But in any event the high, high-tide came late at night; the high tide during the afternoon was not high enough to get the boats through, even with the aid of pushing and dragging.

It happened that the executive aeroplane used by the salt works was on the strip at that moment and Mr McClaughry suggested that if we wanted to make another survey of the situation the pilot would be glad to take us out over the lagoon.

By this time we were getting somewhat worried. The party had been out for two nights and along the water the nights can become exceedingly damp. It was apparent that the boats had been very heavily loaded and were not only drawing a lot of water but that it would have been difficult for the boatmen to unpack sleeping bags and camp stuff. So we got in the plane and made a swing out over the stranded boats.

We found that the two Emerys had waded ashore, leaving Gandara in the boats and it was a rather bedraggled-looking Gandara who waved at us as we went overhead.

So we made a circle and came on the two Emerys far ahead of

79

the boats, exploring the channels at low tide. From the distance which separated them from the boats they must have been walking since daylight. This time I scribbled a note giving them the figures of tide elevation for that particular point and advised them, "You can't get to the post office from here. Go back to the first camp at Scammon's Lagoon and we will meet you there."

We flew low over the Emerys to drop the note and as they saw the plane gliding down towards them until it was only a few feet off the ground, Pat Emery, in a joking gesture, dropped to his knees and elevated his hands as though to push the plane back into the air. We dropped a note and then circled and came back over them to make sure they had it. Later on I assured Pat Emery I had photographed him while he was down on his knees with arms upraised, thanking a merciful heaven for having sent us to the rescue and that this photograph, properly captioned, would be released to the Press on our return. Pat couldn't tell from my dead-pan expression whether I was ribbing him or not. For a while, since I insisted Sam and I be treated as rescuing heroes and kept speculating on whether we would receive medals, I had him worried.

The company pilot, "Mike" (Miguel Angel Marquez), a remarkably skilful pilot, had dropped the note within only a few feet of the Emerys and they waved their hands and the note, signifying that they had it and were in accord with my suggestion.

So we once more circled over the boats to wave reassuringly to Gandara. We noticed that each boat was equipped with a long mast-like pole to the top of which had been tied a red bandana. We found out afterwards that this was so that they wouldn't lose each other in the twisting channels as they went through the sandhills, and would enable the one boat to follow the other. (At the time I was somewhat concerned lest it was a signal of distress.)

Everyone seemed in good health so we returned to the landing strip and Jean, Anita, Sam and I loaded up the cars and again drove back over the submerged salt pans to the place where we had made our first camp.

We felt that the boatmen would have a good thirty miles of travel but could make it in less than two hours. So, with the aid of binoculars, we started looking for them. It wasn't until nearly

Gold-bearing granite country, home of the bighorn sheep

A "baby" whale at close range

In dangerous proximity

The drifting sand dunes on the Virgin Beach

Bahia de Los Angeles

Jean's picture of
a jumping whale

Perhaps the only
photograph ever
taken of a
whale feeding in
Scammon's Lagoon

three o'clock in the afternoon, however, that we first sighted them limping in.

As they came close to the landing we saw that the boats were really too heavily loaded and were, as a result, drawing much more water than they should have. In fact, they even ran aground in negotiating the channel to the camp site.

We found out afterwards that we only knew a small part of it. The boats had been so loaded that it had been hard to manipulate the steering gear by means of the rope which stretched from the steering wheels in front to the engines behind. Because there were two engines on each boat, the rope was pulling on a short leverage and the heavy load put considerable strain on the ropes. They had given way time after time in attempting to swing the heavily loaded boats round short turns. The boatmen had spliced and tied until they had no more slack left for repairs.

I suggested to Emery that maybe we could go back down to the south end of the island and explore the "virgin beach" by Tote Gote. I have never seen people who were less enthusiastic about starting back down Scammon's Lagoon with heavily loaded boats.

It turned out they had had a most uncomfortable night. They hadn't been able to get ashore for fear of having the boats left high and dry when the tide changed. They had therefore tried to sleep in the boats and the damp chill had penetrated their bones. They had spent two cramped nights in the channel and they were not keen about starting out on another thirty-five-mile trip.

Yet if we were going to make a camp on the south end of the island we would have to start at once with the two loaded boats, split up the camp and wait until the next day to make another trip with the second boatload. The boats were out of petrol and would have to be refilled from our reserve supplies, and it would probably take us all the next day to get established on the island. Since it looked as though the next day might be windy, the problem of taking heavily loaded boats thirty-five miles through a windblown chop was not too inviting.

"We can't make it this trip," I said. "That beach is going to have to wait."

Murl and Pat exchanged glances. "Let's go home," Pat said. Murl said, "Okay. We've got our whale photographs, most of

81

the stuff we want. We've done a bit of exploring. We have a good five days of rough roads ahead of us, even if we have the best luck in the world. If there should be another rain storm we'll be marooned in mud around Punta Prieta. It looks as though there is another storm coming and our best bet is to try to beat the storm and get past Punta Prieta while the roads are still passable."

So we decided to unload the boats, put them on the trailers, make an overnight camp and leave as early as possible the next morning.

82

TROUBLE

IT was on the trip home that the mechanical gremlins began to catch up with us. Veterans who knew the country and who had seen us embarking with two nineteen-foot boats in tow had shaken their heads glumly and decided that the boats would necessarily be left by the side of the road somewhere and we'd be lucky if we didn't have to leave the cars as well and try to walk out.

The first mechanical casualty was one of the gearshifts. Something connected with the clutch linkage, which I know nothing about (as a mechanic I'm a total loss; I can't tell the front end of a spark plug from a rear differential), crystallized and gave way. We couldn't shift gears and the road was too rough to tow the car.

Emery crawled under the car, took a look, crawled out, got out his tool box, pulled out a long tent spike, tossed it down to Pat and said, "Fix it."

Pat got out a blow-lamp and a hammer. He and Sam improvised a blacksmithing forge. They heated the metal red-hot and shaped it. They took a portable drill and drilled it until the drill broke. Then they took the stub of the broken drill, shaped it with a file and made another drill out of it and continued drilling.

By nine o'clock that night they had the car repaired and it worked. Moreover, it was such a nice job of part construction that after I got the car into a garage when we got home the man looked at it, shook his head and said, "I can't improve on that. It's just as good as the original part."

The next casualty was Emery's trailer hitch. Because he had lots of room in the boat there was a temptation to keep piling things into it until finally the metal in his trailer hitch gave way and there we were with a nineteen-foot boat and a terrific load of material in it and no trailer hitch. We were still four hard days from the border.

The two Emerys and Sam went to work. They rigged up various and sundry expedients, some of which worked for a few miles, some of which worked longer. Then finally they virtually discarded the trailer hitch altogether. They hammered two pieces of wood into the side supports of the pick-up, they wrapped a chain round and round the supports and down to the trailer, then they put on a "comealong" and tightened the whole thing in such a way that the chain became as taut as a violin string.

It held firmly all the way to the border.

It wasn't until after we had returned and had taken stock of the situation that I realized the extent to which we had failed in our objectives.

One magazine of my coloured films had been lost in transit. Where there should have been seven there were only six. An investigation showed this was the most important fifty feet of all my pictures and it will be remembered that Sam's camera had developed a light leak and shutter trouble as well. All his pictures had a slight fogging, and those which were taken towards the light were ruined, and that included the film of the whale which had been within some fifteen feet of our boat.

Murl Emery had set up his Tote Gote and trailer on the south end of the beach he had wanted to explore but had been so courteous that he had first given everybody a preliminary ride. The girls had found so many of the glass balls that they had gone wild and Emery had spent the only day he had on the beach acting virtually as a Tote Gote taxi driver. We had expected to get back for another trip but weather conditions and business exigencies had prevented.

Despite the fact we had been away more than three weeks, that my desk was piled high with emergency matters and all my business associates were hoping that I now had Baja California "out of my system" and would stay at home, I decided we were going back.

My friend, Mahlon Vail, one of the owners of the 96,000-acre cattle ranch which adjoins my property, offered to put all our stuff aboard a big cattle boat which the company uses to ship cattle back and forth from Santa Rosa Island to the mainland.

Don Douglas, who has always been fascinated by Scammon's

Lagoon and the whales, invited me to come in and look at the moving pictures they had taken on the second expedition, an expedition about which I had known nothing. This was the expedition that had used helicopters instead of boats in an attempt to get the heartbeat of the whale. At lunch with Mahlon Vail, Donald Douglas showed us a superb film. The pictures, taken from helicopters, showed the manner in which the whales swam through the water, the way in which they used tails and flippers. Taken from above, the colour demarcation between whale and water was sharply defined and the pictures represented a thoroughly professional job.

Gandara, in the meantime, had gone down to Ensenada, had contacted some of our mutual friends there, had gone to Mexicali, had conferred with the Governor and the executive officers of Baja California and found that there was a widespread interest in our expedition. Several of the prominent business men of Ensenada had become annoyed that all the publicity about Baja California seemed to settle on vice conditions in Tijuana. No one seemed to know anything about the country around Ensenada, about the country to the south, or about the type of solid, substantial citizens who represent the core of Baja California business and industry. These business men pledged themselves to do anything within reason that we wanted. Almost overnight it seemed that everyone wanted to co-operate.

So almost as soon as we returned we were organizing another expedition for Scammon's Lagoon, but it turned out that insurance difficulties in connection with the Vail cattle boat would delay us five or six days, and there was some question whether the boat drew too much water to get across the dangerous bar at the lagoon. For a while we contemplated going by air, then decided to load our equipment and retrace our steps by car.

Gandara reported that his friend in Ensenada, head of one of the big fishing companies with boats scattered from Ensenada to Cedros Island, had sent wireless instructions to the captain of one of his boats requesting him to have the boat tied up at the wharf at Guerrero Negro on Saturday morning, to await our arrival and to put the boat completely at our disposal. All we had to do was to get to Guerrero Negro by Sunday morning.

This time we didn't take trailers. I had bought a Land Rover and we loaded up our cars and made good time over the road. We were at Guerrero Negro on Saturday morning. We loaded our gear on the fishing boat and arranged for a take-off early on Sunday morning.

It seemed that everyone wanted to co-operate. The salt company placed its best pilot at our disposal. This man, Enrique Romero, knows every foot of water in the lagoons and along the coast. The captain of the boat, Fernando Moreno, a veteran, careful, methodical seaman, quietly competent, knew exactly what could be done and what couldn't be done. I never saw him the least excited during the entire trip. I never saw him when he wasn't watchful, alert and completely on the job.

He was accompanied by his son, Fernando, and a Mexican seaman, Augustin Ortiz, whom we nicknamed "Mucho Ojo", because of his enthusiasm for the venture, the manner in which he would stand watch for whales and his uncanny ability to see everything everywhere. That man had the most wonderful pair of eyes. He could see a whale surface, and then from the top of the mast could tell which direction under water he was going and follow him.

We took along Emery's Tote Gote, and this time we decreed that Emery wasn't going to be courteous to anyone. He had bought that Tote Gote to explore the virgin beach on the island, and, by George, he was going to explore it. He wasn't going to give anyone a ride and he was going to comb every one of those miles of virgin beach without trying to be generous.

The trip by water from Guerrero Negro to Scammon's Lagoon is quite an adventure in itself. One must follow a rather tricky channel out of Guerrero Negro until reaching the open sea, then turn abruptly and, after some twenty miles of water which can be very rough indeed, cross inside a bar in a channel that is marked only by natural landmarks and can be located only by good seamanship. The boat has to go within a stone's throw of raging, roaring breakers that pile up into huge waves, dash across shoals with the speed of an express train and then curl over in crashing spray on the shallows. To make any miscalculation and be caught in those shallows is certain disaster.

However, we had a delightful trip, and entering the lagoon came to anchor at the south end of the island Emery wanted to explore. We dropped the anchor in deep water within a hundred yards of the shore and started unloading.

Because we had brought no trailers on this trip I had suggested to Sam that we should keep our supplies at a minimum. Quite naturally I had been pouring words into a dictating machine while Sam and Emery had been packing. I didn't realize until we arrived and started unpacking the extent to which they had followed my instructions and what they meant by a minimum.

We had one tent as a place in which to eat and store camera equipment in case of inclement weather. We had a couple of "tarps" and that was all our shelter. But we made a hurried camp and then went to work. Emery started out on his Tote Gote and Gandara and I climbed up to the upper pilothouse on the boat.

It had been Gandara's theory that much of our photographic trouble had been because we were too close to the water. He felt that if we could get more elevation and whales could come close to us we could get some good pictures.

I subscribed to this theory, but after seeing the pictures taken by the Douglas expedition from helicopters I felt that the mast of a boat might not be high enough unless we could get the whales to come very close to the boat.

There was one type of picture which we wanted to get as close to the water as possible, and for that reason Emery had brought along his rubber raft and we had brought an outboard motor. These pictures were pictures of whales jumping and standing on their tails. I don't know how a whale stands on his tail, but he does it. Apparently he only does it when he wants to look around, and he prefers to do it during calm weather.

On our previous trip, while we were camped on the island, we would look out, usually in the early morning, and, at a distance of a mile or so, see whales come up out of the water to stand on their tails. By using binoculars and telescopes we could get a pretty good idea of the procedure. The whale would thrust his head out of the water for ten or twelve feet, then very slowly, and presumably balanced on his tail, thrust up another ten feet or so of his body until he would apparently be standing some twenty feet above the water. He would stand there for what seemed to be four or five seconds, then would slowly submerge, and at such times there would be no splash.

On the other hand we had seen whales coming up out of the water at great speed, extending their flippers and then lunging downward with a splash that sent water up in the air for what seemed to be a height of thirty or forty feet.

Our friend, Justo, the turtle hunter, told us that at such times the whales were trying to protect their young and were frightening away sharks. Whether his idea was true or not it certainly seemed that these were aggressive tactics on the part of whales and were resorted to for some very definite reason.

There was still a third manoeuvre which whales made: they would apparently travel at top speed, then come up straight out of the water, not standing on their tails; then they would take a good look round and lunge forward.

We didn't have a picture showing these activities and the question of whether whales fed or not while they were in southern waters was still a matter of debate. We had seen whales engaged in manoeuvres which we thought were associated with feeding, but we couldn't be sure.

At times when the tides would change we would see whales congregating in the eddies where the tides meet. They would swim round in circles and give every appearance of feeding, but we couldn't see under the water and all we could see were occasional fins, parts of tails or a brief glimpse of a back and the dipping circle where whales came up, spouted and went down again. All the time we were learning more and more about whales.

Enrique was still scarred from an experience he had had only a few days previously. He had taken two men out to paint a buoy, one of the big steel channel markers anchored beside the channel and used to guide ships into Guerrero Negro. Enrique was sitting in the boat. The other two men, by means of ropes, had climbed to the top of the buoy. Suddenly two whales appeared close by. One of them thrust his head up in order to take a good look, then both of them made for the boat.

Enrique stood his ground.

One of the whales punched the boat with his nose, then the other one came up and nuzzled it. That was too much for Enrique. He grabbed a rope and scampered up the side of the buoy. He had not been particularly choosy about the method of ascent. He just wanted to get up there fast. He still had evidences of the deep scratches on his legs where he had scraped them in his climb.

The two whales hung around and held the men up on that buoy for nearly an hour. They seemed to enjoy having their quarry treed. From time to time they would stand up on their tails in the water to look at the men from a level stance, then they would go down and swim round the buoy, then they would come up and nuzzle the boat. Then they would swim off and, like cats playing with a mouse, pretend to be disinterested, only suddenly to return.

Enrique had never had anything like that happen before in the eleven years he had been among the lagoons. It was his opinion that whales were absolutely and completely unpredictable, that each whale was a law unto himself and that any whale could attack any boat at any time, although he felt certain the majority of whales were inclined to be peaceful.

Following my instructions, Peggy on her return had ordered every book she could find on whales, and in the brief reading I had done after I returned I found that the authorities seemed to agree that the grey whale was quite unpredictable, that during the mating season the bulls were very apt to charge a boat, that quite frequently baby whales would become confused and think a boat was Mother and would start circling. At such times the real mother would very probably want the boat out of the way and would stage tactics designed to accomplish that purpose.

The truth of the matter was that no one knew very much about grey whales because, from the time the commercial whalers abandoned Scammon's Lagoon until a few short years ago, the grey whale had been presumed to be virtually extinct. Then it had started returning in numbers to Scammon's Lagoon. However, apart from the expeditions by the Scripps Institution of Oceanography and by Don Douglas, little was known about them.

Don Douglas certainly had a wholesome respect for whales. Having been in that boat and experienced the impact of a whale's tail, then having watched the whale turn and charge, Douglas didn't have to read about whales in books. He knew about them. He had been there. No one could tell him a whale wouldn't attack. He had been on the receiving end.

It followed therefore that we realized we had been pretty lucky on our first expedition not to have had a physical encounter with an angry whale and therefore we made certain rules for our safety. One, we wouldn't go out in any of the small boats without lifebelts and without having the big boat standing by for rescue in case of attack. Two, we wouldn't go out in the rubber raft at all unless a rescue boat was standing by. Three, we wouldn't get out in the whale channels without having our lifebelts on and securely fastened.

So far as the big boat was concerned, despite the fact that whales had been known to attack the whaling ships, we felt we were perfectly safe.

So having made these rules, and since Emery was more interested in beachcombing than in whales at that time, and while some of the others were making camp, and Emery was starting up the beach on his Tote Gote to satisfy the burning curiosity which had been eating him for some three years, Gandara and I took our stations on the rocking, heaving platform of the fishing boat, cocked our shutters and settled down to wait.

Here again we found that the whales had a couple of trumps we knew nothing about.

It takes a rather long focal-length lens to get an image of a whale that is big enough to enlarge properly. As before mentioned, a long focal-length lens requires a firm, steady foundation.

Just in order to show us that getting whale photographs wasn't a simple matter, windstorms which kept the boat rocking and swaying came up, and from our platform high above the deck the rocking was so accentuated that it was impossible to find a firm camera platform.

We compensated for this as far as possible by speeding up our shutters, but while we were seated waiting for whales to show up we gradually accustomed ourselves to the rolling and pitching of the boat. When a whale showed up we jumped to our feet, but it always took us several seconds to get our balance and brace ourselves against the rail or hang on to a rope in such a way that we could sight our cameras.

Several times I jumped to my feet, elevated my camera, and just as I was snapping the shutter the motion of the boat threw me off balance so that my picture turned out to be a picture of the rail of the boat or the ocean directly below the boat or a good cross-section of sky.

Moreover, when it came to jumping whales, the whale knew when he was going to jump. No one else did. It turned out that the action is much faster than one would believe, and from the time a whale starts to jump until he is back in the water consumes only a very small amount of time. Getting a camera into action, pointed in the right direction and held steady enough to give a sharp image is quite a problem.

We saw lots of whales. We saw lots of jumping whales. We saw whales that were close by. We saw whales that were in the distance. Strangely enough, however, we saw very few whales standing on their tails on this trip and those that we saw were some distance away.

Once, when we left camp and took the boat out a mile or so away in order to explore a new channel, we looked back and saw a whale come up just where the boat had been and stand on his tail, looking at Emery. All we could do was to watch through powerful binoculars.

Emery, who had been exploring the beach on his Tote Gote, had just returned and didn't have a camera available. We could see him watch the whale and the whale watch Emery. It seemed that the whale was a good twenty feet out of the water and Emery said he felt the whale was standing at least that high.

As above mentioned, whales are utterly unpredictable. However, we did have some luck. Whales began to get accustomed to the boat. They would move by the anchored boat without paying any attention to it after we had been anchored there for a couple of days.

As whales began to take the boat for granted it was only natural that we began to take the whales for granted. And this lulled us into a false sense of security, which is about the only way I can account for the situation in which we subsequently found ourselves.

On one occasion Gandara and I saw that two whales were going to swim between the boat and the shore. We alerted the party on shore and they all ran out with cameras.

It was an awe-inspiring sight to see these two huge mammals

swimming calmly and complacently between Emery, who had waded out up to his knees in order to take a picture from the shore, and Gandara and I, who were standing on the upper deck of the anchored boat, shooting down.

I hoped Gandara's coloured pictures were good. I was shooting black and white and the lead whale submerged just as I was about to take the picture. I had to swing the camera to take a picture of the second whale.

Looking down from his height, the black sides of the whale and the blue of the water mingled together so that the picture contains little suggestion of the thrill of excitement that accompanied the passing of the whales.

On shore, Sam got a very good picture showing the whales passing close to the boat. But, here again, he was handicapped by the fact that only some twelve or eighteen inches of the whale is out of water when he comes up to blow while he is swimming along. And on black-and-white film the result is singularly unimpressive.

Enrique, Sam and I decided to try out the rubber raft, so we got it inflated and then found that in shipment the transom to which the outboard motor was attached had split in two. Emery dragged in a piece of driftwood and by use of a hand axe, ingenuity and the co-operation of the Mexican crew of the boat, manufactured a rough-and-ready transom which seemed to do the job.

So that afternoon, as soon as the new transom had been put in place and the motor attached, Enrique and Sam wanted to try it out and I decided to go along just to see how the raft would work with a full load. Sam picked up his camera and on that trip I was literally wearing my cameras so, as it happened, we had them with us, but nothing was farther from our minds than going out into whale territory or trying to take photographs. We didn't even have our lifebelts. I certainly thought we were going to be cruising between the shore and the anchored boat and I doubt if anyone else had any different ideas.

The bay was calm. The sun was shining and, as it turned out, the motor was purring gently, smoothly propelling the raft at a speed which seemed to me about five or six miles an hour. Sam was adjusting the engine so in place of cruising in a circle we kept the rubber raft pointed straight in order to give him a better chance to make the adjustment.

Because we were all concentrating on the motor and the raft, we got farther from shore and farther from the boat than we had intended. Then suddenly we saw a great commotion in the water about half a mile away. There were huge splashes, great surging black bodies seething and writhing in the water. Clouds of spray were flung up to heights that seemed to be twenty or thirty feet. Occasionally veritable geysers of water would seem to erupt.

Promptly we forgot all about our rules, about the fact that we had no lifebelts, no supporting boat, absolutely no safety factor.

We simply wanted to get closer to have a look—and go closer we did.

The party on shore were watching us with binoculars, waiting for us to turn back, ready to heave up the anchor on the fishing boat and start after us if we got into trouble. They realized what we didn't take into account in our excitement. If the whales sensed our presence and resented it, we were completely helpless in that rubber raft. It wouldn't have taken a charge by a whale to have upset us—just a nudge with a nose or a slap with a tail and we would have been struggling in the water, a tempting meal for any shark that was hanging round.

If, on the other hand, the whales didn't resent us or were completely oblivious of our presence, if the vortex of activity should shift our way no rubber raft could hope to last in the midst of a maelstrom such as that; and certainly no 170 lb. individual could survive having a 30-ton whale drop down on him from a height of ten or fifteen feet.

As we afterwards discovered, the people on shore never realized we were trying to get really close to such dangerous activity as that. They knew that it would be some fifteen minutes before the men on the big boat could raise its anchor, get the engines started and reach us, and they assumed we were going to turn back to safety.

Aboard the raft we had long since quit thinking about rules or the safety factor. We couldn't understand what was causing all this surging and splashing, and human curiosity being what it is, and the zeal of the hunter being what it is, we simply felt we had to get closer so that we could see what was happening. By the time we got close enough to see the whole mêlée swung in our direction and approached us at a bewildering speed. Then the activity veered slightly to one side and again remained stationary.

Sam, so engrossed in hunting that nothing else mattered, shut off the engine and Enrique held the boat in position by using the rubber paddle.

By that time we were close enough to see what it was all about and the minute I found out what it was I became acutely aware of our position.

Three bull whales and an acquiescent, amorous female of the species were engaged in a series of manoeuvres which apparently included a battle among the bulls and coy encouragement on the part of the cow.

I started taking pictures because there was nothing else to do but I felt my enthusiasm draining out of my toes. We couldn't start the engine in time to do any good. Even if we had the engine running at full speed we couldn't get that raft away from there in time to do any good. The rapidity with which the whale vortex of activity had shifted towards us had been sufficient proof of that.

The whales were so intent upon what they were doing they paid absolutely no attention to us, and in that there was an element of danger because if they came only a few feet closer we were likely to be squeezed to a pulp. If, on the other hand, one of the whales resented our being there the situation was just as bad.

By this time it became very apparent even to a casual observer that the whales were in that condition which can best be described as being "emotionally aroused".

Enrique, I think, was as excited as we were and kept protesting that this was a phase of whale activity which had never before been witnessed, either by him or by anyone he knew, and Enrique had spent eleven years in the lagoons.

Apparently one of the male whales would get in complete readiness to consummate his conquest of the acquiescent cow, when another bull, getting under him and charging with all his might, would throw the first bull out of the way and up into the air. The displaced bull, quite apparently all in readiness for what was to have been an amorous interlude, found himself pushed high into the air and rolled over on his back. He would therefore return in angry indignation to find that the bull who had supplanted him was in turn being shouldered out by a third bull.

As to whether any of the huge mammals were successful in their conquest is still an open question. These things were happening too fast for anyone to keep track of what was going on. There was a great splashing. Great clouds of spray and intertwined whale bodies would engage in water-thrashing activities; then one would shoot up into the air and come down with a terrific splash.

The agitation of the water threw our rubber raft into violent motion. It was almost impossible to hold a camera steady. However, Sam got one memorable picture showing a displaced bull while being rolled over on his back at a most inconvenient time —for the whale. This picture was sharp enough to stand enlargement, despite the way in which the raft was being thrown about by the waves resulting from the violent activity.

I was whirring away with my moving picture camera and, as it turned out, have some forty feet of coloured film showing an activity which may never before have been photographed.

Those who were watching us from the shore with binoculars saw that we were so close to what was taking place that they thought we were right in the middle of a maelstrom of whales, of plunging bodies, smashing tails and surging waters. They started shouting frantically to the fishing boat to get the anchor up and get under way. Through the binoculars it seemed that the raft had become disabled.

However, before the boat could get the anchor up the whole surging activity suddenly went into lateral motion again and this time, fortunately, it was away from the rubber raft. The instincts of a hunter being what they are, Sam jerked the starting cord of the engine, attempting to follow; and then suddenly as the engine churned into action we glanced back towards the shore and were surprised to find how small the fishing boat seemed in the distance. Rather sheepishly we exchanged glances as we all three simultaneously thought of the rules we had made.

And then, as suddenly as it had started, the commotion subsided and the water became calm. Our plunging whales had simply disappeared.

I don't know how the others felt but I know my knees were shaking with excitement. I had a hard time getting my voice to work but I pointed to the shore and finally said, "Sam, let's get out of here."

That remark turned the trick. Three rather scared but excited individuals turned the rubber boat and started back to the camp.

On shore some of the party were watching us through binoculars and others were gesticulating wildly for us to hurry back. And back we went.

Despite the fact that I had been frightened at the time and felt even more frightened as we spent what seemed an interminable time in getting the raft to the safety of the shore, I was thrilled with the realization that we had secured photographs which might well be unique.

12

A RACE FOR PLUNDER

WHILE we had been busily engaged in trying to photograph whales, Murl Emery had given his attention to his beloved project of beachcombing. Following my appraisal by aeroplane Murl had convinced me of my mistake. He had shown me enough in an hour on the Tote Gote to make me reverse my opinion and convince me that this beach was a veritable treasure-trove of interesting objects. On our earlier exploration, Peggy had found a bottle with a note sealed in it. This note had been badly damaged because water had seeped into the bottle, just enough moisture to cause condensation and make the note impossible to read. The note was in feminine handwriting and dated ten years earlier. It was written in Spanish, and from the occasional words we could make out and the style of handwriting, it had apparently been written by a young woman who was in desperate need of help. She had put a letter in the bottle and entrusted it to the elements.

It may be mentioned in passing that there were many bottles with notes. Some of them were notes from institutions studying ocean currents, asking the finder to mail the enclosure, together with the date and place where the bottle was found. Some of them were prank notes, obviously inspired by a sense of humour on the part of personnel in the Navy.

Emery had concluded that the part of the beach which was really worth combing was about six to nine miles north of where we were camped. He made one preliminary expedition with his Tote Gote, but didn't have enough petrol to fight his way through the deep sand after the tide came in. He was unable to get as far as he wanted to go and still stay on the safe side; but returned nevertheless with a prize assortment of loot, things which would delight the heart of a beachcomber.

What we didn't know at the time was that we were engaged in one of those peculiar "truth is stranger than fiction" coincidences. On his first trip down to this country, Emery had conceived the idea of getting a stripped-down car over on the virgin beach. Years before Emery had been faced with the necessity of getting a car across the Colorado River. He had stripped the car down to bare essentials and then by using two boats and a lot of ingenuity had managed to get the car across the river. So, when Emery had seen a Mexican with a pick-up that had been stripped down to wheels and engine and not much else, Emery had suggested loading the car on a boat and crossing Black Warrior Lagoon.

The Mexican had told Emery he was crazy, but Emery had expounded his idea at length, telling the Mexican just how he had ferried his car across the Colorado. The Mexican remained firm in his opinion that Emery had polluted a naturally weak mind with too much loco weed, tequila and marijuana. In short, there was no sale.

As we were to learn subsequently, this Mexican, a man named Sande, is a very remarkable individual. Thinking back on our dealings with him, I only wish that we could make him a Secretary of State or a Minister of Finance. Our troubles would be over. We would have a balanced budget, there would be an end of the Cold War and we would be sitting pretty. Sande is a thinker. Sande has an innate ingenuity, and if he had ever taken up chess, would have been a world champion.

Sande's mind started toying with the idea that the crazy gringo had put up to him. The more he thought about it, the more feasible the idea sounded. So Sande looked round until he found a boat of the right size, battered and ancient enough so that it could be obtained at a moderate price. He stripped a truck down to bare essentials. A rather flat petrol tank tilted on its side became the dashboard. A couple of light boards became the seats. There was no such thing as a hood, mudguards or body. The truck consisted of an engine, a petrol tank, a radiator, four wheels and a frame. It was a light pick-up type which had a gear ratio permitting it to go anywhere.

So when there was a low, low tide, Sande parked his boat on the hard sands of the beach at Guerrero Negro and drove the pick-up over the boat. Then he jacked up the pick-up and removed the wheels. He lashed the pick-up firmly to the old battered boat and waited for the tide to come in to see if it would float. The tide came in. The battered old boat did its stuff and Sande had a few inches of freeboard. He found himself in possession of a boat and a truck nicely afloat on the waters of Guerrero Negro.

So then Sande got a skiff and he and his two sons slowly, patiently and laboriously inched their strange load across the water until they came to a place where they could make a landing on the island. They tied up their craft and waited for the waters to subside as the tide went out. Then Sande put on the wheels. Lo and behold, he had the first petrol-powered motor ever to land on a virgin beach.

Now as it happened, within less than two hours of the time that Sande landed his strange assortment on the north end of the beach, Emery was landing his Tote Gote on the south end of the beach, with a determination to explore the beach thoroughly and see what it contained.

It is almost inconceivable that this could happen, but happen it did. It took Sande a little while to get organized, to ferry petrol over and set up a camp. It took Emery a little while to work out a system of carrying spare petrol for his Tote Gote, loading a canteen of water and lunch.

At last, however, Emery's plans were complete. He started from the south end of the beach, determined to go clean to the north end. On that same day, and within a few minutes of the same time, Sande and his two sons started their old jalopy, ran down to the firm sand on the low tide and started south with a determination to see what was on this beach the gringo had told him about two years ago.

Appropriately enough, Sande had christened his skeleton pick-up "Tírame III". (THROW ME AWAY, THE THIRD.)

Emery, going north on his Tote Gote, convinced that he had reached a section of beach where human foot had never trod, looked up and was astounded to see what appeared to be a petrol vehicle bearing down on him from the north.

At the same moment, Sande and his two sons, convinced by this time that they were in a veritable treasure-trove of lumber and shipwrecks, with all the world to themselves, looked up and saw a strange apparition creeping towards them.

99

As the distance shortened and the two vehicles came together, Sande saw, to his amazement, the same bearded gringo who had first proposed his getting a petrol vehicle on the beach two years ago. And Murl Emery saw, to his amazement, the fruition of the idea he had suggested to a Mexican who had at the time dismissed the whole thing as being impractical.

The two men dismounted and proceeded to exchange greetings. Each had the idea that he wanted to be the first to explore the beach, each was somewhat suspicious of the other, each determined to adapt himself to the new situation so that the other didn't win *all* the advantages.

Emery advanced the proposition that, after all, he wasn't interested in lumber. He had only a light Tote Gote and couldn't carry anything. He was interested in exploring and finding what was on the beach, in taking photographs and in getting a few glass balls and other interesting souvenirs. He suggested that his time was very limited. He would only be on the beach for a few days. Sande, on the other hand, had the entire summer ahead of him and could, of course, have all the lumber—and lumber in Baja California is precious.

Emery pointed out that he had companions who were tremendously interested in exploring a virgin beach, but the Tote Gote would only carry one person. His friends had insisted that he should be selfish with the Tote Gote and explore the beach himself. But Emery knew that his companions desperately wanted to see what was on the beach.

So why not capitalize on the situation? Why shouldn't Sande turn his skeleton pick-up, the Tírame III, into a taxicab, come down to our camp, pick us all up and show us what was on the beach so that we could all see it together? This would only delay Sande's operations by one day and there would be money—much money.

Sande was cautious. How much money?

Emery tried to be equally cautious, but by that time it was too late. He had exposed his trump card.

Sande had a considerable knowledge of English which he tried to conceal behind a mask of ignorance. Emery had a fragmentary knowledge of Spanish which he tried to enhance behind a false front of linguistic erudition.

The men sat on the beach and bargained.

At length, Sande made his final proposition. He would come to our camp at one o'clock the next afternoon. He would take us up the beach and back so that we could see it. He would charge us twenty dollars in American money. He wanted a gallon of lubricating oil and five gallons of petrol delivered f.o.b. our camp.

Emery squirmed and twisted, but Sande was obdurate, so Emery made the bargain and returned, still somewhat dazed, to tell us that on this virgin beach which had never been trod by human foot he had hired a taxicab.

The next day we all bundled up against the rigours of a rapid transportation where there would be no windshield, no doors, no mudguards, where we would have to cling to the steel frame of a pick-up by ropes and make improvised seats out of pieces of driftwood. And we waited.

We waited and we waited and we waited. One o'clock came and went. Two o'clock came and went. And then, when there remained only two hours of daylight, Sande showed up.

Emery protested he was late.

Sande shrugged his shoulders and went into voluble Spanish. Gandara wanted to act as interpreter.

Sande didn't want any interpreter. He and Gandara clashed fire right from the start.

Sande had made a bargain. He was entitled to twenty dollars in American money, five gallons of petrol and a gallon of oil. He wanted it.

Emery protested it was too late to do any good.

Sande was indignant. He had made a bargain. Did the gringos want to see the beach or not? There was not much daylight left.

We wanted to see the beach. We bundled up, tied pieces of driftwood on to the frame and started off.

It was a wild ride and a wonderful experience. We had to go about five miles before we came to the place where the beach really got good, and came to our first wreck.

I only wish there had been time really to study these wrecks. Looking at them, one is surprised to find the inherent strength which has been incorporated by the builders in constructing ships. And then, as one sees the wreckage, one is equally surprised at the force of the water which tears down the work that man has done.

Here were old wrecks with oak timbers, reinforced with huge bolts, double hull construction fastened together with steel, and all twisted and battered simply by the force of water. Here were acres of glass balls, miles of intriguing flotsam. It would take many days even to explore the stuff that was there.

As we advanced farther north, however, it became apparent that the reason for Sande being late was that he had been outwitting the gringo with the Tote Gote. He had apparently put in the entire morning and most of the afternoon staking out claims to various interesting bits of wreckage. The entire north half of the beach was staked out with Sande's claims and crisscrossed with tracks from the Tírame III.

Emery noted this circumstantial evidence with an increasingly dour appraisal.

The sun dipped low in the west. A cold wind began to blow in from the ocean. Sande took Emery to one side and expostulated. Emery took me to one side.

"We're late," he said.

"I know we're late."

"It's getting late. It's going to get dark."

"I know that it's late and it's going to get dark."

"Sande tells me that if he is going to show you the rest of the beach up to his camp it will be necessary for him when he returns to bring his two sons with him and spend the night at our camp."

"There isn't any room."

"They will take care of that. They will cling to the truce, in some way. But that's the only way you can see the rest of the island. Otherwise, you'll have to turn back from here, because when Sande gets to his camp he won't have time to drive back to our camp, which is a good fifteen or eighteen miles, and then return to his camp."

Sande stood aloof during all of this argument. He had the trump cards and he knew it.

So it was agreed that we would explore the north end of the island and pick up Sande's sons and they would spend the night at our camp.

We dashed on into the cold dusk, noticing everywhere that

Sande had staked out claims to the most interesting and potentially profitable bits of wreckage.

We came to Sande's camp, and then it became abundantly apparent that this strategy had all been carefully worked out in advance. His sons had their bedrolls all ready and were awaiting our arrival. There was a scene of hurried activity while the sons threw their bedrolls on to the frame, put on stray pieces of driftwood, lashed the whole thing in place and we started back into the teeth of the wind.

That wind became more and more biting. The sun dipped down behind the horizon. The tide was coming in. We had to hurry. Occasionally we went through patches of soft sand where everyone had to get off and push. Then we would get down to the waterline where the wheels would be churning up water.

There was no protection by way of body or by mudguards. Sand and salt water covered my glasses. Sand and salt water covered the exposed side of my face. Sand and salt water got in my ears. Sand and salt water got down my neck. The wind cut like a knife. It got too dark to see anything. All I wanted was a camp fire and warmth.

I realized that we were paying something like a dollar a mile for the experience.

The entire north half of the beach had been staked out by Sande. It was a nice gesture. However, he had apparently left the south half for Emery and his Tote Gote. As it happened, the north half was by far the most desirable, but Sande had camped on the north half and we had camped on the south half. That was the way the cookie crumbled.

So we reached our camp after dark.

The wind began to blow hard and sand began to drift from the big dunes behind the camp, hitting my face so that it stung the skin.

It was a rather bleak and bitter camp.

The captain of the boat suggested to Sande that he and his two sons might want to get out of the wind and so could spend the night in the hold of the boat. The offer was accepted with alacrity.

We suffered through a windy night with fine particles of sand blowing in a veritable sandstorm and covering everything. In the morning, Sande and his two sons emerged from the boat. They had spent a warm night away from the wind, but the boat had been bobbing around quite a bit and one of his sons had been seasick. Sande, however, still kept his poker face. He wanted his twenty dollars. He wanted his gallon of oil. He wanted his five gallons of petrol.

We paid Sande off and he and his two sons started back to camp in their strange vehicle.

We had breakfast and then Emery started out to the north in his Tote Gote. Pretty soon he was back with a wry expression on his face.

Sande had manipulated things in such a way that he had had a good hour and a half start up the beach. He and his two sons were engaged in putting out claim stakes on everything on the *south* half of the beach. Emery had finally caught up with them—at least to a point where he could see them in the distance. Sande and his two sons were stopping the car here and there and running—yes, running—to drive claim stakes into the beach.

Sande had staked the whole beach from north to south. He had completely outsmarted us. He had received twenty dollars and enough petrol and oil to enable him to stay on the job and exploit his claims.

Emery gripped the stem of his pipe in his teeth, filled up a can with an extra supply of petrol, took a canteen of water and a can of beef and said nothing. There was nothing he could say—and he knew it.

He did have one trump card. On the excursion last night he had noted a place where the beach went back for probably a mile and a half into the sand dunes in what had perhaps once been a lagoon. Emery felt certain that the Tote Gote would traverse that, and that the claim-staking Mexicans couldn't get to that section of the beach in their truck.

It turned out Emery was right.

He returned late that night with the Tote Gote literally laden with loot. He had picked up a wooden basket reinforced with woven bamboo strips which had drifted over from China and which had, in all probability, been carried for many miles on the end of a bamboo pole by some coolie transporting night soil to a rice patch. But it was now worn by waves and drifting sand, bleached clean by tropical sunlight.

Emery had, indeed, found a section of virgin beach. Deep tracks in the sand showed that the Tírame III had struggled in vain to get through the sand and had finally been forced to give up. Sande simply couldn't afford to get stuck with the only vehicle on the island, nor could he afford to waste precious petrol in churning his way in low gear through deep sand.

Emery had found a place where there were hundreds of acres strewn with glass balls from the Orient, with bits of interesting flotsam, with glass bottles that the intense sunlight and the passing of many years had burned to a very deep purple. He had also found one glass ball which had become opalescent because of sunlight and salt encrustations. He had found a hand-carved crossbow which had drifted all the way from some tropical island. He had found a torpedo, a wrecked aeroplane of World War I vintage, the helmet of an aviator.

Emery was a happy man, but he had been forced to leave literally thousands of glass balls which intrigued the collector in him, and would have been worth a fortune in the curio stores in the United States. He had been forced to leave dozens of bottles that had been turned, not simply to an amethyst hue one frequently finds in the desert glass, but to an absolutely deep purple by the action of the sunlight. He had encountered shipwrecks of old sailing ships which were more than a hundred years old. He had encountered all sorts of driftage, stuff that he hadn't even had time to examine. But there were no claim stakes, and, just to show that he wasn't to be trifled with, Emery had staked out a claim to the whole beach. Not that he ever expected to see it again, but it would at least let Sande know that the gringos were not entirely dumb.

I don't think Emery knows how to play chess, but he fancies himself as an expert poker player. Somehow or other, however, I have the idea that he wouldn't like to play stud poker with Sande.

13

JUMPING AND FEEDING WHALES

WE wanted more whale photographs. Hollywood wanted me. Everyone knew that Hollywood wanted me. Hollywood was engaged in broadcasting messages on ship-to-shore wireless; and various and sundry boats, picking up those wireless messages, knew that I was encamped in Scammon's Lagoon and that Hollywood wanted me. The script writers were going on strike and it was absolutely imperative that we have enough scripts ahead to finish the season on the Perry Mason show. And those scripts had to be stock-piled and revised before the writers went out on strike.

Moreover, we were now engaged in a battle with the wind. The wind was howling day and night. Sand was drifting from the sand dunes, covering our sleeping bags as though they had been left out in drifting snow. Sand was covering everything, and the waters of the lagoon were rough enough so that it was very difficult to see the whales and virtually impossible to get a good photograph. With such wind blowing it would be an uncomfortable if not a somewhat risky trip back to Guerrero Negro.

One afternoon the wind died down. The captain thought that it would be calm until early next morning, so we hurried out to the boat to take more pictures. We desperately wanted a picture of a jumping whale, so with cameras cocked we sat waiting for one to jump. I did get some rather interesting pictures of whales jumping in the distance, and, as subsequent events turned out, I got one picture that I didn't even know I had because I was using a long focal-length lens and looking through the finder of the camera when I shot the picture. It wasn't until after I got home and developed the picture and enlarged it that I realized I had quite a photographic prize, at least as far as I was concerned. I had a picture of a whale actually feeding in Scammon's Lagoon.

This whale was squirting many gallons of water out of his mouth, trapping the small animal life as the water passed through his "teeth". He was quite a distance away and through the finder I had only a brief glimpse of a whale coming up out of water, then dropping back with a splash. My eye wasn't quick enough to catch what was actually happening through the small image in the finder. But, as it turned out, I applied the shutter at five-hundredth of a second, and at the critical moment when the whale was disgorging the water and before the splash had enveloped everything.

There can be no question that this is a picture of a whale feeding.

So far as I know, it is the only picture of the sort ever taken. I have seen the pictures taken on both of the Donald Douglas-Paul Dudley White expeditions to Scammon's Lagoon. I have studied the photographs in the different books. I have never seen anything quite like this picture of the feeding whale. It may be unique.

However, back on the boat I didn't know what I had and we were waiting impatiently for a whale to jump, looking off in the distance, hoping that if one jumped within four hundred yards we could still get a fair picture.

Suddenly and without warning a whale shot up, right by the side of the boat.

We couldn't tell exactly how high he went. I thought he went about as high as the mast, but he caught us all off base. Gandara jumped to his feet and tried to point his camera. I was on the wrong side of the boat and part of the cabin was between me and the whale. I could see only a small part of him.

The whale submerged and we sat there bemoaning our fate and cursing the luck, wondering what strange hoodoo protected whales from the lens of the camera.

Jean, who had been on the lower deck, was modestly silent. She had only recently picked up photography and no one had paid much attention to her shutter clickings. At length, she modestly proclaimed, "I think I got part of him. I pointed the camera and clicked the shutter."

Still no one paid very much attention.

It wasn't until later, after we had returned and developed Jean's pictures, that we found she indeed had a picture of a jumping whale. She hadn't been able to snap the shutter at the moment of his greatest ascendancy. He was probably about halfway up or down when her shutter clicked. But the fact remains that she had a picture of a jumping whale, and, while I didn't know it at the time, I had one of a feeding whale.

In any event, after it became too late in the afternoon to expect any good photographs we went ashore and started getting the camp together. The captain's prediction held true. It was virtually a windless night and the morning was calm.

With the first streaks of daylight we were rolling things down the beach and aboard the boat, and shortly after sun-up we were on our way.

Three hours later we were unloading stuff on the wharf at Guerrero Negro and considerate hosts at the salt works suggested that the girls and I leave the work of unloading and reloading in the trucks to the others while I went to headquarters to telephone and answer telegrams which had been piling up.

The more I saw of those telegrams the more I felt it would be better not to engage in a lengthy conversation over the ship-to-shore wireless. And, in any event, it was a Saturday afternoon.

It turned out that Mr McClaughry had to go to San Diego the next day and the executive aeroplane was coming down to pick him up. He very kindly offered to take me in with him, knowing that it is almost impossible to get a charter plane over the week-end in Baja California. Nearly all the aircraft are engaged in regular scheduled runs over the week-end, taking sportsmen down to the various resorts that are springing up.

We were anxious to get to the Bahia de Los Angeles because we had been hearing so much about it. We wanted to see it and it was agreed that the rest of the party would start out that afternoon and camp along the road. I would wait overnight and fly into San Diego with McClaughry.

So the others started out, I waited over and shortly after noon on Sunday, found myself in San Diego, hiring a car from the Hertz Company, and I blessed the forethought which had caused me to take my special Hertz credit card along. My appearance was so disreputable that if it hadn't been for that credit card I might have had some trouble even convincing the Hertz people that I could be trusted with a car.

So once again I had a hectic period ahead of me. I drove to the ranch, got busy on the long-distance telephone, told everyone where I was and started work.

Thanks to my battery-powered dictating machine, I already had quite a bit of material dictated and was able to leave those discs for the girls to transcribe on Monday. (Only two of my secretaries are free to travel. The others have "committed matrimony", live within driving distance of the ranch and come in during the day.)

Scripts had been arriving by mail, and after I telephoned, a messenger was hurriedly dispatched from Hollywood with still more scripts. I telephoned Francisco Munoz and asked him if he would be free to take me to the Bahia de Los Angeles where I could join the others on Tuesday morning.

Munoz was very regretful. He was all tied up for Tuesday. He was tied up for Monday afternoon. But Monday morning, early, he could take me.

I had a good two days' work stacked up, but somehow I did it all in one night. Early on Monday morning I jumped into the hired car and took off for San Diego. Never have I seen such a fog! Driving through that fog was a harrowing experience, particularly as I was late in getting started. I wouldn't care to repeat that ride. But somehow I reached San Diego and got there on time. Munoz was waiting impatiently. I asked him about the field being closed in at Tijuana.

He gave me a smile and a characteristic shrug. "It is clear on the other side," he said.

That settled it.

We got down to Tijuana. The field was closed in. Aircraft which should have taken off for Mexico City at six o'clock were still sitting there. The airport was thronged with stalled passengers. Munoz took it all in his stride. He hurried about getting things ready, and while he was doing it the fog began to lift a bit here and there. Munoz is a professional optimist, and his optimism always pays off.

Munoz helped me into the aeroplane, we fastened the seat belts and were off. By this time there was a certain amount of visibility, but if there hadn't been I feel certain I would have been in Bahia de Los Angeles right on schedule just the same.

Francisco Munoz is a careful pilot, but he is one of the old school of lobster pilots who made a living by putting planes down on the beaches at lonely lobster camps, picking up lobsters and flying them back to market. The men who engaged in that work were like the postman—rain, hail, sleet and fog were impediments but never any reason for delay. The lobsters had to be flown. And these men are great pilots.

We broke out of the fog at about 2,000 feet and from there on the trip was beautiful. I always love to fly over the peninsula of Baja California and look down on the roads I have traversed so laboriously. Moreover, on this trip we flew directly over the Sierra San Pedro Martir, a district which I had always wanted to see.

I had heard much about this country, a wonderful mountain plateau on which there is pine timber and lush grass, where there is running water, trout in abundance and any quantity of deer. We were flying at about 11,000 feet and when we came over the mountain plateau we seemed to be within less than 1,500 feet of the plateau. It was a beautiful trip; and then we were over the mountains and out on the Gulf side and I was looking down on the road we had so recently traversed with our motor vehicles.

A very short time later I was leaving the aircraft at the resort of Antero Diaz on the Bahia de Los Angeles. I found that my caravan had arrived only a matter of minutes earlier.

We settled down to living deluxe.

We had rooms. There was running water. The water was not hot except during the middle of the day when the sun would heat five-gallon coal-oil cans on the roofs sufficiently to make the water pleasantly warm. We were sleeping in beds, out of the wind and away from the drifting sands. And we were eating. Holy suffering mackerel, *how* we were eating!

I have eaten in many of the best restaurants in the world. I have arrived at an age when I try desperately to count the calories. I have never had food such as that at Casa Diaz on Bahia de Los Angeles, and I threw the calorie chart out of the window.

Breakfasts are rather conventional: eggs, bacon, hot cakes.

Lunch, however, is really something. It is a big meal. All the meals are big.

A typical lunch may include meat from the huge turtles which are indigenous to the Gulf, a juicy tender meat with a distinctive flavour; frijoles that are cooked as only a Mexican can cook frijoles, wonderful, thin, chewy tortillas and a little fried fish on the side.

There is always fish available.

There are enough fishermen going out in boats to keep the larder and the town, and probably the whole peninsula, well stocked with fish.

Whenever a boat comes back, the truck automatically goes down to load the fish. They are brought up literally by the truckload. A skilled Mexican with a sharp knife spreads the fish out on a cement slab and cuts fillets from the sides, avoiding all bones, avoiding all fins and getting only the strip of fine, firm meat between the skin and the backbone.

These fillets are stacked up on the side of the trough like cord wood.

People who live close to the resort and who want fish simply come and take them. It is a common sight to see a couple of five-year-olds struggling to get their prize home—a fish that will weigh fifteen to twenty-five pounds, which has been freshly caught and is hard to handle.

The fish in those waters represent just about the best eating in the world and the cooks are very, very expert at preparing them. They have been doing it all their lives and that fish, fresh out of the water, is a treat for the palate which simply can't be described.

Or perhaps a meal may consist of abalone and chicken, or some equally interesting combination.

There is always all you want to eat and more in the kitchen.

Clams, oysters? . . . Sure, help yourself.

A man can go out into the clam beds and dig enough clams with his fingers to get a wonderful clam cocktail. Or he can go over to the bed of rock oysters and, with the aid of a stout knife, have absolutely fresh oysters on the half shell.

And then there are the lobsters.

The lobsters usually come with the evening meal; huge platters of lobsters cut in half and drenched in drawn butter.

Those lobsters have a wonderful flavour. They are fresh, well-cooked and the meat is sweet and tender. You don't want to feel like a hog and therefore try to hide the shells so that your neighbours can't see how many you're eating.

Antero Diaz understands that feeling perfectly and he is a considerate host. He will glide unobtrusively behind your seat and pick up the empty lobster shells and remove them so that you can tackle more lobsters with a clear conscience.

There is a rumour that lobsters cause nightmares.

If lobsters really cause nightmares I can assure you I shall have nightmares for the next five years. I have eaten enough of the lobsters at the Bahia de Los Angeles to guarantee my quota of nightmares for that time.

However, the food there doesn't cause nightmares, it doesn't cause indigestion. It does give one a drugged, sleepy, relaxed feeling and, except at weekends when the sportsmen come thronging in by aeroplane, it is seldom one hears human voices after nine o'clock at night.

The cost?

Your room and three meals a day will cost you such a small amount you feel you are robbing the guy.

There were interesting people at the Bahia de Los Angeles—O. W. ("Tim") Timberman and his wife, Pat.

Timberman was an oil executive in Tucson. Came the inevitable day when nerve strain levied its toll. He had always wanted to travel and explore, and his wife had wanted to paint. So Timberman walked off the job, bought a small truck, put a home on wheels, and started for Baja California.

Since that time he has explored the length and breadth of the peninsula. He knows and loves the people and the people know and love him. His wife has developed a remarkable skill with her paintbrush and the two drift up and down the peninsula, familiar with all the roads, visiting people who know them and love them. They have the reputation of being "muy simpatico".

When the Timbermans start along the road the word goes ahead by that mysterious grapevine telegraph which seems to function perfectly in a land where there is little traffic and where one would think news could never travel.

Timberman has written a book entitled *Mexico's Diamond in*

the Rough which is the latest book on Baja California and which contains bits of interesting information which can be found in no other book. It is a book which should be read as it was written, in the quiet relaxation of philosophic leisure. It is a book which tells of roads and adventures, of families and of interesting personalities. It gives little traits of the Mexican character and, not only in the lines but in between the lines, is the picture of two people who have found happiness and contentment after having spent much of their lives in the competitive rat race of a highly keyed-up existence.

Anyone who is approaching the age of retirement and wonders just what he is going to do should read Timberman's book, should read of their wanderings up and down the peninsula; of the table which is supplied quite largely by their own efforts and the generosity of their friends: white-winged doves, fish fresh out of the ocean, lobsters, clams, oysters, roast of venison, and other delicacies.

There were other interesting people at the Bahia de Los Angeles: Faye B. Howard and her companion, Mrs Nina Hartmann.

Mrs Howard is by way of being one of the greatest living experts on shells. She is, however, inordinately modest. To hear her story one would think she was nothing but a refugee grandmother, a fugitive from being engulfed into an existence of perpetual baby-sitting.

Actually she is not only an outstanding authority on sea shells but has had several species named after her. She has made startling discoveries in the field, and as a result of these discoveries some scientific theories have had to be completely overhauled. She has, for instance, discovered shells which had heretofore been found only in fossils and which were supposed to belong to a long past era, not only in the form of non-fossils but actually occupied by the living mollusc.

She and her companion also have one of these houses on wheels; a little home which can be put on the bed of a pick-up and which furnishes protection from the weather, enough room for eating and sleeping; a sort of laboratory; and yet does not have enough weight or bulk to interfere with driving, even over pretty rough roads.

There was one drawback at the Bahia de Los Angeles. We were a little too close to civilization.

Here was a ship-to-shore telephone where we could call people and where people could call us. Here was a regular pattern of aircraft transportation. While we were two and a half or three days from the border by four-wheeled-drive vehicle, we were only two and a half hours from Tijuana by air.

We had some films which I wanted developed and I didn't want to let them out of our possession. I wanted Sam to develop them personally. I was also afraid that I had kept Sam away from his home so long that his family might not recognize him on his return. So I suggested Sam fly back with Francisco Munoz, develop his films, and return a couple of days later.

Gandara found that the Governor of Baja California was very much interested in an exhibit of Baja California which was to be staged at a fair in Los Angeles. We had some very interesting material which could go into that booth, so Gandara hopped a plane for Mexicali and Los Angeles.

Munoz delivered Sam, then flew back to Bahia de Los Angeles with some passengers. He had about twenty-four hours at his disposal so I suggested Murl Emery, Jean and I make the trip to Loreto by air.

A suggestion of this sort to Munoz is instantly acted on. Why wait?

Why, indeed? The words were hardly out of my mouth before we were hurriedly loading cameras and light overnight bags. We fastened the seat belts and were off.

Flying over Baja California is a most interesting experience. It is always fascinating to look down on ground which is virtually untrod by human foot.

Science has uncovered evidence indicating that up to about three hundred years ago Baja California was blessed with a very considerable amount of rainfall. Then within the last three hundred years the creeping cycle of drouth began to make itself manifest. A country that at one time supported many thousands of Indians now has become parched for lack of water. And valleys which must at one time have teemed with human life and abounded with game are now lying deserted in sun-drenched silence.

What would a person find in the way of relics and artifacts if he could get into some of these valleys?

Some of them still remain fairly well watered. From the plane one can see tall palm trees growing in profusion, casting cooling shade. One can see a trickle of water. But there is just about no way anyone can get into those isolated garden spots. There are no roads within miles and miles and miles. One couldn't transport enough water to enable a burro to get there. And so, one can look down on canyons which are probably filled with metallic riches; on dry valleys and mesas which at one time supported much life; on intriguing canyons and natural oases where there is water, food and shade; but there is absolutely no practical method of finding out exactly what is there. It is a virgin country. However, the use of four-wheel drive vehicles is making quite a difference and the influx of tourist dollars is making a difference. Roads are going to be constructed and it won't be too long before adventuresome individuals who want to explore country which has never been touched in modern times can find that country within a few hundred miles of San Diego.

It is an interesting thought.

"Tim" Timberman had suggested that by all means we should go to a point some twenty miles south of Loreto on the Gulf, where we could see the Shangri-La where he and his wife had spent many happy weeks; a gulf within a gulf, completely surrounded by protecting hills, with an opening only a few yards wide leading to the waters of the Gulf itself. Timberman told me it was about six miles via the shore line, and from the air it looked to be all that. It is a paradise for the hunter and fisherman and the deep, tranquil blue of the water lying serene, protected from winds from any direction, a shoreline ringed with sandy beaches alternating with deep water along sheer mountains, offers limitless opportunities for leisurely existence and quiet exploration.

Timberman told me that once I had seen it I would never be happy until I managed to get there, and I am afraid he is right.

Loreto, one of the first cities of Baja California, was just beginning to recover from the devastating effects of a terrific *chubasco* (the Baja California version of the tropical hurricane).

There had been winds up to well over a hundred and twenty miles an hour. Rain had descended in torrents, had spread down from the hills in a flood. Adobe bricks had dissolved like sugar lumps in hot coffee. Palm trees had been toppled like broken toothpicks, and many lives had been lost.

Here and there rubble and wreckage was slowly being cleared away; but the town, with indomitable spirit, was carrying on. In the course of its long existence it had survived flood and earthquake and the people were philosophical. They had taken refuge in the old mission, and the handiwork of the ancient priests had again justified their faith. The stone structure had stood while trees were crashing and buildings were collapsing.

New construction was springing up from piles of rubble, and I was impressed with the schoolhouse. Despite the surrounding wreckage of disaster the schoolhouse was new, modern and the pupils were bright and alert. No matter what else had to be done, the school had priority.

As we walked past, school was just coming out and one of the teachers was marching the pupils round for a period of exercise. I came along with a camera and started snapping pictures. Then, after the class was dismissed, I shook hands with the teacher and became acquainted. He was of Chinese-Mexican descent, and had that wonderful patience which I have found so frequently in the Mexican school-teacher.

There is something about the Mexican school discipline that inspires obedience and respect, yet leaves the individual free to manifest and develop his own individuality. It is as though teacher and pupil were in partnership.

My arrival with a camera naturally interfered with the drill, if it could be called such, but both teacher and pupils took that in their stride. The pupils had a desire to co-operate and the teacher knew they had that desire. They were also curious about the photographer and about the camera.

I have never heard a harsh word in a Mexican schoolhouse. I have never seen a pupil who seemed insubordinate. I have seen many who made faces, who smiled, who took liberties, but I have never seen one who was insubordinate or insolent and I have never seen a nervous Mexican school-teacher.

It is in comparatively recent years that Mexico has learned to emphasize the importance of education, and within the next few years we are going to see some remarkable results.

Also in Loreto I found an enthusiastic reader fan, a tomato grower named Al Green, who took me into his house to show me a big supply of Gardner books translated into Spanish.

He had at one time read *The Land of Shorter Shadows* which had been loaned to him by a friend and was very anxious to get a copy of that book—however, as previously mentioned, it is a book which is now out of print and which has become a collector's item.

Jean had two treasured copies of the book and, before we left, Green's enthusiasm was such that she had agreed to send him one of her two copies.

When we departed Green was on hand with plenty of ripe tomatoes neatly packed in cartons so that we would have enough tomatoes to last us on our trip to the border—big, luscious, ripe tomatoes and, as we later found out, sweet and flavourful.

Many parts of the United States were being gripped in blizzards at the time but Al Green was shipping tomatoes to California and had been shipping them all winter.

It was quite an operation. He and members of his family had ranches where they grew the tomatoes. They were brought in to a packing house, sorted and packed, then shipped by aeroplane to the United States. The operation was expensive but the tomatoes commanded a premium because they were so well grown and well selected, and Al Green told me that the Safeway Stores took his entire output, willingly paying the premium in order to get such choice tomatoes on their shelves.

It was hard to tear ourselves away from his enthusiastic hospitality, but we were really travelling on a tight schedule and we were somewhat concerned because the fog had now descended on the Gulf side, and Loreto had low visibility and, wonders of wonders, a drizzling rain.

But Munoz took all this casually and we were off on schedule and soon out of the clouds and into the bright sunlight.

We returned to the Bahia de Los Angeles and then Munoz promptly took off for Tijuana to bring Sam back the next day.

I should of course have known what was going to happen when Sam came back. Fortunately, I didn't.

Leo Roripaugh, a neighbour of mine in Temecula, an adventurous sportsman and a skilful aviator, was taking a holiday at Bahia de Los Angeles—a place he had learned to know and love—and we sat through a leisurely evening in the warm, velvety darkness watching the stars reflected in the water and saying how nice it was to be completely relaxed, and free from the evils of too much nerve strain.

The next day Munoz was late in arriving and we were somewhat worried but about four o'clock he came in and touched down on the landing strip with that deft skill which comes with years of flying. He taxied up to the place and Sam emerged from the plane with a whole file of important messages: there were more scripts in Hollywood; the strike had been moved forward; I must get back *at once*.

My publisher had two books awaiting proof-reading; the Detective Book Club was in a hurry for one written under the pen name of A. A. Fair, and a Perry Mason book was scheduled for immediate printing. There were stacks and stacks of important mail—vital matters which needed immediate attention.

I tried to charter a plane to get back, but to no avail. Munoz had a full load for the next day. It was now getting late. All the charter planes were filled up for the week-end.

So we dashed into our rooms and hurriedly threw things helter-skelter into the cars. We had only an hour before darkness but an hour was an hour. We hastily shook hands and were off, engulfed once more in the exigencies of civilization.

Baja California is a land of serene charm. There are rugged places in the road. It is a land which is still largely unexplored. There are ghost cities and abandoned mines. There are places like Las Flores out of the Bahia de Los Angeles where ambition and capital started a great mining town and imported machinery and even a railway engine, cars and track.

These things were all brought in by water. Then they were landed and laboriously taken apart so that they could be transported by human power and on the backs of burros. Then they were reassembled. A city sprang up some seventy years ago. For a while there was great prosperity and buildings were erected. The town even needed a jail, and that jail, constructed of stone, not only still stands, but etched in the stone one can find places where the repentants scratched a tally of the time they had served as each day of their sentence became a yesterday.

There were graveyards; one graveyard for the rich on the west side of the town; another graveyard for the *peon* on the east. Now the distinction between rich and poor has been obliterated by the passing of time. It is as hard to find one graveyard as the other. We did find one grave with an iron marker still in place, grown over with desert plants.

We found old machinery and dilapidated wreckage. We found the remnants of an old civilization, but the once teeming city was now wrapped in the dignity of death; the mysterious, quiescent period which is as much a part of life as birth itself.

There are quite a few such ghost cities in Baja California. There are the ruins of old missions which were established by the padres when they sought to convert the teeming population of Indians. There is adventure in Baja California, and there is something even more rare. There is serene tranquillity; and there can always be found the touch of human humour.

When we were returning from our first trip, as we approached the border we stopped at one of the "swanky" restaurants which are beginning to appear here and there.

This was a magnificent establishment, with subdued lighting, the soft strains of gentle hi-fi music, waiters resplendent in white shirts, dinner jackets and coloured bow ties. The menu had an impressive array of items covering the gamut of sea foods, wild game and various cuts of steak.

We were tired and hungry. We had had a long, hard day and we wanted something good to eat.

I took a look at the menu and suggested to Gandara that he speak to the head waiter and find out what was the best dish that we could get without too much delay. I rather suspected that with such a wide variety on the menu some of the dishes were more staple and in instant readiness.

So Joe called over the head waiter and there began one of the most spirited conversations in high-speed Spanish I have ever listened. Words were rattling like hail on a tin roof. The conversation developed into an animated argument.

After it had gone on back and forth for some two or three minutes, Jean caught my attention. "Look here," she said, "I don't want Joe ordering for *me*. *I* want to pick out what *I* want.

It's all right for him to find out what is best in the kitchen but I want to do my own ordering."

Joe heard her, nodded his head and motioned with his hand that she wasn't to worry, everything was well, and then plunged once more into rapid-fire conversation with the head waiter.

The head waiter gestured emphatically with his hands. Joe raised his eyebrows in incredulity. He barked staccato questions and the head waiter answered volubly.

It was late and I was afraid the dining room would close before the conversation terminated, so I kept nudging Joe to speed it up.

Joe would nod over his shoulder, so to speak, and then resume the verbal barrage.

Finally it got down to a point where it was apparent there was a meeting of the minds. Joe's questions became shorter and while the note of incredulity still remained in his voice it was apparent that he was getting at the gist of the thing.

The head waiter became more and more emphatic but his statements were shorter.

It was apparent that he and Joe had established a basis of friendship and the head waiter was answering Joe with complete candour—a candour which was, perhaps, too complete.

Finally Joe sighed and turned to us and picked up the menu.

"Well, Joe," I asked, "what did he say?"

Joe said, "He told me, '*Here, I would order nothing except beans*'."

With one accord we looked at the long menu and burst into uproarious laughter.

The head waiter, who understood very little English, looked at us with a puzzled expression. There was no accounting for the vagaries of American tourists.

Once the land of Baja California has stamped its charm upon you, you can't remain away very long at a time. Those who have known this peninsula continue to love it and to return to it—and those who have hunted whales in Scammon's Lagoon are marked men. Whale hunting is too exciting not to leave an indelible mark.

Too few people know anything about Baja California. The roads in places are bad. The climate is wonderful. The marine scenery is unsurpassed, and there are literally thousands of potential resort sites within a short distance of the heavily populated centres of Southern California.

As my friend, Donald Douglas, pointed out in a recent conversation with me, the technical and scientific developments in the field of converting sea water into good drinking water are destined to have a terrific impact on the future of Baja California.

In the vicinity of Los Angeles there are hundreds of thousands of sportsmen who are fed up with the fished-out streams they so frequently encounter, who would give their eye-teeth to drop a line in virtually virgin waters, well populated with hungry fish. Yet within one or two hours' flying time of Los Angeles there are these blue waters, literally filled with fish. There are white sand beaches, a relatively gentle, curling surf, a climate which combines the dryness of the desert with the cool, moist breezes blowing off the ocean.

It seems inevitable that Baja California is on the threshold of a great expansion.

I know some of the prominent people who are in business in Baja California. They are interested in promoting better international relations and in making the country more accessible to the tourist. As air transportation becomes faster, safer and more economical, more sportsmen are going to become familiar with this country, and as tourist traffic justifies it, roads are going to be built and improved and resorts are going to spring up.

Baja California is a land of adventure, and more and more people are going to become familiar with the charm of a country where dry air, warm sunshine, cooling breezes and blue waters present an irresistible combination for sports and recreation.

PART TWO

Hovering over Baja

14

INTRODUCING THE PAK-JAK

I HAVE been exploring Baja California for many years, and from time to time have made excursions down the rough, narrow roads of the peninsula to the various points of interest: to Bahia de Los Angeles, the fishing paradise; to Scammon's Lagoon, the breeding place of the whales; to the fabulous Hattie Hamilton Ranch a hundred-odd miles below Ensenada; to the Sky Ranch at San Quintin, the home of the most wonderful clams, and then on beyond to Santa Rosalia, Mulegé and El Coyote; to San José del Cabo, La Paz and to the Cape. In short, I have pretty much worn a series of ruts in the road and thought I knew the country pretty well.

Then at a time when I was looking for new adventures, my friend J. W. Black, of Paradise, California, designed the Pak-Jak, which is something of a cross between a motor-cycle, a scooter and an army tank.

At the time Black designed his machine there were other devices on the market, but they didn't appeal to Black as being just what he wanted. He wanted something that was so rugged in construction that it would be almost indestructible. He wanted something so thoroughly dependable that a man could rely on it in places where his very life would be forfeit if there should be a mechanical failure. He also wanted something that had enough power to go just as straight up as a rider could sit in the saddle without having the whole contraption fall over backwards. And he wanted something that weighed under 175 lb. gross. It took quite a bit of inventing to produce a machine that satisfied Black, but eventually he did so and called it the Pak-Jak.

Because Black was a friend of mine, I was in on the ground floor, so to speak, of all the experimentation and designing, and almost immediately I dreamed up an idea for an adventure de luxe. We would take half a dozen of these machines. Black would design a two-wheeled trailer which could be pulled by the machine and which would carry 5-600 lb. of camping equipment on reasonably level ground.

We would go by boat down the coast of Baja California, taking these Pak-Jaks with us, would unload the outfit at Guerrero Negro and would then start moving up the beaches. We would travel with the trailers at low tide, keeping to the hard-packed sand. Then, as the tide came in and we had to move up the beach to where the sand became softer, we would disconnect the trailers and use the Pak-Jaks to explore the back country until once more the tide went down and we could find a sandy strip of hard beach sufficiently wide and firm to enable the trailers and camp outfit to be transported.

The idea was simple enough and sound enough, provided the beaches would adapt themselves to this type of exploration. We knew, of course, that the extent of sandy beaches was the vital factor in our plan. We realized that from time to time there were jagged promontories cropping out into the ocean which would present effective barriers to further progress even at low tide. However, after seeing the versatility of Black's contraption and the terrain over which he was able to navigate successfully, I had high hopes that by picking the right stretch of beach we could perhaps have as much as fifty miles of exploration, and that our excursions into the back country would unearth material which would be of great interest: evidence of prehistoric Indian villages, perhaps even an unexpected water hole. We also wanted to make a survey of the country to see to what extent it was populated by game.

At that time I was under the impression that Baja California was pretty much of a desert. Certainly anyone who traverses the road is entitled to reach that assumption. While there are a few well-watered oases such as the beautiful palm-covered country of San Ignacio, the road for the most part goes through a dry, arid country where anyone on foot would almost inevitably perish of thirst before he could reach any human habitation or any source of drinking water.

I had seen enough of the beaches near Guerrero Negro to know that it would be possible to go some distance with our Pak-Jaks and trailers and I felt certain we could have some adventures and probably explore country where no tourist had ever set foot. However, we wanted to make certain.

J. W. Black constructed his trailers and tested them out so that he was satisfied we could carry quite a supply of camp goods, drinking water, petrol, sleeping bags and provisions along reasonably level country. All that was needed now was to pick out the particular beach that we wanted to explore. Quite obviously the best way to do that was by air.

Baja California has generated a breed of pilots comparable to the bush pilots of Canada and Alaska. These men bring lobsters from the lobster camps into the market, and the lobsters have to be transported when they are ready to go and the market is ready to receive them. Adverse weather conditions, including wind, must not be a deterrent, yet Baja California is often the scene of great turbulence in the mountains and fog on the beaches. So these Baja California pilots learn to fly by instinct, the seat of their pants, an inherent skill and a daring resourcefulness which puts them out in front as among the world's best and most daring fliers.

My friend Francisco Munoz is one of these pilots. He has now graduated from flying lobsters and has a regular passenger service from Tijuana to the Bahia de Los Angeles, but he also has time to do some charter flying. So I contacted Francisco Munoz and made arrangements for an exploratory trip at a time when he would have two full days at his disposal.

Sam Hicks, my assistant and ranch manager, J. W. Black, inventor of the Pak-Jak, Murl Emery, and I crowded into the plane with Munoz and we took off from Tijuana.

There are two sections of Baja California: the north and the south. And the northern state is, in turn, divided into two further sections, although there is no actual demarcation other than the one political boundary which is merely a surveyed line.

Mexicali, the capital of the state, is a thriving, prosperous city that is growing so fast it is bursting out at the seams. Over to the west, Tijuana is becoming a centre of legitimate entertainment, with its race track, bull ring and jai-alai, and it, too, is growing like a mushroom. When I first knew the city, it consisted of only a few adobe buildings and one unpaved street. Today it is a prosperous city of 165,000 people with scores of legitimate tourist attractions. There is a constant flow of commerce back and forth across the border and it plays an important part in the economy both of California to the north and of Baja California to the south. Heaven knows how many tourists go to San Diego simply to make the trip across to Tijuana in Mexico—tourists who would never have gone farther south than Los Angeles if it hadn't been for colourful Tijuana.

Munoz has a single-engined aircraft, which he keeps in the pink of condition since he spends much of his life flying over mountains so rough that an engine failure would mean almost inevitable disaster.

There are two schools of thought about flying over rough terrain: one is that two engines are better than one, and that is undoubtedly sound reasoning. The other, however, is that with a single-engined aircraft its slower landing speed gives one a much better chance, if one has to make a forced landing, of walking away from the craft. And, of course, there are other factors involved, such as operational economies, etc.

In any event, Munoz has a single-engined aeroplane and since he realizes the importance of keeping it in good condition, I always feel pretty much at ease when I am flying with him.[1]

On this trip, Munoz was going to take us exploring. We weren't going to follow any established routes, nor were we going to play it safe. We were going up into the mountains to the south of Tijuana and to the east of Ensenada in order to see some country that Munoz thought we might be interested in, although I felt at the time that it had to be the beaches or nothing. We weren't interested in mountain canyons. However, since the country between Tijuana and Ensenada is traversed by a paved road, we didn't care about the beaches until after we had passed the Hattie Hamilton Ranch some 120 miles to the south of Ensenada.

Ensenada, by the way, has emerged from a sleepy little Mexican village and is now a thriving port with facilities for both large and small craft, excellent accommodation for the tourist, and is populated by some of the most forward-looking, alert businessmen one could hope to meet anywhere.

This is a good thing for the economy of Baja California and a good thing for the United States. Yet I look back with nostalgic

[1] Since this was written, Munoz has added a twin-engined aircraft to his equipment.

128

Our Pak-Jaks on the boat

Emery and Lee during the second day of the storm

Lowering Pak-Jaks
down a rocky cliff

The burro fails to
negotiate the rocky
slope

memories on the time when Ensenada was merely a very colourful Mexican town, with its fuel delivered daily by burros who were driven in from the hinterland where wood choppers loaded them with firewood, made the long trip to Ensenada and then turned the burros loose at night to clatter along the sidewalks looking for shrubs on which they could browse.

However, as has been so aptly remarked, "One can't eat his cake and have it too."

As the Mexicans say, "One door never closes but another opens," and over on the gulf side of the peninsula 120 miles below Mexicali, the fishing village of San Felipe will give the tourist all that he wants in the way of local colour with quite good motel and restaurant facilities thrown in. There are also fishing boats that can take the tourist out into semi-tropical waters where there is first-class fishing.

One of the outstanding citizens of Ensenada is David Zarate Zazueta. (Usually when a Mexican gentleman has three names, he is called by the middle name. The last name is the name of his mother.) "Dave" Zarate has for many years been a colourful and influential figure in Baja California.

There is a custom that the mayor is not to be re-elected for a second consecutive term. The next most influential position in the city is that of president of the chamber of commerce, so for many years Zarate has alternately been mayor of the city, then president of the chamber of commerce, then again mayor of the city.

Dave is virtually bilingual and has a polished charm which is distinctive, yet difficult to describe. While there is a certain formal undertone, yet it is so utterly sincere and natural that it fits the man's personality as easily as a well-worn shoe or perhaps it would be better to say a well-worn glove. It is to some extent quite typical of the Mexican gentleman.

Dave is one of those individuals who has what can only be described for want of a better name as intellectual perspective. He meets everyone on the common ground of mutual understanding. I have known him for some thirty-five years and find that his name inspires tremendous respect both in Baja California and among the people who know him north of the border.

Above all Dave Zarate is a great friend, warm, loyal and interesting. It is always a pleasure to visit him. Yet Señor Zarate is only one of the outstanding citizens of Ensenada. I mention him particularly because of my long years of friendship.

This little city of Ensenada has some of the most progressive citizens of any of the Baja California cities. As one of my friends recently expressed it, "If you want to get something done in Baja California, go to Ensenada. If it's anything worth while they'll back it, and if they back it they'll get results."

In retrospect, I think Munoz realized that our dream of exploring the beaches of Baja California was impracticable, and wanted to direct our attention to some of the other country which was completely unknown so far as the tourist was concerned. In fact, this country is completely unknown to everyone except a small handful of people: aviators who have flown over it, mostly at great height because of the rugged nature of the country beneath; a few prospectors who have apparently been in some of the country at one time or another; and one or two ranchers whose cattle have strayed into some of these canyons and who have followed them at least for a short distance before giving up the chase.

So after leaving Tijuana, Munoz set a course which would bring us into country which I never knew existed.

Years ago, my friend Goldbaum of Ensenada, who was a great Mexican patriot and an enthusiastic booster of the peninsula, had assured me that Baja California had a lot more water than people realized, that in unexplored sections of the peninsula were palm-lined canyons where there was running water, deep crystal-clear pools carved out of the solid granite, and a land of virgin fertility.

Goldbaum had made several mule-back trips into the "back country" trying to find out more about it. He carried a sextant with him and would shoot the sun at noon, pricking his position on a chart and then taking photographs which were identified by longitude and latitude. He had a museum at Ensenada in which he had many curios, many Indian artifacts and books filled with photographs.

Much of what he had told me was more or less hazy in my mind because at the time I was more interested in the very remarkable man than in the things he had found; but some of the things he had said had stuck in my mind and now began to come back as Munoz, flying over country where no single-engined aeroplane had any business, began to show us far, far below, canyons that undoubtedly were studded with palm trees and in which there was a plentiful supply of water. These things simply weren't supposed to exist in Baja California. It was supposed to be an arid desert region with an incomparable climate; warm, dry air; plenty of sunshine; and more days of sunlight than any place in the south-west other than the arid desert regions.

Munoz knew we wanted to fly low enough to see the canyons, but he is also a prudent flier and he knew that he couldn't afford to take any unnecessary chances. Flying over that country in the first place was taking plenty of risks.

So we broke out our cameras and started taking photographs, incredulously studying the terrain below and wondering how we could possibly get into it.

Munoz circled and flew us to a point where we could see the nearest road. Then we took photographs of landmarks, fixing the locations in our minds and on photographic film so that we could find our way back by four-wheel-drive vehicles to the end of the road, and then by using Pak-Jaks could take to the game trails which led from the dry mesa country down to the watered canyons.

By the time we had finished exploring the country at the back of those mountains and had headed for the ocean below San Quintin, we were so tremendously excited that when it began to be apparent our dream of exploring the beaches with Pak-Jaks was impracticable, we weren't too badly disappointed. So we asked Munoz if there were any more canyons that he knew about and he told us there were vast sections of the mountain country which were virtually unexplored. He had, he said, flown high over other canyons where he felt certain there was water and in one place had seen what looked like ruins of a huge building. Then he told us about the canyons of La Asamblea and Sal Si Puede.

I don't know what is the significance of the name La Asamblea, but Sal Si Puede being literally translated means "get out if you can". These are two main canyons in a series of canyons to the north of Bahia de Los Angeles and there are some interesting stories connected with them. From the air, the canyons look like branches of coral, winding perhaps twenty-five miles up from the gulf into the granite mountains.

No tourist has ever explored these canyons. A few hard-bitten Mexican prospectors have from time to time landed at the beach on the gulf side during periods of calm weather and by walking up the sandy wash have covered the four or five miles of terrain to the place where the canyons begin. Then they have gone an undetermined distance up the canyons, but no one has ever gone very far, at least up Sal Si Puede. There is supposed to be a spring of good water in La Asamblea about twelve miles from the ocean, and there are stories of people who have reached it and managed to return. There are also stories of people who lost their lives in the attempt.

So having flown down to the south along the coastline until we became convinced that there were no beaches to the north of Guerrero Negro of sufficient extent to satisfy our ambitions, we asked Munoz to fly us over the gulf side of the peninsula so that we could take a look at the palm-lined canyons to the north of Bahia de Los Angeles.

We spent that night at Bahia de Los Angeles, a resort operated by my friend Antero Diaz and his wife; a place which is utterly unique. It is only some three hours' flight from the congested district of Los Angeles and San Diego and is known to scores of sportsmen having private planes, and on weekends plane after plane brings in adventurous fishermen or people who simply want to make the trip and relax in the warm sunshine off the gulf; but above all, to sample the fabulous cooking prepared under the direction of Señora Diaz.

Of late Diaz had added an eight-foot twin-screwed diesel boat to his fleet. This boat is a converted sub-chaser and there are reasonably comfortable quarters for sportsmen who wish to go far out into the gulf, over to the east side of the island of Angel de La Guarda where there are some of the most flavourful oysters in the world to be had for the taking, where there are big clams and where the fishing is out of this world.

We had an enjoyable night with our friends there at the Bahia de Los Angeles and then the next morning Munoz started us on a flight which was to have far-reaching effects. We flew up to the palm-lined canyons and explored them as well as we could from the height we had to maintain to have any reasonable standard of safety.

Looking down on those canyons, it was easy to see why they were unexplored. On the gulf side was a rather rugged beach where breakers stretched far out whenever there was any wind. Only during periods of dead calm would it be practicable to land a boat laden with supplies on this beach. Behind it was a stretch of some five miles of deep sand running up a barren wash where some of the most colourful mountains I have ever seen were spread haphazardly on each side of the wash. Striated in a variety of colours—red, pink, green, and various pastel shades—they were for the most part completely devoid of vegetation. Down in the wash below where one must walk through ankle-deep sand the sun beat down with pitiless intensity and the sand threw back the rays and the heat so that even in mid-winter a person who would walk up that wash must wear heavy dark glasses, carry plenty of water in his canteen and move slowly.

The canyons began about five miles up from the ocean, starting out as two main canyons and then branching out into dozens of canyons which ran back into the granite mountains which were great piles of granite boulders varying in size from small rocks to those the size of a skyscraper, tumbled in confusion with precipices to trap the unwary traveller.

It would be impossible for any man to walk over these mountains. If he carried plenty of ropes, he could, of course, make a mountain-climbing expedition of it and eventually and gradually get down or up the slopes.

However, there was not just one single range of mountains but wave on wave of ranges, consisting of granite, and in places mile after mile of tumbled malpais boulders, a particularly hard iron-coloured, exceedingly heavy volcanic formation. The mere sight of them even from high up gave one the shivers. Apparently the only practical way into the canyons was from the wash on the gulf side.

However, Munoz wanted to show us a route he had worked out which he thought might be practicable for Pak-Jaks.

Some fifteen miles back from the gulf there was a series of dry lakes, and Munoz thought that four-wheel-drive vehicles with skilful drivers could manage to get into them. He also thought that he could arrange to land on one of the lakes, particularly if a car on the ground marked out a smooth strip that was free of "pot holes". From that point, it was only some six miles to a section of the Sal Si Puede Canyon and the mountains were rather low and not quite so precipitous.

Munoz thought we might be able to establish a base camp on this dry lake and get our Pak-Jaks over the mountains and down into the canyon. Munoz was about the only one who thought so.

Yet the canyons represented a continuing challenge. I couldn't get them out of my mind. People who lived in Bahia de Los Angeles and were familiar with the country assured me that no one had been among them for at least eighteen years to their positive knowledge. From time to time, people landed from fishing boats during periods of calm and explored the wash and an occasional hardy soul had even got up to the canyons themselves. One man was reputed to have gone up La Asamblea Canyon to the spring of good water and had managed to return the following day.

There was one most interesting story about La Asamblea Canyon. Twenty-eight years ago two prospectors landed on the beach and trudged up the sandy wash until they came to the mouth of the canyons. Then they started prospecting up the canyon. It was agreed that one man would take all the food and water and try to prospect while his companion went back to the boat to replenish supplies and return to join forces with the prospector.

On returning to the place selected as a rendezvous, the man who was laden with provisions and all the water he could carry found no trace of his companion. He waited impatiently with time rapidly running out, then started exploring trying to find the tracks of his companion. Eventually he found his partner. He had been bitten by a rattlesnake and had died a horrible death. The story was pathetically told by the man's rolled-up trouser leg, the tourniquet he had contrived above the bite, and the knife slashes he had made in his leg.

It should be mentioned parenthetically that this section of the country is the home of a very rare, very vicious and very deadly rattlesnake, a red diamondback, which attains lengths up to six feet. The poison is so deadly that there is no known instance of anyone who has been bitten surviving to report the symptoms.

There is one exception: some time ago a herpetologist, handling one of these rattlesnakes in a museum, received a glancing blow on the leg. Nearly all the venom ran down his trouser leg to the floor, but a small amount got into the blood stream. This man was in a hospital within seventeen minutes of being bitten and was given all the treatment that modern science knew about. He had anti-venom serum; he had antibiotics; medicine for the heart; morphine for the nerves. He had everything. Yet this man nearly died. He had taken with him a pad and pencil intending to write down his symptoms, because he recognized the scientific value of doing so, but he was too ill to make even a single note. And it is to be realized that this snake struck only a glancing blow. He struck blind through the folds of a sack, all but missed the man's leg, and spilled nearly all the venom on the floor. Any man bitten by a red diamondback rattlesnake whose fangs penetrate deeply and inject a full dose of venom into the blood stream might just as well give up.

To get back to our prospector, however, when his body was discovered, it was found that he was without his prospector's pick. Since a prospector's pick to a prospector in that canyon would have been at least as important as his canteen of water, it was assumed that when the snake had buried its fangs in the man's leg the man had lashed down with the prospector's pick, breaking loose the snake's hold. And as he had done so, the pick had slipped from his hands. The snake presumably was killed, or at least its fangs had been removed from the man's leg and the man had no time to pick up the prospector's pick, but was engaged in trying to save his life.

It is interesting, however, that round the man's shoulder was a sack containing ore. Stories vary as to the richness of the ore. Some people say simply that it was very rich; others say that it was almost pure gold.

The surviving partner had hurried back down the wash, had got in his boat and gone to Behia de Los Angeles for help. Then because the weather was calm they were able to return to the canyon and bury his partner. And, of course, there was a great deal of excitement over the sack of ore that had been on the man's shoulder. He had discovered a mineral deposit of fabulous richness. Thereafter, four people lost their lives trying to get into this canyon to search for gold.

Would the Pak-Jak enable us to get up these canyons and explore them? Could we use this interesting device to get into places where no tourist had ever been, or could ever hope to go by using ordinary means of transportation? We made several surveys from the air and became convinced that if we could land on the beach, the Pak-Jaks would pull our trailers loaded with provisions up to the canyons themselves. We could establish a base camp here and have at least one or two days of exploration ahead of us before having to get back to the beach.

And, of course, we realized that we couldn't land at all during periods of high wind and that when we got ready to come home, we might find ourselves marooned on the beach. There was also the realization that if anything went wrong, we were going to add our names to the list of those who had given up their lives trying to explore the deadly canyons.

So after Munoz had circled the canyons several times and we had taken pictures, we headed north, where Munoz showed us other parts of the peninsula which he felt certain had never known the foot of a tourist and many places where, apart from prehistoric Indians, it was quite probable no human foot had ever trod. All in all, when we returned to Tijuana with a map showing dozens of places that we wanted to explore, we were filled with excitement.

We all agreed that the first objective should be that of the twin canyons of La Asamblea and Sal Si Puede and the numerous branches that fanned out into the granite country. So we arranged with Antero Diaz to charter his eighty-foot boat on which we could load our Pak-Jaks, trailers and provisions, and we wanted some smaller boats equipped with powerful outboard motors to keep with us, so that in the event of an emergency we could launch a speedboat and get back to the Bahia de Los Angeles.

Antero had a healthy respect for those canyons. In addition to our other precautions, he insisted that we carry with us a compact, battery-powered, but very powerful, radio so that he could keep in touch with us at the Bahia de Los Angeles. Every day at noon we were to try to call him and report whether we were okay and whether we needed anything. If, because of static or other trouble, we couldn't get him at noon, we were to try again at five o'clock in the evening and, if that failed, we were to try at six o'clock the next morning.

In addition to all these other precautions, Munoz was to fly over us if we ever actually got into the wash, keeping an eye on us, and in case we got into any real trouble and needed anything, we worked out an elaborate system of signals by which we could make our wants known.

So we hurriedly assembled a caravan to go down the road from Mexicali to Bahia de Los Angeles; a caravan that would carry Pak-Jaks, trailers, sleeping bags, food, petrol, water cans, some tents for our base camp, and, of course, cameras and films. Then we started out, filled with determination to get into those canyons, or else.

15

THE ROAD TO BAHIA

BAJA CALIFORNIA is the scene of an ancient civilization. It is a fabulous country, rich in history, rich in mystery. It is a land of almost perpetual sunshine; the ocean is warm and blue, while the air, despite its proximity to the ocean, is dry and clear.

While cars with two-wheel drive *have* been taken over the road from Mexicali to Bahia de Los Angeles, it is not advisable for anyone to start out on the trip unless he is an experienced desert driver, has a car equipped with four-wheel drive, *or* a pick-up with four-speed transmission, a properly balanced load, and is accompanied by a car which has four-wheel drive and a tow chain for short sandy stretches or emergencies. Nor is it really advisable for one person to make the trip alone, nor for any number to make a trip in one car. It is better to have two cars and one should carry plenty of drinking water and petrol.

We paused in Mexicali long enough to say hello to Joe and Emily Gutierrez. Colonel José Gutierrez is typical of the best of Mexico, a man with driving energy, a keen sense of humour, shrewd business acumen and devoted loyalty to his friends. He lives a very rich life and for many years has been my friend. He and Emily (born in the United States) have contracted a marriage that has really worked out. Whenever I go to Mexico via Calexico and Mexicali, I look forward to visiting these friends.

Gutierrez is always building up a business of some sort. The man is a dynamo of creative and executive energy, and I sometimes think he likes to engage in new enterprises for the sheer pleasure of overcoming seemingly insurmountable obstacles.

His hobby is training jumping horses. He loves horses and is skilful in training them. Recently a friend of his had an "outlaw" horse that he was threatening to kill. Colonel Gutierrez said he thought this a mistake, so the friend said, "All right, I'll give *you* the horse. Let's see what *you* can do with him."

So Joe took the horse and a few weeks later the animal would allow Joe to climb all over him, crawl under him, ride him anywhere.

Recently Joe has gone into the bottling business—having a licence for Orange Crush. This is something of a side-line with him, but his plant is a huge modern bottling works sparklingly clean. The drink is distributed by a fleet of trucks and the plant is a credit to Mexicali. It was therefore only natural that when we left Mexicali our cars should be loaded with case after case of Orange Crush—a "going away" present from Joe Gutierrez who had taken a half day out of his busy schedule to see that we got across the border without undue delay and started on our trip under favourable auspices.

From Mexicali the road is surfaced to San Felipe, which is 120 miles south of the Border. San Felipe is a fishing camp-tourist resort, which is becoming better known and more popular day by day. There are boats to be hired here, there are good stores, there is a very fine motel, a superb restaurant and a most interesting curio store specializing in leather goods.

The road from San Felipe to Puertecitos, a distance of about fifty-two miles, is subject to more change than any other road in Baja California that I know of. There are places where the road runs over a hard, rocky alluvial plain and where the surface can be washboarded so it will jar your eye-teeth out. Then it crosses long stretches of sandy wash and I have seen this road so churned up that if you are forced to get to one side to let some other vehicle pass, the chances of getting stuck are very good indeed.

Moreover, American tourists insist upon towing trailers with boats down this stretch of road, and when the road is bad there are tourists stretched all along it in various kinds of trouble—broken trailer hitches, blown-out tyres, overheated engines, vapour locks; and, in fact, almost every kind of mechanical ill to which the average motorist is prone, including being just plain stuck in the sand.

However, the Mexicans work this road regularly, and if you come along after it has been repaired it is a joy. You drift along, averaging almost thirty miles an hour, wondering what would cause anyone the slightest concern in negotiating *this* road. Two months later you jolt your way over the harder places, churn your way through the sand and think this must be a terrible way to travel.

Puertecitos is an interesting little fishing camp resort. There is a restaurant and a bar built from native rocks which were harvested from the adjoining mountains. On the outside these rocks have been left rugged and jagged, but inside they have been cut, smoothed and varnished.

There are boats here and a limited number of people can get accommodation. There is good petrol and a petrol pump, and this is the last place at which one can get petrol until one comes to the Bahia de Los Angeles, about 150 road miles farther south.

Below Puertecitos one suddenly realizes that one is in a country where road conditions are somewhat unpredictable. However, here again, I have seen all sorts of changes in the road from time to time. There are times when one can very readily make it in a two-wheel-drive pick-up with a four-speed transmission. There are times when I wouldn't want to tackle it with anything except a four-wheel drive.

For some thirty miles south of Puertecitos there is a succession of short, steep pitches and a few rather long, narrow grades which are very steep indeed.

The really expert dirt-road driver on coming to one of these grades shifts into low gear and moves slowly and steadily up the road, and if the road is smooth he can get over the summit. The average driver, however, charges at the road with all the speed he can muster, drops into second gear as soon as the pulling gets tough, and then, just before he gets to the top, when he encounters the real test of his engine, throws the gear into low and steps on the throttle. The result is the wheels start to spin, making a little depression in the road for the next car; and, since the second car will find the going getting tough at approximately the same place, its driver will shift his gears and the spinning wheels will make just that much more of a hole. By the time enough cars have been over the road it is all but impassable for two-wheel-drive vehicles.

After a while one encounters a whole succession of these holes, the cars will stall, and the unhappy motorists have no alternative but to back slowly, painfully, laboriously and dangerously down the narrow hairpin turns of the grade to a place where there is good footing in order to try again.

Recently a couple of volunteer road workers have taken over on this stretch and have done marvels with it.

On this trip I had anticipated some difficulty with my two-wheel-drive pick-up south of Puertecitos, but the road had been smoothed so that we didn't need to surge on the power. We could keep an even, steady pace and we went over the steep grades without the slightest difficulty; although on our way back we did encounter a party that was having lots of trouble. Their plight represented one of the tragedies of Mexico; the lack of capital which besets willing, energetic men who would like to better themselves.

The people in this party were enterprising, willing workers. They had pooled their resources to buy a second-hand truck. Then they had mortgaged the truck to get a stock of staple provisions and with these provisions they had left Mexicali to drive down Baja California, hoping to sell the load at sufficient profit to enable them to pay out and make a good return on their investment.

Unfortunately, unfamiliar with the roads, when they hit the first of these long grades they realized that the truck probably would not be able to pull the load up the grade, a distance of perhaps a mile of winding, narrow, very steep road. They also saw the wreckage of other trucks down in the canyon at the bottom—a grim reminder that the road could take its toll. So they played it safe. They unloaded the truck at the bottom of the grade and took it empty to the top. Then by manpower they started carrying the load up the grade. That would have been an almost endless task, and probably would have been more than the men could have hoped to accomplish.

Yet when we came on them they had carried the first part of the load about two-thirds of the way up the grade. There were sacks of potatoes that weighed over two hundred pounds. There were hundred-pound sacks of flour and tin tubs of lard; things which couldn't be divided and which were exceedingly heavy.

There is one thing about the Mexican driver, when he gets into trouble he has no respect for passing traffic. If *he* can't go, there is no reason why anyone else should. So we found the road blocked at the top of the grade by the empty truck, and at the bottom of the grade by the pile of foodstuffs which had been taken from the truck and left there to be carried up by man-power. We also found the first back-aching consignment of goods about two-thirds of the way up the grade.

Sam Hicks and J. W. Black are rough, rugged individuals. They wanted to show these Mexicans that they could do a job when a job needed to be done, so they walked down and each picked up one of the 200-odd-lb. sacks of potatoes, hoisted it to his shoulder and started walking up the grade; a grade so steep that cars with two-wheel drive sometimes stall on it.

It was soon apparent, however, that this method of transport-ing the load of the truck was going to be out of the question. So Sam got the men to move the empty truck at the top, then he turned one of the four-wheel-drive pick-ups round and backed it down the grade.

The Mexicans watched this operation with awe. Backing a truck is an operation Mexicans are not anxious to undertake, nor do I think they are very good at it. Backing a truck down this steep grade made them apprehensive and they wouldn't even consider riding down the grade but ran all the way so that they could help load the truck at the bottom.

Sam, who is an expert driver, manoeuvred the car round all the sharp turns, down to the bottom of the grade, then they loaded about a third of the stuff on the pick-up, Sam ran it up with the aid of the four-wheel drive, transferred the load to the Mexicans' truck and then repeated the process on two additional trips to finish up the load that was at the bottom, leaving the Mexicans jubilant and the road clear. However, we had to point out that there were grades ahead equally formidable.

I am wondering how the Mexicans got over the rest of that road, where they are now, and what happened to their load. Even when we found them, two of the sacks were punctured and flour was leaking out.

When one considers the days of heartbreaking labour that went into amassing the capital necessary for this venture, it is easy to see the inherent tragedy, the almost inevitable financial disaster, which lay in wait for these men in the miles of steep, rocky road ahead.

Now may be a good time to take a look at the people who are going to be with us on this trip.

Sam Hicks, something over six feet, slim, long-legged, long-armed, calmly competent, in the early forties, has been coping with any emergency he has ever encountered during an adventure-filled life. He started out as a rancher, cowpuncher, bronco rider and trapper in Wyoming.

He and his father began outfitting hunting trips during the hunting season, as well as operating a string of ranches during the rest of the year. I first met Sam on an elk-hunting trip and Sam is conceded, even by his competitors, to be just about the most skilful elk hunter in the State of Wyoming.

Sam came down to visit me and bit by bit a friendship developed until finally Sam let his ranching interests in Wyoming go and started working with me.

He is a great friend, a wonderful assistant. He is a good writer and on occasion writes articles which he sells under his own name to various magazines. He took quite a few of the photographs in this book. He is a skilful investigator and has worked with me on cases for the Court of Last Resort, knowing instinctively where to look for evidence, what evidence to look for, and can recognize evidence when he sees it.

He is a good all-round outdoorsman, a wonderful shot, has a keen sense of humour, is always good-natured and makes an ideal camping companion.

Murl Emery is a law unto himself, and you have already met him in the first part of this book.

Murl went through a period when he wanted to be a business-man. He had a boating concession on Lake Mead where he sold thousands of tickets every day; tickets ranging from 75 cents to 25 dollars, depending on the trip. He had a whole fleet of speedboats and a background of water knowledge which is encyclopaedic.

Beneath a rugged exterior of simulated indifference, Emery has one of the most probing minds I have ever met, remarkable powers of observation, a basic knowledge of geology and a know-ledge of how to live in camp that is surprising.

As Emery once expressed it to me, "Most people go on camping trips. I spend most of my life in camps."

And there are lots of things that a man must learn if he is going to camp. It is nice to have a fine tent with a stove in it when one is camping. If the stove is properly designed it can be used for heating and cooking. But, as campers have painfully learned, the stovepipe sucks up hot coals from the stove. These coals, under certain conditions, float briefly through the air, then settle on the tent, burning little holes the size of a pinhead, or, at times, setting the top of the tent afire, so that before the fire can be extinguished there is a great gaping hole with a perimeter of charred canvas.

Emery blithely takes a .22 revolver and shoots the stovepipe full of holes, then he builds his fire and forgets about the problem of a burning tent.

Why does this work?

I don't know. I assume that it somewhat lessens the velocity of the draught so that there is not enough suction to pull burning embers from the stove beneath and I assume that once a burning ember does get in the stovepipe there is enough oxygen-laden air coming in to make the ember consume itself before it spews out of the top of the stovepipe. All I know is that it works.

Murl Emery has one quality which has probably done more to bring about his success in mining than any other trait he has. As he explained it to me at one time, the average miner is too much of an optimist. He gets a prospect, he has a good showing of gold and he keeps on following this prospect. It doesn't get very much bigger but the miner has convinced himself there is a big vein just round the next bend or behind the next few feet of rock. So he puts in all his spare time and all his money following this prospect. Emery says every mine was once a prospect but that doesn't mean every prospect is destined to become a mine.

So Emery is completely hard-boiled about these things. He looks on a prospect with a professionally jaundiced eye. He refuses to waste his time and his operating capital on something unless he can prove it is good within a very limited period of time. Emery may have passed up a few fortunes in his life but he has certainly conserved his time and operating capital so that the mines he has developed are solidly based and he feels, moreover, that he is able to go out in the desert and find a new mine any time he wants to.

Emery has something close to scorn for money and the responsibilities that go with it. He is a whimsical, outdoor, two-fisted philosopher, a very good mechanic and a wonderful companion.

J. W. Black is a young man who is going places. He is something of a mechanical genius. He regards the world with the good-natured tolerance found only in people who are big enough and strong enough to know that they can lick any individual or anything that happens to get in their way.

I doubt if there is any mechanical problem Black can't overcome, and his strength is such that he can pick up pieces of iron I cannot even budge, and handle them as though he were juggling confetti. Black's mind is going all the time and what he sees he remembers and what he remembers he correlates.

Lee Sine, one of the other members on the trip, saw Black's Pak-Jak and with his partner, Ray White, made him a proposition to manufacture a consignment of them on a commercial basis. They took over the distribution and guaranteed to sell them at a minimum price.

It soon became apparent, however, that the problem was not going to be one of demand, but one of supply. Those first few machines were snapped up by the public and Black found himself forced to work nights, days and weekends in order even to begin to keep up with the demand.

Black, however, made one resolution: that after he had completed a specified number of these machines he was going to close the plant temporarily and take a trip somewhere, regardless of demand or pressure from the outside. He had remained firm in that determination and since Lee would have no machines to sell until Black got back into production, both men were able to take time off to accompany us to Baja California.

However, I doubt if wild horses could have kept them away from the trip; even if Black had been in production and Lee Sine had had machines running out of his ears, I think they would have somehow managed to come along on the trip.

Lee Sine is a man who does his own thinking, absorbs new experiences in silence, digests them thoughtfully, then reaches conclusions and is quitely likely never to express an opinion until after his thoughts have crystallized into convictions.

It will be clear, therefore, that we had some useful individuals on this trip; a combination of men who had a knowledge of camping and of woodcraft, mechanical ability of a high order, versatility and ingenuity. One couldn't have asked for a better collection for tackling a difficult assignment.

Since we had all agreed that the most feasible route was by water and that it would be best to land at a point below which the whole network of canyons came together into a broad wash some four or five miles from the ocean, we were hoping for calm weather.

At this particular part of the coast, Angel de la Guarda Island, some fifty miles long, ends with high, rocky promontories veering at a sharp angle to the north-east. Some fifteen miles away the shoreline of Baja California, with high mountains, angles sharply to the north-west. The result is that there is a wind trap which compresses the prevailing winter winds into a natural funnel; and this particular part of the gulf is apt to be rough when all the rest of it is smooth.

However, we felt certain that if we could only get good weather we could land our stuff on the beach, establish a base camp there and then have little trouble getting up to the canyons. Of course it would be quite a job. We would have to get far enough up the canyon to find water, establish a camp there, then return to our base camp on the ocean and arrange to transport enough petrol, food and sleeping bags to enable us to get by. Then we would move up from there a step at a time, making another assault on the canyon.

Both Munoz and Antero Diaz, however, had been sceptical about our ability to land our machines on the beach at the mouth of the wash. And a survey showed that if we landed them anywhere else we still had the problem of crossing mountains so steep and precipitous, and so strewn with huge boulders, no wheeled vehicle could get over them.

However, the last days of December, 1960, were warm and balmy in Baja California and the gulf was flat calm. We camped on New Year's Eve in a spot in the granite country where we had camped on several occasions.

That granite country needs a word of explanation. The peninsula of Baja California seems for the most part to be a mass of

146

granite. In places the terrain has been worn and eroded until there is no soil visible—nothing but the granite and the sand formed by decomposed granite.

As one approaches the backbone of the peninsula the wind-worn granite takes on fantastic shapes. In places the rock has weathered and checked as the seams of softer material have weathered out, and great square boulders which look as though they must have been shaped by human hands, weighing thousands of tons, have either tumbled into confused piles or have balanced themselves precariously on some foundation which, in turn, has been worn away until it seems that even a slight breath of wind must send the great boulders toppling down, leaving a path of roaring destruction in their wake.

There are also smaller boulders where the eroding effect of sand-laden winds have blasted away softer material, leaving the granite looking for all the world as though it were part of a man-made wall.

Elephant trees, those distinctive trees which are indigenous to Baja California and are found in only a few other similar places, seem to like the decomposed granite, and grow in profusion. There are also various other types of cacti and a species of greasewood growing here in the granite country. And just beyond it one encounters the cirio tree, a tree which is found only in Baja California and on the mainland near the gulf.

Our first camp a few miles south of San Felipe had been hastily made as darkness approached, and was simply a place for a fire, a hurried sketchy meal and a night's sleep. But our second camp up in the granite country was one where we had a big campfire, where we brought out folding chairs and spent an hour or two of de luxe companionship. It was New Year's Eve and we were mindful of that fact—not that we intended to sit up to see the New Year in.

Camping out in the open during the long winter nights inevitably changes one's sleeping habits. At home I have difficulty sleeping more than three or four hours a night. I am usually working late at night and again early in the morning, and at times when I get really nervous I have the most irritating of all habits —that of being tired, going to bed, falling asleep, and then wakening with a start about two or three hours later, hopelessly wide awake and as stimulated as though I had been drinking a gallon of coffee.

Once I get out camping in the still, dry air of Baja California, however, the situation is different. To begin with, any seasoned camper thoroughly detests cooking after dark. Emery always insists on making camp by four o'clock whenever possible so that the camp fire can be made and the meal cooked before dark. Then the dishes are washed and put away and we sit round the camp fire. We have a powerful radio and we are almost always able to bring in news from somewhere at six o'clock, with a weather forecast which may or may not be of value. Then we sit round to talk.

By six-thirty we are getting up and turning our backs to the fire for a while, to warm them up, then returning to the folding chairs for a few minutes, then again getting up and circulating round the fire. By six forty-five I usually decide that it would be a little more comfortable to crawl into my sleeping bag and listen to the conversation from the down-filled warmth of my bag and the soft cushion of an air mattress. The others decide to follow my example. Conversation continues for a few minutes then, like the camp fire, begins to die down.

Some comment will come to my mind during a long period of silence. I will start to put the thought in words, then realize that after all it isn't quite worth the effort. The next thing I know it will be midnight. The stars will be blazing steadily overhead, the camp fire will have burned down to a few red coals gleaming fitfully through the ashes, and the outer atmosphere will be cold and silent.

Rounded rolls of white canvas, gleaming in the starlight against the darker ground, will mark the places where my companions are sleeping. I will feel awake but not alert. I will roll over into the warmth of the sleeping bag, heave a deep sigh and look up at the stars for a while. I will be thoroughly convinced that having slept more than five hours already there will be no more sleep for me that night. So I will reconcile myself to remaining awake, watching the constellations. I pick out the location of the various nebulae, marvel at the blazing brilliance of the stars in the crystal-clear silent atmosphere. I will settle myself into a slightly more comfortable position and then awaken to the realization that the east is a streak of colour and that the stars have receded until only the brightest ones have become mere pinpoints which are rapidly fading into oblivion. After a few nights one accepts the fact that normal bedtime is somewhere round six-thirty, and lets it go at that.

On one trip when we were interested in the news there was a very good broadcast that came on at seven-fifteen. Each night we made up our minds we would be up for that news broadcast. We never made it, but had to content ourselves with the six o'clock news the following morning.

In our complex civilization we are whipped into an artificial rapidity of pace that strains our nerves to the limit. But down in Baja California one suddenly sees things in a new perspective. Those business deals that were so terribly important a few days ago are now relegated to the background. The tranquillity of the silent, peaceful country is a soothing benediction to tense nerves. The calm satisfaction of having had a complete complement of sleep is, in itself, a soul-satisfying feeling. And while the camp-fire is made, breakfast cooked, the dishes washed and put away, the air mattresses deflated and the bedrolls tied, all with swift efficiency, there is no feeling of fighting the second hand of the watch. There is efficiency without haste.

One of the dividends of a trip by road down Baja California is the thrill of rising each morning with the knowledge that adventure is lurking somewhere ahead. It may or may not be just round the next bend in the road. Perhaps it is not within the next hundred miles. But somewhere along the road ahead one is certain there will be a real adventure and that each day will present problems which while perhaps not dangerous enough and unexpected enough to be listed as real adventures, will nevertheless be something out of the ordinary requiring the exercise of a certain amount of ingenuity and on-the-spot thinking.

The trouble with civilization, or perhaps I should say one of the troubles with civilization, is that our lives are taken too much for granted. The very conveniences which we have invented to increase our efficiency, decrease our ability to cope with un-expected problems. Our meals are cooked on electric stoves or gas ranges which have various automatic temperature controls; bread is converted into toast in an electric toaster which pops the slices out golden brown and piping hot when they have reached just the peak of perfection. The ice-box enables us to reach in for milk and cream which has been kept perfectly fresh in handy-sized containers ready for pouring.

Every morning endless streams of humanity flow down to places where they take trains or buses. The buses, in turn, wend their way through congested traffic while the passengers are reading the morning paper, until finally all these human ants have converged into a vortex of seething activity at a time when a succession of carefully adjusted springs and cogwheels, turning minute and second hands at a uniform rate, point to the hour of eight-thirty or nine o'clock as the case may be. Here these human beings, by this time transformed into the component parts of some huge economic machine, are whisked upwards in elevators to the proper floor and arrive at offices which are heated by thermostatic control to exactly the right fraction of a degree for human comfort.

All this is very nice, but there is something symbolic about it, like a watch. Each one of these individuals is wearing attached to his wrist one of these cogwheel devices actuated by a spring which moves minute and hour hands at a uniform rate so that at a given instant every one of these individuals sees the hands in exactly the same position as the hands which are attached to the watches on the wrists of all the other hurrying, jostling individuals converging towards the common centre. If the hands aren't uniform in their position, the owner hurries the watch to a jeweller who cleans and adjusts it so that the man is once more in step with the remorseless march of time.

Down in Baja California you can throw your wristwatch away, and you can throw your calendar away. You rise in the morning when it starts to get light. You gather the wood to build the fire. You let the fire die down to coals and on those coals you cook your breakfast. Your time guide for the day is the sun, and the shortening and lengthening of the shadows. Since the only purpose of a watch would be to tell you how much daylight was left in the day, it is easier to look at the shadows themselves than to estimate the time of sunset by consulting minute and hour hands. You are independent. You are on your own. Your activities are not co-ordinated with those of other people. There is, in short, no routine. And always there is the knowledge that the day will bring interesting events, many of which will be completely unexpected.

I have taken many trips down the roads of Baja California and I have never yet taken one where something didn't happen that was worth while chronicling. It is this feeling of having left the routine of civilization behind, of being on your own, of encountering each day as a challenge, that makes the exploration of Baja California roads such a delightful thrill. To have the benefit of a restful sleep in the open, to rise in fighting trim ready to meet the challenge of a new day—this is life!

While we had intended to wish each other a Happy New Year and perhaps have a New Year's drink the night before, sleep had stalked each one of us and caught us unawares. So we somewhat sheepishly wished each other a Happy New Year on January 1st, 1961, and having got the chores over and the camp loaded, were on our way a little after seven-thirty.

16

WE SET OUT FOR THE PALM-LINED CANYONS

FOR the most part one can only make from eighty to a hundred miles a day in Baja California, if one is not driving oneself to the point of fighting the road. And if one tries to fight the road and cover a few more miles the road is very likely to prove the victor in the conflict. In fact, it is almost axiomatic in Baja California that haste not only makes waste, but complete destruction.

As Emery remarked from time to time during our stops, "Let's slow down so we can get there quicker."

After one has poked along at five to twelve miles an hour for several hours it is a welcome relief to come to the broad expanse of Dry Lake Chapala where, when the lake is dry, the soil is smooth as cement, and one can open the car up. Even so, at such moments, shooting the car up to such breakneck speed that one feels positively reckless, one is apt to find on glancing at the speedometer that one is going perhaps forty-two miles an hour. In contrast to the pace one has been maintaining, this seems dare-devil speed.

When, however, the lake is flooded, which it is at intervals during the winter season, and it becomes necessary to go round the lake, the experience is annoying. The soil surrounding the lake is a silty combination of sand and loam. Every mud puddle in the road represents a bottomless trap which must be detoured. And the road itself is rutted almost hub deep. The slightest impatience is apt to result in a broken spring.

Arturo Grosso lives at Laguna Seca Chapala. He has not only a series of small typical ranch buildings but a well which gives good water. It was only recently that Grosso was able to find water he could use. He could put down a well and get water all right but whenever he tried to irrigate a garden with it everything curled up and died. There was something in it which killed vegetation. On this occasion when we stopped to visit him, he was jubilant. He had secured water, he said, which was good water and which he felt certain would enable him to grow a garden.

Grosso is an intelligent man, an energetic man, and, by Baja California standards, a rich man. He has many head of cattle and he has the ability to look and plan ahead. He has sufficient cash margin to hire cowboys and all through this section of the country Arturo Grosso is a power. Grosso is friendly, speaks good English and is keenly interested in people and in events. He likes to chat for a few moments with travellers who pass by, but since he is a busy man with extensive interests it is usually difficult to find him when he isn't in the midst of some big undertaking such as rounding up cattle, shipping cattle or on some other ranching operation. We stopped and paid our respects to Grosso, chatted with him for a few minutes, then moved on down the road.

We paused briefly at the ruins of the ghost city of Desengaño and then went on to Bahia de Los Angeles, arriving there about two o'clock on Sunday afternoon, just in time to be invited by Señor and Señora Diaz to participate in the fiesta.

It was quite a fiesta, with turtle soup and barbecued turtle. The turtle—a big gulf turtle some three feet long—had been barbecued over mesquite-wood coals, by the simple expedient of cutting the turtle in two, propping the shells on rocks, building a fire in between and letting the meat along the inner shells cook to moist tenderness while the juices melted and ran down over the cooking meat. Then the meat is cut into cubes, the shell turned into a kettle and the meat allowed to simmer in the juice while peppers, garlic, lemon, onion and herbs are added.

We were in a spell of unusual calm and we were jubilantly anticipating being able to land without difficulty and establish a base camp. But one doesn't do things hastily in Mexico and this is particularly true during the celebration of the New Year. Antero explained that he couldn't possibly get the boat ready before Tuesday morning at daylight, and in the light of subsequent developments it seems that getting things rounded up for Tuesday morning must have meant the application of quite a bit of pressure.

Antero said that we could load our things aboard the boat on Monday afternoon and be prepared to start at daylight Tuesday morning. So we settled ourselves to a period of relaxed waiting which, in my case, meant following the custom of the country by taking a siesta.

Sam, J. W. and Lee took Pak-Jaks and rode up a trail to an old mine high up on the mountain at the back of Bahia de Los Angeles. From this point of vantage they were able to get a breath-taking view of the entire bay, and they wanted me to go up there the next day with cameras to take some coloured photographs.

However, after listening to their description of the trail, zig-zagging in a series of hairpin turns up the side of a steep mountain, I decided to let the opportunity pass. While a Pak-Jak "will go anywhere", it is no better than its rider and when it comes to negotiating the sharp hairpin turns of a steep trail with a canyon precipice on the down side, I am willing to do it if the necessity arises but I don't want to do it just for fun.

The Bahia de Los Angeles is wonderfully photogenic. It stretches in a great crescent with islands out in the gulf protecting the bay itself from most of the bad weather. The water is an intense blue, the sand a dazzling white and the entire place is soaked in an atmosphere of friendliness.

The Mexicans who live there are dependent upon Antero Diaz for livelihood and Diaz is dependent for the most part on American tourists. The result is a friendly background of personal warmth which matches the balmy warmth of the climate.

Heaven alone knows how many people Antero can put up at a pinch. There are many cabins scattered around and the cabins have wide porches. When occasion requires, Antero can put up cots along these porches. He never has the slightest idea how many people are coming. A few people negotiate the road and come by car, but for the most part his patronage comes by air, sportsmen who have discovered the place and realize that within a couple of hours' flying time from the border they can be in a fisherman's paradise where they can have marvellous food, accommodation with indoor plumbing, comfortable beds, and all at a cost that is absurd when compared with American prices. The result is that at weekends plane after plane comes winging in from the United States and groups of excited tourists pull out fishing tackle, personal baggage and cameras.

Antero is on hand to greet them with genial hospitality, and to assign them cabins. On Saturday night one is likely to hear excited voices in a veritable babble of conversation and the high-pitched sounds of feminine laughter until Antero brings about a curfew by stopping the Diesel motor which generates electric power.

On Sunday tourists are triumphantly holding up fish in front of cameras, guides are busy cutting fillets from freshly caught fish and stacking them like cord-wood.

Sunday afternoon one hears the roar of engines being warmed up. By Monday the place is back to normal with only those who have come in overland by cars and the passengers Francisco Munoz has brought in on his flights from Tijuana besides a few more-or-less permanent guests who have come to stay for one or two weeks.

Antero takes everything in his stride. Nothing bemuses him. He always has his good-natured smile, his quick, energetic competence; there is always plenty of food, plenty of help, and you are somehow given the feeling that while there may be other guests you are number one on the list. It is little wonder that sportsmen everywhere talk about the charm of Bahia de Los Angeles.

Dr Gordon Carman, a dentist of Beaumont, California, has made Bahia de Los Angeles almost a second residence. He has leased some ground from Antero Diaz and has erected his own house. He has an aeroplane and flies back and forth from time to time, virtually commuting between the place where he has his practice and the relaxing environment of Bahia de Los Angeles.

On Monday morning Dr Carman dropped in to shake hands and suggested that since he wasn't leaving until noon it might be a good plan for us to make another survey of the canyons by air.

Since Lee Sine had not seen the canyons from the air and since Murl Emery had been up enough to have a pretty good idea of the terrain, and because Carman's aeroplane would hold no more than four passengers, it was decided that Sam, Lee, J. W. Black and I would accept the generous offer and do a little more aerial exploration.

Lee Sine had flown in planes over the Himalayas during the war, so we assigned him the role of co-pilot and Sam and I took over the photographic assignment, and we were off.

It was a beautiful day for aerial observation and Dr Carman, a skilful flier, took us down into the canyons so that in places we seemed almost to be skimming the top of the palm trees. Here were places within fifteen minutes' flight of the Bahia de Los Angeles where we could look down on a country where no tourist had ever been; perhaps where no human being had been for the last three hundred years.

From the aircraft we saw grove after grove of interesting palms. We saw long stretches of smooth canyon lined with palms on each side. We studied the whole labyrinth long enough to realize that there were miles and miles and miles of country in which there would be novelty and adventure. Here we could see game as it existed in primitive surroundings. We were likely to find mountain lions and mountain sheep which had never had the slightest contact with a human being. While we were exploring we could bear in mind that no one knew what was just round the bend, because no one had ever been there and returned to tell the story.

We returned to the Bahia de los Angeles, impatient to leave while the weather was still a flat calm. There had been fiesta and celebration on New Year's Eve. We knew that there had been celebrations the night before because we could hear the stringed instruments, the sound of soft Mexican voices singing from time to time during the night. We had hardly expected, however, that Monday night would also be a fiesta night, but it was. All during the night when we wakened we could hear music and singing. It seems that virtually everyone in Mexico can make music of sorts. They can strum a guitar and they can sing. And there is a softness, a plaintive something about the Mexican music which blends with the temperament of the country and the velvety softness of the Mexican nights.

It was soothing to waken from time to time during the night and hear the sounds of the celebration—never the boisterous, raucous noises which emanate from an American celebration, but always the soft, controlled cadences of melodious voices and a harmony of mind reflected in the tempo of the music and the type of singing. All in all they made quite a band, with violin, guitar and a musical instrument which apparently took the place of our bass viol.

This consisted simply of a big inverted lard tin with a hole punched in the top and a cord running through the hole and knotted on the end. The other end was tied round a broomstick to which the worn-out broom was still attached.

The musician would put the lower end of the broomstick near the perimeter of the tin can, then would tighten the cord by pulling back on top of the broomstick. He would pluck at this cord and the result would be a deep percussive note. By tilting the top of the broom a little more and putting a little more tension on it, or relaxing it somewhat, this note could be changed noticeably, and the instrument gave out a throbbing undertone which caused the music to pulsate in hypnotic rhythm.

We wondered if our crew would be able to prop their eyes open with toothpicks so as to make the trip the next day, and I began to feel that the daylight start was simply a figure of speech.

However, we were up before daylight and Antero Diaz got up to turn on the Diesel motor so that we would have light. We got everything packed and all our personal baggage ready to go and transported to the edge of the ocean. Reassuringly, there were lights on the big boat indicating that it had started its generator and almost as soon as it was light enough to see, the crew came to fetch us in boats and take us aboard.

Once aboard, there were some delays in getting the engines warmed up and the anchor up, but within a reasonable length of time we were under way, creeping slowly out of the harbour.

It had been a beautiful night. The moon, very slightly past the full, had risen to send a narrow ribbon of light over the bay. Then, as the moon got higher, the ribbon of light became broader, until finally the whole bay was a silvery sheet of illumination with the boats at anchor silhouetted in dark outline. Now, in the early morning, the moon was just setting over the mountains behind the settlement; it made a beautiful picture.

After we started crawling out of the harbour I took time to get acquainted with the two people Antero had selected to work with us on the trip: Ynes, who was to be something of a guide and general factotum, and to run the speed-boat in case of necessity; and Juanito, who was to act as cook.

At the time I didn't appreciate the remarkable characters of these men. Juanito, quietly self-effacing, was a Tyrolean who had for some reason become a political refugee from Europe. He was a thoughtful man who spoke four languages (if one could count English), stooped with years and with much work, but quietly capable.

Ynes was essentially an adventurer and a hunter. Apparently, as we learned later, he was somewhere in his forties but he gave the impression of being much younger. He was powerfully built and, as it turned out, had about the keenest pair of eyes I ever encountered. He had acute powers of observation, virtually no knowledge of English, and I think perhaps somewhere in the back of his make-up, a certain amount of scorn and perhaps pity, for the *gringo touristas* whom he must chaperone from time to time, and who were fat, soft and, according to his standards, enormously wealthy; and, also according to his standards, completely helpless.

He carried his prize possession, a .30-30 rifle along with him, and it wasn't until an hour or so later that someone noticed that a crude record had been scratched on the stock of the gun. The word *borregos* was preceded by six straight lines; then came *venados*, signifying deer, preceded by seven straight lines; then coyotes, preceded by six straight lines.

But we noticed there were some other scratches near the top of the stock and we twisted the gun so that when we finally got the light just right we could decipher what had been written there. It was *Gringoes*, preceded by two straight lines.

This was to be the day of our great adventure. Our spirits were buoyed up enormously. We were on pins and needles, thrilled with excitement, impatient to get where we were going. The boat seemed barely to crawl along the gulf.

Juanito got down in the galley and cooked us breakfast: French fried potatoes, fried eggs, tortillas and coffee. Then we were back on deck, studying the shoreline with binoculars, talking in tense tones of suppressed excitement.

Our Pak-Jaks were tied along the chain which served as a rail for the boat. Our gear was safely stowed in the hold. We had a lot of provisions: apples, oranges, flour, bacon, tinned goods, beans. We had petrol, drinking water, cameras, films, sleeping bags, air mattresses, clothing.

We were loaded—so was the boat.

The first gusts of cold wind began to come in our faces and we bravely assured each other that this was just a mild sea breeze. Then the breeze began to freshen. Soon there were whitecaps and we then assured each other that this was just a local squall, that the weather was perhaps changing but that we would get to our landing place early enough to take advantage of a relatively calm sea.

The wind freshened until it began to howl through the superstructure of the boat. Someone reported another boat on the starboard bow and we swung the binoculars round to see a shrimp fishing boat still farther out in the gulf making heavy weather of it while it came cruising shoreward at an angle which would intercept our course about three or four miles ahead.

Then suddenly, while we watched, the boat abruptly changed course and headed directly for us. It came to within a few hundred yards, then veered off while the crew studied us intently, then forged on ahead. Apparently they had seen our deckload through binoculars and had wondered whether they were having a nightmare or whether it was possible some boat, headed towards this trackless country where there was not even so much as a trail, could be carrying a deck-load of motorcycles.

It soon became clear that the fishing boat was headed into a bay where a headland gave limited protection against the wind. However, we were still brave and optimistic, but by the time we reached this bay we were slapping spray into the air as we hit the waves. The whitecaps were racing past, the wind was howling a gale, and it was obvious we were going to have to enter the bay and take advantage of what protection it had to offer.

Binoculars showed that several other fishing boats were also headed our way, indicative of the fact that they all expected heavy weather. Moreover, the barometer was falling rapidly.

We clawed into the best protection we could find and dropped anchor but the force of the wind was such that the anchor dragged and we had to keep the engines turning over to hold our position.

By this time several more of the shrimp boats were coming into the bay, dropping anchor and trying to hold against the wind. Most of them gave it up and, hoisting anchor, went just as far into the bay as they dared and as close to the shore as they could get, dropping anchor in the area of maximum protection.

It was at this point that we all became weather experts. Sam was positive the wind would go down at about three o'clock that afternoon and it would be flat calm. He based his opinion upon what he had observed at the channel on prior trips. Others hoped it would go down by two o'clock but we were all sure it would be flat calm by dark. The moon was full enough so that we could, if necessary, make a landing by moonlight.

That left us a day with nothing much to do. So we started killing time, and I think the crew took advantage of the situation to get caught up on some much needed sleep.

We soon found that by moving baggage in the hold we could establish comfortable quarters there, spread out our sleeping bags and lie in relative ease, protected from the wind.

I realized of course that if I slept during the day I wouldn't be sleeping at night but I couldn't resist the drowsiness of inactivity and from time to time would doze off in naps of an hour or so. I had brought along two battery-powered dictating machines: the Audograph, which I had had with me on previous trips to Baja California and which had given me such good service; and one of the new Webcor Microcorders, a transistor-powered tape recorder which is remarkably sensitive and which is invaluable for a writer who wants to record conversations. I used both these machines as I dictated from time to time.

For the most part, however, I slept.

Then came the wind-blown night. The Diesel was stopped, the lights went out and we were left to our own devices in the hold of the boat, snuggled into our sleeping bags, the wind screaming overhead, the boat rocking in the waves.

Shortly after dark we had changed our anchorage, gone into the bay as far as we dared go, and managed to get enough of a holding ground for the anchor so that we could shut off the motors.

The boat was silent save for occasional creaking and the screaming wind. Our place in the hold was well ventilated through the open hatch but because of the tightly joined, insulated walls there was no suggestion of a draught.

We had all been sleeping and we all felt certain that we were

We make camp and relax

A canyon which has never before known North Americans

The author

going to be awake most of the night. Much to our surprise, everyone had a perfect night's sleep.

I think there is quite a lesson here. We knew there was nothing we could do if we were awake. We were in the only comfortable place on the boat; whatever was to come next would be the result of developments due to forces other than anything we could personally control. In fact there was nothing to do except sleep, so sleep we did.

Emery was the first one up the next morning. He poked his head through the hatch and exclaimed jubilantly: "We've got it made! The weather has changed. It's overcast. That means the wind is going to be from the south and during the period of change there'll be a flat calm."

All of us jumped up, dressed and waited impatiently for the crew to get up and in action. What we didn't realize was that the crew had taken an earlier look at the situation, just at the first streaks of daylight, and not being quite as naive or quite as enthusiastic as Emery, had decided we were beaten and gone back to bed. Eventually the crew got up and Juanito started making coffee.

It should be mentioned at this point that we were in radio communication with Antero Diaz, who had a ship-to-shore radio installation, and who had telephoned us at about nine-thirty the day before, apparently ready to suggest that we go back and try to get into the canyons over the mountains. In his opinion the water approach was going to be impossible for a rather extended period of time.

Sam, however, had been the one to talk to him and Sam, filled with optimism, had assured Antero the weather wasn't at all really bad where we were; that is, it was windy but it could be a lot worse. Antero reported that the bay was calm but binoculars showed him that the gulf out beyond the islands was whipped into a turmoil of raging whitecaps. Quite clearly he had wanted us to turn back but Sam had pooh-poohed him for being chickenhearted. We were going to the canyons or bust and we weren't going to get there by turning back.

When the wind began to come up in the morning all of us felt pretty discouraged. The crew got up, took a look, and it was possible to see from their facial expressions what they felt the weather was going to be. We didn't need an interpreter or a Spanish-English dictionary. And the faces of Lee Sine and Murl Emery were pretty darn good barometers of scepticism. As they sat huddled in the lee of the cabin, I couldn't resist taking a photograph which was even more eloquent than words.

By nine-thirty Antero Diaz was on the phone again. This time I insisted that, as time was dribbling through our fingers, we yield to his superior judgement. He thought we had better go back to Bahia de Los Angeles and try to get over the mountains. He felt certain the weather was going to be rough for some days.

It was not a popular decision but we made it. We got the anchor hoisted and started back with a tailwind pushing us on, and arrived shortly before noon.

Antero Diaz was all apologies. In true Mexican fashion he wished to assume all the blame. The cursed weather had betrayed him, but he couldn't refrain from pointing out that we must expect wind this time of the year. He had warned us. "No?"

We reminded him there had just been four or five days of clear calm and Diaz nodded vehemently. It was too bad. We had just missed it. If we had only been a day earlier perhaps. He eloquently shrugged his shoulders. But he felt certain we could get in through the dry lakes. After all, there was only one little hump to get the machines over and he was certain we could do it.

That, however, brought up another problem. We certainly couldn't get trailers over those mountains and we couldn't carry enough on the Pak-Jaks to establish a base camp in the canyons, if we ever got there. So we were going to have to get a string of mules that could pick their way into the canyon somehow.

Antero was certain that a mule could go wherever the Pak-Jak could go. J. W. wasn't quite so certain. But it was finally arranged that Antero would locate Pepe Smith, who had a string of mules and burros. Smith and Sam would round up all the mules and burros on the ranch, and Pepe would take off, prepared to join us somewhere at the head of the dry lake.

I wanted to arrange a definite rendezvous and Antero smiled tolerantly. We didn't need to worry. Pepe would find us.

Wherever we were, that was where Pepe would come with the mules and burros.

Since Pepe was going to have to go some forty miles, we started him getting his stuff together and then took a quick trip with the cars and the Pak-Jaks down to the ghost town of Las Flores.

Seventy years ago Las Flores was a flourishing mining community with great prosperity and great hopes. The promoters had even shipped in a locomotive and put up a narrow-gauge railway line, running from the mine to the town where the mill was to be located. For some years the mine had been in production and then it had closed down. Now the buildings were in ruins, the rusty locomotive had been partially dismantled and the tracks had been left to rust to pieces.

We inspected the old rusted locomotive, and then, using our Pak-Jaks, prowled round the site of the village, picking up little discarded bits of evidence of a bygone civilization.

17

WHERE NO HUMAN FOOT HAS TROD

THE next day we were off for the dry lakes. We had a great assortment of Pak-Jaks, tents, water, petrol, sleeping bags, provisions and cameras. Ynes and Juanito were riding on top of the load, and since they were the official guides it became necessary from time to time to confer with them. So we would stop the car and Sam would climb up one side, I would climb up the other, and we would have our conferences.

We crossed the first dry lake, ploughed along in four-wheel drive into the rough country on the other side of the lake and began to see wild burros.

Whereas the tame burro moves along in calm patience, apparently only mildly interested in whatever new vicissitude of fortune life has in store for him, these wild burros hold their heads high and are proud of their freedom. They swish their tails in nervous indignation at the approach of a vehicle and then take off across the desert in that peculiar half-trot, half-gallop which is characteristic of the species, and which can cover ground at an astonishing speed.

The wild burro is esteemed as remarkably good eating by everyone who has tried it, and while I think perhaps I have eaten wild burro on occasion without knowing it, I have always tried to discourage the killing of wild burros.

I had two pet burros once who gave me their confidence, and in turn received my confidence. We had a wonderful companionship. Moreover, I learned a great deal. The burro can understand just about everything he wants to and he is adept at pretending not to understand the things he doesn't want to understand, but which you want him to. He can look at you with patient lack of comprehension yet at the same time not only know what you are saying to him, what you want, but what you are going to say and what you are going to want, and exactly what he intends to do about it. And heaven help the human being who pits his restless impatience against the mind of a burro.

On some of the old-time cattle ranches where there was a great distance between headquarters and the outlying grazing country, when they found a steer that was too "snaky" to drive in a herd, one who would break away at the first opportunity and head into the brush, they had one cure which always worked. They would drive a burro from ranch headquarters out to the brush. They would corner the steer, rope him and then tie him firmly to the burro. Then they would go away.

In the course of time the burro would show up at the ranch with a steer that weighed five times as much as he did. From the viewpoint of the burro there was nothing to it. When the steer started moving away from the ranch he would have to drag the burro. Whenever the steer moved towards the ranch the burro would move under his own power. At first the steer would drag the burro wherever he wanted to go, but eventually the pair would show up at the ranch. Such is the power of patience. Never underestimate the burro.

Juanito had prospected over much country and had a general idea of the lay of the land. Ynes had hunted over much of the country and knew a good deal about it. Sam, J. W. Black, Lee Sine and I had flown over the country looking for landmarks and getting the country "firmly fixed" in our minds. Sam insisted he could pick out landmarks on the ground that he had seen and noted from the air.

So far as I was concerned, I had carefully studied the terrain, and I was lost. Looking at the country from the air was one thing and looking at it from the ground was another. However, when it comes to argument I'm damned if I'm going to be left out of an argument simply because I don't know what I'm talking about.

So we drove and argued and argued and drove, and eventually came to a spot where we pitched our tent in the very late afternoon of an overcast day.

That night I awakened to look at the moonlight. It was a cold, windy night and the shadows were coming from the wrong direction. Incredulously I took another look. The camp was facing in the exact opposite direction from what I had thought it was the night before; either that, or else the moon was coming up in the wrong direction.

In the morning we had an argument as to directions and Sam impatiently traced a cross on the floor of the tent, marking north, south, east and west. When the sun came up it came up in the west so far as I was concerned, and to the south as far as Sam's diagram was concerned. In fact everyone was turned round and I am inclined to think that that is one day that the sun got tired of coming up in the same old direction day after day and decided to have a little variety.

We had a hurried breakfast, then Sam, Emery, Lee Sine, J. W. Black and Ynes all swarmed aboard the pick-up which contained the Pak-Jaks and started exploring the country, headed towards a mountain which Sam swore he could recognize from his observations on the aeroplane. In view of the fact that he hadn't known where the sun was coming up I was inclined to take this with what is known as a pinch of salt and a barrel of pepper.

I decided to stay in camp with Juanito and we had a leisurely talk during which Juanito gave me much of his history. He never talked about the Old Country or what had happened there, but by using sign language, English and fragmentary Spanish, I gathered that Juanito had spent some two years shark fishing, making his headquarters at a spring known as La Botica, which was near the wash which we had wanted to explore by boat, and where we wanted to make our base camp. We had heard from others that there was a spring near there and that fishing boats sometimes put in to replenish their store of drinking water.

Juanito had also had some interest in a ranch which was near the site of the old mission of Calamajue. He had from time to time walked back and forth from his camp on the beach to this ranch and in doing so had traversed one of the canyons. I gathered it was the most northerly canyon of the system we wanted to explore. He said no one else had ever been there.

Juanito said there was a spring of water about twelve miles from the ocean and about thirteen or fourteen miles from the ranch. He used to make the trip in two days, trudging through the long, hot, sandy canyon, until he reached this water; staying there at night, then getting up the next morning and moving back to his camp.

166

This had been seventeen years ago when, one gathered, Juanito had pushed himself to the limit, walking as rapidly as possible so that he could leave the ranch in the afternoon and get to the spring, then leave the spring early in the morning and get down to his camp in time to go to work shark fishing.

Juanito was now seventy-one. He was stooped somewhat and he had lost many of his teeth, most of which he had apparently been forced to extract himself. He was now having another toothache and intimated he would probably have to extract another tooth in the near future. But there was no complaint in Juanito's nature. He was like a burro. He took things as they came and he wasted no time in wishing that they might be otherwise.

As I came to know him later, here was a man in his seventies, who could ride all day on a burro after cooking breakfast and helping to pack the burros, who could come into camp at night bone tired yet quite ready to get out the pans and start cooking over the fire, then, in the light of the campfire, clean up the dishes and get everything put away shipshape before going to bed.

It is something of a job riding a burro hour after hour in the sun, particularly if a man is heavy and Juanito was carrying a good deal of weight.

Ynes, the hunter, stocky build, thick-chested, with short arms and legs, was a walker. He wasn't built to walk but he walked anyway. Now, Sam Hicks is a natural walker. He has long legs, a slim waist and lean flanks. He devours the distance with long, easy strides. Ynes, on the other hand, being short-legged took a step and a half to one of Sam's, but he used those short legs of his like powerful pistons. As I got to know the man better I was surprised to find the extent of his endurance. He would stand up to a day which would leave the ordinary man as limp as a dishrag. He would cover ground which even a good walker would have considered a long day's work, and then he would be ready to pitch in and go to work when we were making camp.

Shortly after noon Emery came back filled with excitement. They had explored the mountains and decided we couldn't get over them. Then, just as they were about to give up, Lee Sine had found an old, old trail.

This trail apparently went back to the time of the missions. Along the sidehill many of the huge boulders had rolled down in the last hundred years or so until the trail was in places virtually obliterated. But farther on one would come to places where the trail was again fairly open. And up on the mesa above the first mountain ridge the trail was in good shape.

By working on this trail and moving the rocks that could be moved from the trail, and for the rest relying on the rugged hill-climbing ability of the Pak-Jaks, Sam, Black and Sine were trying to move the machines up the hill.

Ynes had started back earlier before they had found this trail and had said that he would be in camp at two-thirty. As soon as he arrived we were to move the entire camp to a point near the start of the trail.

Since Ynes carried no watch and the route he was going to take was a long, arduous walk along the ridge of mountains, I was somewhat apprehensive that he would be late. He was going to have to tell time by the sun. I could have spared myself the worry. Ynes showed up in camp at exactly two-twenty-eight.

Moving the camp was some little chore. But Ynes and Juanito tackled the job with skilled efficiency. Emery furnished both man-power and direction and within a surprisingly short time we had the camp loaded and started out, following the tracks in the deep sand, getting up to our new camping place shortly before dark and pitching the tent—again in a cold wind.

Sam, Black and Sine came down the trail, three tired men. But they had moved the four Pak-Jaks which they had with them up to the top of the mountain. (My Pak-Jak had been left behind in camp in case I wanted to do some exploring on it. Otherwise they would have had it with them.)

So, while everyone was tired that night, they felt that they had the hardest part of the job behind them and that they were going to be able to get the Pak-Jaks down into the wash early the next day so that we could start out.

Sam insisted that this was the wash which led down to the other wash by the ocean and eventually, by using it, we could reach the canyon we wanted to explore. He pointed out landmarks he had seen from the air. These were also landmarks I had seen from the air, but they didn't look like anything I had ever seen before.

We started fixing up light packs of bare essentials. Pepe Smith would bring eight mules and burros. That would leave four burros for packing because we had to have riding burros for Smith, his twelve-year-old son Nenny, and for Juanito and Ynes; although Ynes insisted that he would be able to walk right along and keep up with the burros.

It is interesting to note parenthetically that on this trip Ynes did so much walking he wore a pair of shoes to shreds. By the time the trip was over the soles were flapping loose from the uppers. I am reminded under such circumstances of a remark made by Bill Sullivan, an Idaho outfitter who has taken me on several trips into the primitive area. "My shoes were so damned thin," Sullivan was wont to state, "that whenever I'd go to town and step on a piece of chewing gum I could tell what flavour it was."

Early in the morning Sam, Lee Sine and Ynes started up the hill to move the Pak-Jaks down to the flat on the other side. J. W. Black took my Pak-Jak to "ride" up to the top of the hill.

"Riding" these Pak-Jaks over obstructions such as huge boulders calls for much skill and, at times, considerable strength. The rear wheel of the Pak-Jak keeps revolving. You can put the front wheel up against a building and the rear wheel will keep revolving slowly and steadily until it has dug a hole or worn all the tread off the tyre. When one comes to an obstruction in the trail one is supposed to put one's feet down on the ground, give a gentle push and open the throttle slightly. The Pak-Jak leaps forward and up, and then you either drop on the seat as it goes by or partially close the throttle, take another step and give another little burst of power. At times you have to reach back and pick up the rear frame of the Pak-Jak and lift it over some obstacle which is so spaced that the frame of the Pak-Jak gets "hung-up".

However, given a big rear wheel which continues to revolve no matter what happens, it is surprising what one of those things can do.

The terrifying thing, however, is when one loses one's footing or perhaps gets a foot tangled in a rock and the Pak-Jak, with that steady, remorseless power, keeps on going. Even if you are only moving at the rate of a mile and a half an hour that can seem to be a terrific speed under some circumstances. It's difficult to co-ordinate one's reactions fast enough to synchronize wheel, throttle and brakes and keep up with what is happening—I know because I've experienced it and have the scars to prove it.

Pepe Smith showed up with the mules and burros a little after nine o'clock. Don't ask me how he had found us. He knew where we were and came unerringly to the place where we were camped. Not to the place where we had been camped the day before, but to the place where we were camped now. Smith is a tall, taciturn individual who has known his share of tragedy. He had a large family and then recently his wife died, leaving him with all the children and the necessity of making a living as well as keeping the home together.

Pepe was accompanied by his twelve-year-old son Nenny, an alert, intelligent lad who was as full of bounce as a rubber ball. That boy did a man's work all during the trip. He rode from daylight to dark, he helped pack burros, he would hobble the burros at night, had sufficient skill to track each individual burro the following morning, knew how to saddle pack and unpack, and always tackled every task—not with the attitude of trying to do a chore—but with enthusiasm and endless energy.

Looking at him one could only wonder at the responsibilities he had had to take on, both at home and out in the field; remembering that there were seven children, and that five of them were younger than he was, one could realize something of the situation and appreciate more fully what it meant to have a young man so competent, so cheerful and, above all, so quick to get into action and accomplish what he was called on to accomplish.

Even travelling light we had our pack burros pretty badly overloaded. One burro in particular had to carry two five-gallon cans of water, two five-gallon cans of petrol and a bag containing other equipment. With water at ten pounds to the gallon and the cans weighing three or four apiece, that burro was carrying well over 200 pounds. And he was carrying it over country that was rough, steep and rugged; then down into soft sand where a man's feet sank with every step. The poor little burros, carrying this amount of weight, sank several inches every time they put down a hoof.

We left all our surplus supplies in the tent; most of our cameras, the dictating machines, films, provisions, drinking water, petrol and some of our bedding.

I started out at about ten-thirty to walk up the trail and over the mesa to where the Pak-Jaks were waiting on the other side. It was a long, tough climb just pushing my way up and it was more than two hours later that I got down to where I could see Black and Sine had the other Pak-Jaks waiting.

It turned out to be quite a job getting the mules and burros over the mountain, even with the trail which the men had cleared up as much as possible. Once, one of the burros got all tangled up in the rocks and was smart enough to know that he couldn't dislodge himself without breaking a leg, so he simply stayed put until everything had been unpacked and rocks had been moved and he had been lifted to his feet. Then he was repacked and consented to move on.

At length, however, we had the whole expedition together at the start of a broad wash leading in the general direction we felt we wanted to go, and started off.

We on the Pak-Jaks were so impatient that we cruised far ahead of the burros and then either waited for them to catch up or doubled back to make certain everything was coming all right.

It was a wonderful thrill going down that wash. Not only was the scenery beautiful but we had the knowledge that within the last twenty or twenty-five years no one had been there. Pepe Smith, Juanito and Ynes were the men who would have been there if anyone had been, yet none of them had ever set foot in this country. Pepe Smith hadn't known about the ancient trail we had uncovered and was pleased to have learned of it. In short, we were exploring brand-new country.

After two or three miles the wash broadened out into a sort of amphitheatre with granite cliffs closing in on three sides and a gentle up-slope on the other. It looked very much as though we were hemmed in but we realized that in times past, during periods of storm, quite a bit of water must have run down this wash and it had either found some outlet or would have formed a lake, and there were no signs of a lake. So we kept on going.

Abruptly the wash turned into a canyon between granite cliffs, but the floor remained sandy and it was easy to keep going with Pak-Jaks.

After several miles of this it began to get late in the afternoon and I felt we should make camp where there would be feed for the mules and burros.

These hardy little creatures feed on mesquite, or if there is a verde tree available and a few limbs can be chopped down, they will browse on its leaves and seem to get along all right. It was destined to be a dry camp for the animals and I understood the preceding night had also been a dry camp. It is remarkable what these mules and burros can do in dry country, particularly if they are not worked too hard or encounter too much hot weather.

Pepe Smith was, however, anxious to press on just as far as possible before dark, so he suggested we move on for another half hour.

The burro which was overloaded—the one carrying the water and petrol—knew somehow that I was looking for a camp site and that my voice indicated I was sympathetic. He started following me round like a dog. If I got away from the main wash to investigate what I thought might make a good place to camp and sat there waiting for Pepe to come up, that burro would spot me and come up to me, then turn and stand so that his left side was to me and all but thrust the knot of the pack rope into my hands.

At length, just as the canyon was bathed in a deep pool of shadow, the riders who had been on ahead came back with alarming news. They had reached a place where there was a sheer drop of forty or fifty feet. During periods of flood there must have been quite a waterfall there. In the meantime the bed of the canyon simply came to a steep rocky barrier, dropped fifty feet and then resumed its way towards the sea.

This was disturbing news indeed. It looked as though we might have to turn, retrace our steps, fight our way back over the mountain and give up all hope of getting into the palm-lined canyons. We ate a rather gloomy supper although Sam was confident that we were within a few miles of the place where the canyon merged into the wash we wanted to follow.

I suggested that Sam try to scale one of the canyon walls so that he could get to the top and see if he could spot the ocean and see how far away it was. But Ynes, who had been looking round, motioned to Sam and they vanished into the late afternoon shadows.

I learned afterwards that they climbed down the rock wall,

walked about half a mile and then came to a place that Ynes knew—a place he had found in his walk up from the ocean on a previous trip. With that landmark once established Ynes knew the whole country.

So, just before it got completely dark, Sam and Ynes were back with the encouraging news that we could probably get up to the palm canyons if we could only find some way of getting our Pak-Jaks down the face of that cliff.

Nevertheless I was worried. We might use ropes to lower our equipment down the cliff, but could we ever get up again? We had food and water for a very brief trip. I could never have walked back to base camp.

I didn't do much sleeping, yet I will long remember the beauty of that night. This air, despite the fact it is near the ocean, was free of humidity and clear as crystal. I could look up and see the stars in great profusion. The Milky Way was a silvery star stream, and I could pick out individual stars which could never be seen at all in the more polluted atmosphere of the cities.

I slept and then wakened as the slightly lopsided moon came up over the canyon wall. There were smoke trees in the canyon. Having a light, silvery blue shade and lacy, spine-like leaves, they look for all the world like drifting smoke. As the moon came up over the rim of the canyon the mountain was a silhouetted black of intense shadow. The wash turned to brilliant silver and these smoke trees, outlined against the black of the shadow, were turned by the magic of moonlight into silvery clusters. Over all was the blanket of absolute, complete silence. I knew that the following day would hold adventures—many adventures.

I dozed off and slept soundly until the first streaks of daylight, when we were up and getting camp organized. By broad daylight we went down to take a look at the face of the cliff.

Some of the others could negotiate it by lowering themselves down on the waterworn rocks, then angling along through a fissure and then finally moving slowly down a steep ledge only a few inches wide with a straight drop behind it and only a precarious handhold. I might have done it, I don't know. And I might have been seriously injured. I had to have help to get down there and I didn't make any bones about it.

Just now the problem was whether we could ever get our camp

173

equipment and our Pak-Jaks down this ledge. If we could, we had it made. If we couldn't, we were beaten.

Pepe Smith surveyed the surrounding country, and finally found a route by which he thought he could get the burros up on to the wall of the canyon, inch his way round to a point below the barrier, then descend to the lower canyon and lead the mules back up to the rocky wall. We, in turn, could roll all the camp stuff into bundles and lower it with ropes over the face of the cliff.

The Pak-Jaks, however, presented quite a problem. They weigh about 170 lb. apiece and they have two wheels and are precariously balanced. If we could find some way of keeping them upright so that we could use the wheels to ease the load we felt we could make it, but they would have to be kept upright and everything would have to work like a charm.

So we got all the rope we could and started working our vehicles down the cliff a few inches at a time, holding them snubbed with a rope, letting them roll for a few inches, then straightening them; letting them roll for a few more inches until finally we came to the last fifteen or twenty feet which was a sheer, absolute drop. There was nothing we could do except snub a rope and trust to luck.

It was touch and go for a while but we finally got the first Pak-Jak lowered down to the floor of the canyon below and after that the others came faster. Whether we could ever get them back again was another question—one that gave me increasing concern.

We didn't wait for Pepe Smith to get the burros all reloaded but, impatient as we were to see what lay ahead, started the Pak-Jaks and moved on down the canyon.

A mile or so on down the canyon Ynes indicated we were to take a canyon which went to the left. We did so and came to the unmistakable indication of water. There was a yellowish type of coarse grass ahead, completely covering the canyon. And there were bones. Heaven knows how many bones there were. These were the skeletons of mountain sheep and they were there by the dozen.

There were indications that the canyon had been used by the Indians as a hunting ground. There were typical Indian hunting "hides", so constructed that hunters could shoot a bow and arrow through openings so placed that the game must pass within fifteen to twenty-five feet of them.

We found a pile of bones which could have been covered by a good-sized blanket and in that one pile we counted the remains of thirty different sheep. Some of these undoubtedly had been killed by mountain lions—we saw many lion tracks—some few probably by bullets and perhaps some by Indian arrows. And it was possible some of them had died of old age.

Ynes insisted that when the mountain sheep became too old to forage in the hills they came down to this spring to live out their old age, and finally to die. The bones would certainly so indicate.

Native hunters could hardly have accounted for these skeletons, nor for the very good heads of horns which were lying there in the sunlight—although we had now reached a point so near the ocean it was possible some hunters had found this spring. We tasted the water in it. It seemed to be strongly flavoured with soda, as though someone had put a teaspoonful of baking soda in a glass of water.

I have a feeling that it would have been possible to have found many arrow points here in this canyon. Undoubtedly the Indians had rigged up "hides" almost from time immemorial and had ambushed the mountain sheep as they came to drink. Some day I hope to return and make a search for arrow points and again study this canyon, but at the moment we had no time for that. We were determined to get to the canyon of the palms, go up past the first few intersections and see just what the situation looked like from the ground.

We got our Pak-Jaks and started down the canyon which speedily widened into a wash with towering cliffs of pastel pink, orange and a bluish green. The pink seemed to predominate and there were whole mountains of it. We didn't climb up to see exactly what materials composed these various strata. In fact the sides were virtually sheer in places. However I did inspect some of the cliffs where the coloration came down to the floor of the wash. The material seemed to be of compressed ash, coloured a delicate, uniform pink with no streaks in it at all. This formation ran for miles along the coast, cropping out here and there in various places.

As we descended towards the ocean the wash became wider and wider until finally we reached its intersection with another wash and saw an outcropping of the same pink formation thrust up out of the canyon floor at the junction of the washes.

We knew now that we were on the right track, since we had previously spotted this same pink outcropping from the air and knew that it marked the place where the palm canyon wash joined the others. So we waited for the mules and burros to catch up to be sure we were all headed up the right canyon, then turned and started up this other wash.

Within half a mile or so we began to realize that this canyon must have lots of palm trees in it. There were evidences of floods and the trunks of palm trees were scattered about like matchsticks.

It is difficult to account for the floods. They must have been within modern times. Yet it is a land of little rainfall. However, occasionally during the summer months a chubasco or Mecian hurricane comes roaring up the gulf. At those times there is a tremendous amount of rainfall and there are many indications that because of local conditions these canyons and the surrounding country get rainfall when the rest of the peninsula is bone-dry.

We pressed on hurriedly now, eager to get up into the clusters of palms we had seen from the air. The sun was intense and looking down at the reflected sunlight from the white sand was agonizing. Yet I put off wearing dark glasses because I find that these ruin my sense of exposure in photography.

As we worked our way up the wash the mountains on each side began to press together until we had the beginning of a wide canyon looming ahead of us. And here we began to encounter rough going. There were spots of a few hundred yards where the sand had been washed away, leaving rocks piled in confusion which we had to fight our Pak-Jaks over. We pressed on for what seemed to me to be an interminable distance and found the mountains coming closer together until we were very definitely in another canyon.

Then along in the afternoon we saw our first palm—a stately tree standing in solitary splendour.

Just before we came to this palm, however, there was a branch in the canyon and our aeroplane explorations had indicated that we should take this right-hand branch because it seemed there was a veritable oasis, with water, some few miles up it. Moreover, Juanito had said this was the canyon which had the good spring —"Agua Buena".

So while we went up a half mile or so to look at the lone palm tree, Pepe Smith with the mules and burros went on up the right-hand canyon.

The chips were down now and we were gambling for keeps. This was the third day the mules and burros had been without water and they simply had to have water that night. If they didn't get it, they couldn't get out of the canyons and if they couldn't get out of the canyons, we couldn't, because the burros were carrying petrol for the Pak-Jaks, as well as drinking water for us.

We had seen, up this right-hand canyon, what seemed to be an oasis from the air, and Juanito had told us of the spring that had been there seventeen years ago, but springs have a habit of drying up and there was always the possibility that Juanito could have been mistaken.

It is an uncomfortable feeling when one realizes that one has left the comforts of civilization so far behind that one's very life is dependent upon some little thing. Juanito was well past seventy. It was quite possible that his memory had begun to play tricks on him. We were staking our lives on the accuracy of his memory and on the fact that a spring which had existed seventeen years ago would still be in existence today.

As the heat of the canyon gradually dehydrated our tissues, and as I began to realize more and more the importance of reaching water sometime that afternoon, I began to take stock of the situation. Or, as Emery expressed it, take a good, long look at my hole card. So we paused only briefly at the lone palm tree, then turned, retraced our steps and started up the right-hand canyon. Here we again encountered a little rough going for a spell, then came a smooth stretch, and then we came to four large palm trees where we stopped for photographs and a little well-earned rest in the cool shade.

However, since we could see the glistening fronds of other palm trees up the canyon, we cut short our rest. As we went up the canyon, cluster after cluster of palm trees appeared and the shade became more and more welcome.

We were also encountering tougher going, with places where the water had formed riffles as it fell rapidly during periods of flood and had left great barriers of water-worn rocks. These were not too serious an obstacle but we realized that excitement and a very, very strenuous day, following a whole series of strenuous days, had brought about a certain amount of emotional fatigue as well as just plain physical weariness. We had had too many experiences crowded into too short a time.

As we pressed onward the canyon narrowed and again we found more palms. I kept thinking that each cluster of palms we were approaching must be the place where we had seen the oasis from the air. It seemed that we must have gone past our destination.

However, Sam and Ynes were on ahead—Sam had fixed up an improvised seat on the back of his Pak-Jak and they were riding double. We knew that Sam and Ynes would have turned back if there had been any serious trouble and felt that they were probably resting by a spring of cool water.

Such is the process of the human mind, that as we encountered more and more palms in the canyon we began to take them for granted. I was hungry, thirsty and too dog-tired to appreciate the marvellous scenery.

Finally after fighting across a rocky bar and coming to a level stretch, suddenly we saw ahead such a tremendous growth of palms that we knew it must be the oasis. Sure enough, we found Sam and Ynes waiting for us, the mules and burros hobbled, and good old Juanito, despite the long strenuous day, busying himself with cooking.

We had the luxury of a wash, then a long cooling drink. Then I settled down in the shade to rest.

Despite the fact that I was physically tired, I got up in a short while and started looking round. I couldn't rest, and I know the others felt the same way. Here we were in virgin country and we might find anything round the next bend in the canyon.

Ynes decided he would take a walk and Lee Sine went with him. I watched them go, wishing I had the energy to join them; but knowing that Ynes's short legs were going to be pounding up that canyon and that Lee Sine, an expert hiker and deer hunter, was going to be hard put to keep up with him, I sat down again.

I dozed for half an hour, then awakened to watch the long shadows in the canyon and suddenly knew that I simply had to take a walk. So I told the others I wouldn't be going far, would keep in the canyon and would be careful not to get into any trouble.

In most of the country where I have travelled with Pak-Jaks, game has become accustomed to the sound of petrol motors. There are enough through highways, enough car traffic, so that wild game has come to take engine noise more or less as a matter of course. Deer will stand and look at a motor-car and not become frightened so long as the machine keeps going. Let it come to a stop and the deer are gone.

The same is true with the Pak-Jak and the other principal motor-scooter, the Tote Gote. People who rode those during the hunting season told of riding right up to deer who watched the contraptions with mild curiosity and didn't start running until the hunter brought his machine to a stop. This, despite the fact that the air-cooled engines make a considerable racket and the game must have heard the vehicle approaching for many minutes before it came in sight.

The situation, however, was different down in this canyon in Baja California. It soon became evident that game down here, unaccustomed even to the sight of human beings, knew nothing about petrol engines, and as our five Pak-Jaks came roaring up the canyon, the sound echoing from the walls, the game simply took off.

As I walked up above our camp I became painfully aware of what had been happening. The story was all too plainly written in the sand. In places the sand was quite damp where water was just beneath the surface. In one or two places there were pools. Everywhere the story was the same. There had been all sorts of game in the canyon earlier in the afternoon. The game had suddenly taken off in fright and this had undoubtedly been due to the noise of the Pak-Jaks.

There were the tracks of mountain sheep, cat tracks, fox tracks, deer tracks, and, in the softer sand, tracks that I couldn't be sure of but which I thought were mountain lion tracks. But there were lots of tracks. The canyon was alive with game.

It is interesting to note that Lee Sine and Ynes, who were on ahead of me, not only saw these tracks but after they had walked far enough to get away from the noise of camp and Pak-Jaks, found five mountain sheep standing watching them curiously. They also found a ledge with faint Indian writings on it—writings that were all but faded out by wind and weather. They reported that they were getting into a really interesting part of the canyon when it became so late they knew they would have to turn back, and even then they arrived in camp after dark.

I was bone weary that night as I crawled into my sleeping bag and I drifted off to sleep almost instantly. Later I wakened to watch the stars and marvel at the dryness of the air which brought so many stars into view that the whole heavens seemed to be one massive Milky Way.

I went to sleep again and wakened with a start. Some big animal was moving cautiously within a few feet of me. I could hear the soft footfall of a cautious foot on gravel, then a rock moved under the weight of an animal that must have had some size. I thought of the stories I had heard of mountain lions and lay motionless, listening.

The animal was also motionless for a moment, perhaps because it realized I was holding my breath. Then it moved on again through the darkness, perhaps thirty or forty feet from my bed, walking along the loose rock which had tumbled down from the mountain, making just enough rock noise for me to be sure that it was an animal of some weight. But apart from those little noises of moving rocks and the previous noise of crunching gravel there had been no sound. Whatever the animal was, it was moving on padded feet and was keenly aware of the fact that I was lying awake, listening.

I lay there trying to determine whether the animal had gone and in the middle of my listening must have fallen sound asleep because when I wakened again the lopsided moon had turned the fronds of the palms into silver reflectors. The shadows were black in the canyon and here and there was a glimpse of moonlit sand. There was complete silence—no sound of any sort—just the silence stretching from interstellar space down to the earth.

I enjoyed the sheer beauty of the spectacle, then closed my eyes again and was almost instantly enveloped in warm slumber.

18

THE MYSTERY OF THE BURNED PALMS

WE were up at the crack of dawn and after a hurried breakfast we left the others to get the camp packed up and loaded. We Pak-Jakkers went down the canyon to the intersection, then turned at the intersection and went up past the lone palm tree, and on up the other canyon.

Here we found varied scenery of breath-taking beauty. There were palms of all ages and all sizes. In places the canyon was nearly choked with palms.

And there were places that needed exploring badly; interesting branch canyons, outcroppings of rocks, veins—apparently of quartz—and a silent, majestic beauty.

As the canyon twisted and turned the light came from different angles and each clump of palms seemed to be more beautiful than the last. We knew that we should turn back in order to meet the mules and burros, but we kept on and on until finally we *had* to turn back.

There are some facts that definitely limit one's choice of conduct. Hunger is one. We were out of provisions. Because we hadn't known if we could find good drinking water, we had gone light on groceries in order to carry water. Even so, the dangers of the trip being what they were, we were still just a little apprehensive as we started back.

However, Lee Sine, J. W. Black and Emery opened their throttles wide and went tearing on up the canyon for another mile or so in a last-minute sprint.

The sheer beauty of those canyons held us entranced. Looking at the palms on the way back gave us a different view from the one we had had coming up, and the difference in lighting made each view seem completely novel. Only the tell-tale tracks of the mule train and our Pak-Jaks in the soft sand showed that anyone had ever been that way before.

It was somewhere along here that Emery, who is intensely observant, made a discovery which was destined to assume a great deal of significance later on, although at the time we simply considered it a puzzling find.

As has previously been pointed out, Murl Emery is quite an individualist. He does things his own way, at his own time, in his own manner, and while we were exploring the canyon Murl made short side trips, stopped to look at rocks, fell behind and usually caught up with us about the time we were stopping to take pictures.

Murl's find on this occasion was a geologist's pick, a characteristic tool which has a hammer on one end for knocking specimens off rocks and a sharp pick on the other for prying or digging. This particular geologist's pick, or miner's pick, had been drawn to a point in a blacksmith's shop, and the sharpening of the end of it must have taken place very shortly before it had been lost by whoever had left it in the canyon, because apparently it had been used very little since.

At that time we hadn't heard the story of the two prospectors, the lost gold mine or the fatal rattlesnake bite. We didn't realize we had found the missing link—the prospector's pick.

From the way in which the handle had been split by the dry air and the intense sunlight we knew the tool had been there for many years, mute evidence that some prospector had gone at least that far up the canyon.

It was only after we returned to Bahia de Los Angeles and saw the excitement Emery's find generated that we got the whole story and knew that the pick had been lying there for twenty-nine years—lying in plain sight—and that four men had lost their lives trying to get to where the pick had been lost.

At that time we only knew that Emery had made a most puzzling discovery. Any prospector who had managed to get that far up the canyon would have considered his prospector's pick as important as his canteen. It was unbelievable that such a person could simply have "lost" his pick.

Later, as we sat round the camp fire, we tried to visualize what must have happened. We had all sorts of theories: The man had perhaps managed to get a burro into the canyon. He had tied the prospector's pick to the pack and it had fallen to the sand.

Despite the fact we explored what we felt were all the possibilities our imaginations stopped far short of the real story. It proved to be a startling demonstration of the old saying that truth is stranger than fiction. Somewhere near the point where Emery found that prospector's pick there is a fabulously rich gold mine.

And now we encountered another major mystery. The men who had been with us knew these canyons. That is, they knew the country surrounding the canyons. They had known this country intimately for eighteen years. During that time they were positive no one had ever gone into the parts of the canyon we were exploring. They couldn't have even made an attempt to reach the mountains which buttressed the canyons without using a known point for the initial supplies of water, food and animals for transportation. Yet we found a great many of the palm trees had been burned.

As the palm trees grow, the leaves which constitute the fronds wither and droop, forming a yellowish tinder-dry "skirt" round the trunk of the palm. Sometimes during periods of high wind these dead leaves are broken off and form a litter round the base of the palm trees. Under ordinary circumstances, however, the palms generally develop a "skirt" which stretches almost from the ground to the top of the palm, perhaps fifty or sixty feet up, and the older part of this skirt at the bottom of the tree must be of great age.

A palm tree has a porous, resilient trunk. During the last war, bunkers made of palm logs proved to be more resistant to certain types of cannon fire than concrete.

There was plenty of mute evidence in our canyons that the trunks of the palm trees were so constituted that even when the skirts had been fired and had become a roaring inferno of swirling flames, the palm tree, although badly damaged, would eventually "come back" and again start growing.

So, when we saw numerous palm trees that had virtually no skirts but fire-blackened trunks, we came to the conclusion that regardless of what the others had said someone *must* have been in those canyons within the last few years and fired the palm trees.

Juanito was very bitter about the burned palms. He said that too many of the Mexican prospectors would gleefully set fire to palm trees in order to watch the spectacle, having no concern for the beauty of the country—yet he was also absolutely positive that no one had been up these canyons for eighteen years.

On the other hand, Juanito's theory, if true, couldn't account for all the burned palms that we saw. As Emery expressed it, "There aren't that many matches in the country."

Studying the terrain through binoculars, we found isolated palm trees growing high on ledges in the boulder-strewn mountains where it was unthinkable anyone would have climbed simply for the purpose of setting fire to a palm tree. In fact, some of these palms grew in places where it seemed almost impossible for any human being to travel. Yet these isolated palms were the ones that were almost uniformly burned.

Experimenting with some dead palm trees and with some of the older leaves which had dropped to the ground we found the material was all but explosive. Touch a match to the bottom part of the skirt of a dead palm and almost within the winking of an eye the whole tree would be enveloped in flame.

Not only are the palm leaves like tinder but the skirts are so arranged that there is a natural updraught. For a second or so smoke will come swirling up through the palm leaves, as though through some big chimney, then flickering flames will dance through the white smoke and then the whole tree becomes a roaring inferno and all this takes place within a second or two.

Not only do the palm leaves burn, but the burning generates a highly inflammable gas which goes up high above the tree and is then ignited, so that the column of flame is many times higher than the tree itself. Quite obviously, any material as explosive as this is a natural fire risk.

We subsequently learned that lightning accounts for many of these burned trees. In this granite country there are thunderstorms of great violence. Some are accompanied by rain, but as a rule the lightning comes first, the rain afterwards. And in many instances the electrical storm is a dry storm with little or no rain.

We collected evidence indicating that there is still another way in which the trees catch fire and this probably is due to static electricity, and the sparks generated by this static electricity.

There are winds in this country, dry winds, and so much static electricity that one must be careful, particularly if wearing

184

rubber-soled shoes. Just the act of walking will build up quite a static charge and if one touches metal, or even another person, a hot spark will leap from the finger-tips.

Apparently during periods of high wind the rubbing of the palm fronds generates a charge of static electricity which at times can result in a spark, and one spark is all that is necessary to start this highly inflammable material going up in roaring flame.

Francisco Munoz told us that many times on his flights he has seen palm trees burning when careful inspection had convinced him there was no person anywhere about. He had studied these burning palms and the surrounding terrain sufficiently to convince himself that there is some form of spontaneous combustion which sets the trees afire.

The fact that some of the burning was due to lightning was all too evident in trees where one found only a portion of the skirts burned. These skirts are so highly inflammable that if the initial spark hadn't been followed almost immediately by a veritable deluge of water, as from a cloudburst, the entire skirt of the tree would have gone up in flames.

Apparently some of the palms can't "come back" after one of these devastating fires. We saw quite a few tall palms whose trunks had been denuded by fire and the tip of the tree was a barren, fire-blackened point. Some of these were standing, some had been blown over. Of course we had no way of knowing that the denuded trees which were still standing wouldn't eventually come back, since the palm is certainly tenacious and the porous moisture-absorbent trunk seems able to withstand almost any kind of abuse.

Juanito's familiarity with the canyons was, as I mentioned earlier, due to the fact that he had worked on a ranch up in the mountains and had simultaneously carried on his shark fishing operations at the mouth of the wash. I learned later of some of the things Juanito had done, some of the things he had been forced to do. The story made me squirm just to think of it, yet it is authenticated although it seems utterly incredible.

Juanito and one companion went up into a wide wash near Bahia san Luis Gonzaga and prospected up to the point where the wash became a canyon. They found indications of gold at the surface and Juanito and his companion started to sink shafts. The soil was gravel and decomposed granite. They had no timbers with which to wall the shaft. They had to walk twelve miles to get their drinking water. They rigged up a windlass and a bucket and tried to get down to bedrock. Juanito was the underground man. The other fellow turned the windlass. The holes were as small as they could be made, and Juanito, pushing down the hole, would have to stand with his feet on each side of the bucket as he filled it with gravel. Then the gravel would be raised, sifted, and the gold extracted by a dry cleaning process.

Juanito got down forty-two feet before he had to give up. He wasn't at bedrock at that time. He had reason to believe that bedrock might be another forty feet below him. At a depth of forty-two feet he felt that he was deep enough to be able to risk driving lateral tunnels without too much danger of a cave-in, so he branched out with lateral tunnels. They put down other shafts and connected the lateral tunnels. These tunnels were very small. Juanito burrowed, as he expressed it, "like a rat".

They had no means of getting fresh air down the shafts. Moreover, much of the oxygen was consumed by an acetylene miner's lamp which Juanito was using.

Slowly, laboriously, facing the constant danger of a cave-in which would leave him buried alive, Juanito gophered in the soil, scraping out a bucketful at a time which his companion, a strongly built, powerful man, would raise on the windlass, put the dirt through a screen, process it in a dry washing process and extract the gold.

It can be imagined how these men lived. Their food consisted of tortillas and frijoles and very little else.

All in all they spent six weeks at this work and emerged with a pound of gold. As Juanito aptly remarked, "I have worked hard —too hard perhaps."

It is surprising what human beings can do when they have to in order to survive, when, as Emery expresses it, "the chips are down". Now, at the age of seventy-one, his short body bent by age and hard work, Juanito continues to work hard in order to make a living—too hard.

On this trip he used to be up at the first streaks of daylight, building a little campfire, getting out his frying pan, cooking breakfast, then washing the dishes as best he could in the limited amount of water which we dared to allot for the purpose; then he helped with the packing, climbing aboard a burro, riding all day, then, as we made camp just before dark, got his fire going, his frying pans out and cooked a meal for nine hungry men over a campfire in the dark, hunkered down on his knees bending over the coals as he cooked.

Then later he would gather up the dishes, take the frying pan half full of water which was all we dared spare for dishwashing and get the dishes as clean as was possible under the circumstances, putting a few drops of water in the dish to rinse it out, then cleaning the dish and putting it out to dry.

After that, Juanito would get up from his knees, wearily walk over to the place where he had his blankets spread on the bare ground, crawl into "bed" and go to sleep.

Ynes, the younger of the two men, was really in the prime of life. He had the energy of a bouncing ball, and as I have said, the keenest pair of binocular eyes I have ever seen on anyone. Ynes could not only see objects with his naked eye almost as plainly as I could see them with a pair of binoculars but he could, and did, see everything. Everything that moved Ynes saw, and I think he saw most of the things that didn't move, but the faintest flicker of motion anywhere and Ynes's eyes were on the spot, cataloguing what was going on.

Ynes not only made the long daily journeys and helped pack and unpack the burros, but he made innumerable side excursions. He walked, he rode burros, he doubled with Sam on the back of Sam's Pak-Jak.

I think what happened on the last day of our canyon trip is probably as indicative of the character of Ynes as anything I can use as an illustration.

We were travelling rapidly now, and we retraced our steps up to the sheer rock wall. We were carrying ropes with us and were quite a distance ahead of the mules and burros.

Those Pak-Jaks weigh 175 lb. apiece in the raw. In addition to that we had saddle-bags which were pretty well loaded but which could of course be removed as we came to this vertical portage.

Ynes worked his way up the rock face with all the facility of a mountain goat. Sam Hicks joined him. Lee Sine followed.

J. W. Black worked the Pak-Jaks, one by one, up to the bottom of the rocky wall. Then Black picked up the front end of each Pak-Jak and knotted round it the rope which the others had lowered from above. Then Black picked up the lower part of the Pak-Jak, braced himself, heaved his powerful muscles and lifted the Pak-Jak to a point where it was in the proper position for the others to start hauling on the rope.

There were five Pak-Jaks in all. They had to be raised up the perpendicular face of the rock. Then our gear, stowed in the saddle-bags, had to be lifted up.

By that time the train of mules and burros had arrived and all the camp gear was unloaded and it had to be hoisted up by ropes. Then the unladen burros were taken back down the canyon to a point where they could scramble up the rocky slope and be guided up over the high ridge until they were able to get down into the canyon above the rocky barrier. Here they were repacked.

Ynes assisted in all this, working at top speed. Sam Hicks, J. W. Black and Lee Sine, all rugged outdoor men, kept pace with Ynes and the Mexicans and in so doing earned their respect.

By the time we had our equipment assembled at the top of the rocky wall it was well along in the afternoon. Sam Hicks and Lee Sine started ahead on their Pak-Jaks. Ynes, using his coat as a cushion, climbed on behind Sam and they started off up the wash at top speed.

By that time it was apparent we weren't going to be able to get too far before we had to make a camp, and we were completely out of provisions. We had no coffee, no frijoles. In fact we had nothing.

I tried to keep up with Sam and Lee, but they were going too fast. Not only was the gear ratio of their machines such that they were a shade faster than mine, but these men with their perfect sense of balance, rhythm and co-ordination could take many of the rough places at full throttle, whereas I had to slow down. So I came along behind moving as rapidly as I dared, but taking no chances since a broken bone in that country would have presented us with an almost insurmountable problem.

Some distance behind me J. W. Black was keeping pace with Murl Emery and behind them came the mules and burros. Sam and Lee hoped they would be able to get to the mountain barrier early enough to be able to "ride" their Pak-Jaks over the trail, down to camp, get emergency rations from the stock we had left in the tent, and hike back over the trail to a point where they could join the camp.

As it happened, I wasn't fully familiar with the plans. All I knew was that Sam, Lee and Ynes had gone on ahead, that the rest of the camp was somewhere behind me. So I just kept plodding along.

Quite late in the afternoon I reached a point in the sandy wash where I could go no further. I was in a cactus country where balls of cactus spines on the ground would puncture a front tyre if we ran over them—as we had earlier found out to our sorrow. I was also in a country where the rocks which had rolled down from the mountain barrier were getting bigger and bigger and at times it was necessary to lift the rear end of the machine when it got straddled over a big rock.

Lifting the heavy rear end of a machine which weighs nearly 200 lb. time after time, is simply too much of a good thing for a man who is not accustomed to heavy lifting of that sort, who has had a full day of Pak-Jak travel and the excitement of exploration. I decided that I could make better time walking than I could on the Pak-Jak so I simply abandoned the Pak-Jak, knowing that somehow or other I had missed the trail—not knowing exactly where the trail was, and with my lifting muscles pretty well worn out.

So I walked up the mountain barrier. I never did find that darned trail. I simply climbed the side of the mountain, a few feet at a time, until I came to the mesa on top. There I knew the trail was plainly legible so I moved along until I saw the characteristic sign of the trail, one or two rocks piled on top of a really big rock, making a sort of rude monument. I worked my way over, found the trail and wearily continued along the mesa, then started down the "trail" on the other side.

Halfway down the trail I met Sam and Lee coming back. I was surprised to see them. I thought they had planned to spend the night at the tent. They had a pretty good-sized sack of provisions, which Sam was carrying over his shoulder.

It was then only fifteen or twenty minutes before sunset and night comes quickly in that country. There was, moreover, no moon until round about one or two o'clock in the morning. So it was quickly decided that Lee Sine would go back to the tent with me and we hoped we could find enough covering there to keep us warm during the night. If we couldn't, there was a stove in the tent and we could rustle firewood and so keep warm so long as we stayed up to stoke the stove.

So Sam, with the heavy sack over his shoulder, his long legs devouring the ground, walked rapidly on up the trail.

I asked where Ynes was and Sam told me that he had decided to stay "on top" for a little while. Ynes had of course simply stepped off the Pak-Jak at the foot of the mountain trail, had walked up to the top, and was up there in the top country somewhere, his keen eyes surveying everything that had happened. He had of course seen me come up on the Pak-Jak, wrestle it for half a mile or so over a series of rocks where I had to keep lifting and straining, and at the same time keep in mind the necessity of avoiding the balls of spines on the ground.

These particular balls of cactus had stiff, unbelievably sharp spines some three inches long, which would go through shoe leather as if it were paper, and had given us a couple of punctures in the front tyres.

I explained to Sam where I had left my Pak-Jak and told him that when he came back he could pick it up and ride it down to meet the others. In that way he might get there before it got too dark to see any obstacles that might be in his path.

When Sam got over the top of the mountain barrier and started down the trail on the other side he met Ynes pushing my Pak-Jak. It is difficult to explain what this means so that a person who is not familiar with the machine can realize what Ynes was doing.

When one starts pushing a machine of that kind it is necessary to push against the engine, and while at times the belt can be loosened enough to avoid full compression, there is always a drag.

Moreover, when one is standing on one side holding the handle bars and trying to push the machine, it is necessary to exert a great deal of strength in order to keep it balanced. It weighs 170-odd lb. and if it gets too far to one side it is likely to topple over and carry a man with it.

Now Ynes had been *pushing* my machine for over half a mile across a cactus-infested country, and lifting it over great lava rocks, in order to reach the trail at the foot of the mountain barrier. Then he had started pushing it *up* the trail. Riding a Pak-Jak is difficult enough over these rocks when one has enough traction to keep the rear wheel turning. Then, the machine has only to be lifted over rocks which are big enough to leave the frame suspended with the wheel off the ground; in such a position there is no traction. But to *push* a machine over these rocks is something very few men could do.

Ynes had been pushing my machine for more than half a mile to get to the foot of the mountain barrier and now he was *pushing* it up the trail—and all this after a day of arduous labour, a day which would have left most men physically exhausted.

So now Sam climbed on my machine, Ynes folded his coat and got on behind Sam, and with the sack of provisions they started back over the half-mile or so of rough, rocky terrain strewn with boulders and cactus spines, then down the soft, sandy wash for some two or three miles until they could see the glow of the camp fire which guided them into the camp where hungry men eagerly pounced on the provisions Sam and Lee had hurriedly thrown in the sack.

I subsequently found out that on several occasions Ynes had been up "on top" so that he could watch me as I explored the country. He kept me under almost constant supervision. As he was heard to express it to one of his companions, he never "bothered" me because he saw that I was "all right".

I know now that if at any time I had sprained an ankle, broken a leg, or had any other mishap, Ynes would have been at my side within a matter of minutes. And if I had a broken ankle I know very well that Ynes would have piggy-backed me over the roughest mountain terrain and got me back to camp. It is loyalty of this sort that gives a man a choking feeling. It is a loyalty that was far above and beyond the call of duty connected with employment. These men had given us their friendship and it was remarkable to see the extent of their loyal devotion.

19

ENTER THE HELICOPTER

LEE SINE and I went on down the trail to the tent. It was a rather dispiriting sight as we arrived in the late dusk and picked up one of the electric torches. The wind had been blowing through the mountain pass almost constantly. One side of the tent had broken loose from the anchoring stakes and had been flapping back and forth, whipping the desiccated soil into a flour-fine dust which had covered everything in the tent with a layer that seemed to be a quarter of an inch thick.

We built a fire in the stove. We dusted off some of the boxes. We cleared off a space on the table. We found that there was no petrol in the petrol lantern and we were just too damned tired to try and get a petrol can open, find a funnel and fill the lantern.

We used electric flashlights to cook a small dinner. We scouted round and found what covering there was in camp—a part of a sleeping bag which had been left by Emery, a quilt which had been left by Juanito, and some canvas. We made up a couple of beds and, keeping all our clothes on, rolled in to sleep before six-thirty.

We wakened during the night thoroughly chilled. We built a fire in the stove and got the tent warm, drifted off to sleep again, then woke up sometime around midnight and repeated the process. This time we had the stove pretty well filled with coals and the chill was broken until about four o'clock in the morning when we again built up the fire.

By daylight we cooked a breakfast and then went to thaw out in the sun while we waited for the others to show up.

Soon we heard the familiar roar of Pak-Jaks and Sam, J. W. Black and Murl Emery came into camp. Shortly after, the mules and burros arrived, and we started hurriedly breaking camp, throwing things into the pick-ups, getting the tent down and rolled up, and then started the long, dusty grind back across the

A palm-bordered wash and its first modern explorers

The machines are hoisted step by step up the rocky wall

We land by a water hole

sandy washes, through the narrow canyons, down to and across the dry lakes, and towards the road.

We arrived late in the afternoon at Bahia de Los Angeles. We were dirty, dusty and tired. I had a two weeks' growth of grey whiskers, I was grey with dust, I hadn't had a bath for more than a week. I was downright dirty, and the others were in the same condition.

We found a palatial yacht at anchor in the bay with a group of famous people on board. They were expecting our arrival because they had been told by Antero Diaz that we were about due. (Diaz had the news from the observations of "Faithful Francisco", who had kept us under fairly constant observation from the air.)

The party included a multi-millionaire and some notable literary people. One of them was Joe Krutch. As well-known for his nature writing as he is for his literary criticism and philosophical essays, he has a wonderful talent for describing country —a real eye for detail. His book on Baja California, for which he was collecting material at the time, has now been published.[1]

There was also Roger Tory Peterson, the artist and author of *A Field Guide to the Birds*. Peterson had just completed a new edition of *A Field Guide to Western Birds* and was then engaged in gathering material for still another book.

There were other people aboard the yacht, people who were friends of friends of mine, people who knew Murl Emery well, people who were friends of friends of J. W. Black and Lee Sine.

It would have been hard to have imagined circumstances under which we were less presentable, and after shaking hands and acknowledging introductions we got away as rapidly as possible to the luxury of a cold shower bath.

As I have previously mentioned, the shower baths at Bahia de Los Angeles are at times rather sketchy affairs. Not only is the "heating" of the water a problem, but there is no reserve supply of water. When several people take showers at the same time the water dwindles to a trickle and then without further warning the trickle vanishes.

So, during times of peak activity, if a person doesn't move swiftly he is very apt to find that he has covered his chilled skin

[1] *The Forgotten Peninsula.* Joseph Wood Krutch (Sloane, 1961).

with a thick lather of soap only to have insufficient water to wash it away. By the time I could get into the shower the water was quite cold and all of us making simultaneous ablutions had reduced the flow of water to a trickle, a dribble, and all I could get were a few scattered drops which I collected in cupped hands and applied where it would do the most good. Nevertheless, I remember that cold shower as one of the nicest, most luxurious I had ever had.

Then came dinner at the Casa Diaz. The showers at Bahia de Los Angeles may be rather primitive but, as I've said before, the food is just about the best in the world. This evening, it was not only there in abundance, but it seemed especially succulent after our recent camp fare.

After having existed on lukewarm water which had been swished around in canteens until it had acquired a metallic taste, the luxury of the carbonated Orange Crush which had been given us by Colonel Gutierrez as we left Mexicali was beyond description. Our dehydrated tissues soaked up the tangy beverage, and stomachs which had known only frijoles and tortillas for many days welcomed the flavour of citrus fruits. The dinner at Casa Diaz was out of this world, and what with one thing and another we didn't get to bed until nearly eight-thirty that night. That was dissipation!

In the morning the people from the yacht came over to break-fast. They had a twin-engined aircraft and were taking off for a quick flight down the peninsula, covering distances that would have taken us six or seven days by four-wheel-drive vehicles. They expected to be back at Bahia do Los Angeles by noon and then up-anchor and down the gulf on the yacht. We saw them off on the aeroplane, then loaded our gear and took off from Bahia de Los Angeles headed north.

It was with a real pang that we said good-bye to our friends, at the Bahia de Los Angeles, people whom we had come to know and to respect, people who had shared risks with us and who had been devoted to our welfare. I looked back as we left. Antero was waving good-bye. Ynes, who is largely Yaqui Indian, was trying to be as expressionless as possible. Juanito was trying to smile a farewell but the tears were trickling down his weather-beaten cheeks. At the time I had no idea we would ever go back.

In a limited way, we had achieved some of our objectives. We had gone into the canyons and we had made hasty explorations. On the other hand, there was so much we hadn't achieved and it looked as though we never would. Transporting petrol, drinking water, food and personnel by mule pack into a base camp in the canyon called for more equipment than was available.

We might have established a base camp on the dry lakes and had Pepe Smith go back and forth carrying supplies with mule and burro, but the mules and burros couldn't have stood the strain. Those hardy little animals can go for two or perhaps three days without water while they are being worked, but they can't keep up a pace of that sort, living off the country and being rationed on water. Moreover, even with our four-wheel drive trucks we couldn't have carried enough water to the dry lakes to keep the livestock supplied with their needs.

However, while we hadn't covered more than a small percentage of the canyon system, we had gone a good many miles up and down the canyons. We hadn't been able to do more than hit the high spots and hadn't had time for detailed exploration, but we had had adventures and we had experienced the satisfaction of knowing that we had reached places other men had never explored.

So, as we pulled out of Bahia de Los Angeles, I didn't expect to see Juanito, Ynes or Antero Diaz for many, many months, if ever. We had made our assault on the canyons and had probably reached a point where we could call it a draw. We hadn't conquered the canyons but, on the other hand, the canyons hadn't conquered us. We had been in them. We had actually gone for some miles up the dreaded Sal Si Puede (Get out if you can), and we had got out.

But those canyons were in my blood. I kept thinking of them. I kept dreaming about them. We got home and I developed my pictures. I found I had some striking photographs, which I studied, and from them made a rough map of the canyons. I plotted out about where we had been with our Pak-Jaks by checking the photographs taken from the air.

The daughter of Louis Roripaugh, who is one of my closest friends, was married to a helicopter pilot who spent his time during the summer months piloting a helicopter for one of the big companies engaged in mining activities in Alaska and in Canada. This young man came to visit us and brought pictures that he had taken from the helicopter. It was only natural that he should start talking about what a helicopter could do.

Instantly I became fired with enthusiasm. What were the chances of getting a helicopter to explore Baja California, to ferry supplies back and forth to a base camp in the Sal Si Puede Canyon? The young pilot, Ron Frame, thought our chances were pretty good, *if* I wanted to spend the money. Helicopters, as it turned out, were darned expensive.

At first I decided that the idea of exploration by helicopter could be nothing more than an air castle. But that night as I tried to sleep I realized that expenses are, after all, only relative.

A man might think nothing of spending three thousand dollars on a trip to Europe where he would be following the beaten trail of tourist routine. Or if some business situation arose where I had to go to New York, I would unhesitatingly bundle a couple of secretaries, typewriters and dictating machines into an aeroplane and take off on a trip which would cost much more than three thousand dollars, and three thousand dollars was the standard rental rate for the helicopter for two weeks. After all, I was only young once, so what the heck.

I rose in the morning after a more or less sleepless night, during which I had been haunted by dreams of canyon exploration, and grimly determined to see the thing through. So I rang up Ron Frame and asked him if his company would consider a charter trip to Baja California. Frame said he would find out and started putting through telephone calls.

A couple of days later Frame advised me that his company had turned it down. Their equipment was all too far north. They didn't want to transfer it to the south; but he gave me the names of other companies that were engaged in helicopter rentals.

I got busy on the telephone and found companies that were quite willing to charter helicopters—until they found out the terrain I had in mind, then instantly the warmth of cordial salesmanship was replaced by the cold chill of indifference.

Instead of having them try to sell to me I found that I was trying to sell to them, and as buyers they were unbelievably cold —cordial personally, but officially very, very cold.

A helicopter needs careful attention. It needs supplies and watchful maintenance. And a helicopter needs insurance. That is, a company chartering helicopters must have insurance. Since Baja California is a country of very poor roads where little is known about existing conditions other than the fact that it is currently supposed to be a country of barren mountains, of arid deserts, of great winds and considerable turbulence, no one wanted to be the first to pioneer a helicopter exploration, and apparently the insurance companies regarded Baja California with jaundiced eyes.

Then Ron Frame paid a visit to the Hiller Aircraft Corporation which manufactures the Hiller helicopter. This company considers their product to be a long step ahead of any competitive helicopter. They believe they have more power, more lift, more dependability; in short, just about more of everything, and they were interested in the idea of using the helicopter to lift our Pak-Jaks from a base camp on the dry lake to a spike camp in the canyons. They were also interested in hovering over country which had never before been explored. In short they were interested.

After some telephone conversations Bob Boughton, the young man who has charge of foreign sales, decided to come down and have a talk with me. The result was to have been anticipated.

By this time my coloured slides had been processed and I had the story of the canyons in colour; pictures taken at a great height from aeroplanes; pictures a little lower in aeroplanes; pictures showing the manner in which we had made our limited assault on the canyons; and a few precious pictures of the interior of the canyons, the beautiful palm trees, the intriguing rock walls, some of the veins of quartz. Slowly, steadily, remorselessly, the story of those canyons as portrayed in my coloured pictures started working on Bob Boughton. By the time he was ready to start back to San Francisco, the canyon fever had fired his blood. He was all for it.

A couple of days later Bob was on the telephone. The company had decided to work out a deal for joint exploration. It wasn't in the business of chartering helicopters, but it was in the business of demonstrating what its helicopters could do. The challenge of Baja California, the very things that had kept other companies from being interested, the wind, the turbulence, the difficulties, all were a challenge the Hiller Company wanted to meet. It was thought that we could work out the financial details and other problems and go in for a joint exploration.

So once more I threw my writing schedule out the window. I got busy on the telephone. J. W. Black closed up his Pak-Jak shop in Paradise. Murl Emery, who was engaged in an important mining deal, threw the whole thing overboard announcing that he never had cared for money anyway. Leo Roripaugh (a brother of Louis Roripaugh and an enthusiast on Baja California) offered to come along with a four-wheel-drive pick-up capable of carrying seven fifty-gallon drums of aviation petrol.

Almost before I knew it and certainly before I had had an opportunity thoroughly to air my sleeping bag and unpack the dust-impregnated kit bags I had brought back from my other trip, I was getting things together for just about the most exciting expedition I could imagine.

This one was going to be *it*. We were going to meet those canyons head on and beat them on their home ground.

It was decided that we would send ahead three four-wheel-drive pick-ups, one Land Rover station wagon, all loaded with petrol and supplies so as to enable us to cover the first leg of the trip as expeditiously as possible. Bob Boughton, Pedro Rivas, the helicopter maintenance man, and I would leave some hours later, pass the pick-ups on the road and fly on to the Hattie Hamilton place where we would rendezvous the first night.

Since I have an hour-long weekly television show it is almost necessary that no matter where I travel I keep one foot in Hollywood. So I had arranged with Francisco Munoz to come along with his aeroplane, to shuttle back and forth from the closest landing field to our various camps, to fly in scripts, important mail, extra supplies and secretarial replacements as needed. All my portable office equipment, portable typewriters, dictating machines, tape recorders, etc., were sent on ahead with the pick-ups.

Everything was set for departure early on Monday morning and Bob Houghton promised to have the helicopter at the ranch sometime on Sunday.

That Sunday was a day of hectic activity. Not only had I

started dictating at three o'clock in the morning, trying to catch up on my more pressing work, but I had been up at four o'clock the morning before and had been pouring words into a dictating machine most of Saturday, taking only enough time off to do some rather hurried and sketchy packing.

On that Sunday, whenever I heard the sound of an engine I convinced myself that this was the helicopter coming in for a landing, and dropped everything to run out and take a look.

As it happened, that Sunday there were numerous aircraft flying over the ranch, and I must have gone hurrying out at least fifteen different times, each time firmly expecting to see the helicopter hovering overhead.

By four o'clock in the afternoon I was certain it would be only a matter of minutes, and then after an hour or so of waiting, as the sun finally set, I found my disappointment giving way to very definite annoyance. I felt that Bob Boughton could at least have telephoned if he had encountered any unforeseen difficulties.

I quit work at five o'clock, left my study and walked up the hill to the main house. Murl Emery, Sam Hicks and J. W. Black were sitting in the front room having drinks. I joined them. Dusk was deepening into darkness. We gave way to the blues. Then suddenly we heard the sound of an engine, approaching rapidly and at a low elevation.

We rushed to the door, looked out, saw nothing, and then the helicopter burst into view coming in at not over a hundred feet above the ground. As we stood there, the landing lights came on.

There were high voltage wires running across the yard by the house, and it had never occurred to me that anyone would try to land a helicopter there in the yard, but now with darkness blanketing the country it was quite apparent from the way the helicopter hovered briefly that it was contemplating a landing.

I made a dash for a flashlight that had a red warning light on it, but before I had made more than half a dozen steps the helicopter settled down, not in the yard where we had expected it, but at front of the house and almost on the doorstep—a place, as it turned out, that Bob Boughton had scouted out on his earlier trip as being a safe landing spot.

It was an unusual experience. Five minutes earlier we had been moodily contemplating the wreckage of our scheduled trip. Now we were escorting Bob Boughton and Pedro (Pete) Rivas the few short steps from the helicopter into the living room.

I think it was perhaps at that time that I first began to realize the extent to which these canyons had been dominating my life. I wanted to get into those canyons and explore them from one end to the other, and when it looked as though our helicopter trip was going to be delayed or perhaps cancelled, I had felt such a keen sense of personal failure that it seemed someone had pulled a plug and plunged my mind into darkness. Now that the helicopter had arrived, the revulsion of feeling showed me how much the exploration of those canyons meant to me.

Long before daylight the next morning there was a great deal of activity at the ranch. Leo Roripaugh came over with his pick-up and the machines pulled out for San Diego and Tijuana.

Bob Boughton, Pete Rivas and I, who were to go in the helicopter were able to wait for what was planned as a leisurely breakfast. I gave a lot of last-minute instructions, got in the helicopter, strapped myself in and heard the roar of the engine as the machine started. I braced myself and waited.

Suddenly we shot up into the air. Contrary to my expectations, there was no feeling of rising, none of the "cold stomach" of an elevator ascent. I felt that the ground had simply dropped away beneath us, and we poised for a moment, hovering over the ranch, then took off across the roofs of the ranch buildings just above the power lines, headed for the steep mountains at the back of the ranch.

There was one persistent and peculiar sensation connected with riding in that helicopter. I felt as if I were floating inside a huge soap bubble, and I'll admit there was a great feeling of insecurity. I kept waiting for the bubble to burst.

Looking down between my feet through the plexiglass I could see the ground not over forty or fifty feet below me. Above and to both sides there was only plexiglass. Below me the mountainside was a streak of half-blurred panorama: the fire trails I had cut so arduously, the steep, precipitous, rocky slopes, the clumps of trees, the old spring, and then more rocks, all flowing past in a vast moving spectacle of unreality. I had climbed so laboriously up this very steep mountainside that I couldn't adjust myself to skimming up it at such speed so effortlessly.

Abruptly the ridge of the mountains was directly ahead. It looked as though we could just about clear it. Clear it, we did—and suddenly the whole country dropped away beneath me. I found myself suspended in space in a fragile soap bubble with a straight drop of a thousand feet directly beneath my seat. It was for the moment a terrifying sensation.

We crossed the wide valley, hovered over the motor road, then left it as we took a compass course for Tijuana. Mountains loomed ahead. We made no attempt to get over the top of the mountains, but instead roared into the canyon.

I felt that I knew enough about flying to know that no mechanical contraption designed to take men through the air had any business going up this steep mountain valley; and, particularly when Bob swung the machine over to within a few feet of the canyon walls, I felt my time had come.

I learned afterwards that this is good helicopter technique. When entering a canyon where there is a wind blowing, one hugs the steep slope up which the wind is being pushed by the pressure of currents and simply rides the updraught to the top of the mountain, thereby saving fuel and power.

I finally realized that we were being buoyed up as we came so close to this steep slope and the air cushion sent us zooming upwards, and then just as I had relaxed and had accustomed myself to the feeling of being lifted by the wind, we were over the top and again the country fell out from beneath me. Again I was poised over a sheer drop.

It was hard to keep from tensing one's muscles under those circumstances. I darn near pushed the floor out.

By the time we had reached the outskirts of San Diego, however, I had adjusted myself pretty much to the sensation and was beginning to look about and enjoy myself.

Skimming along so close to the ground gives one the true feeling of flying and discloses things that would never be visible to a person travelling in a conventional aeroplane.

For instance, as we came up the slope of one of the hills we encountered a big hawk sitting in the branches of an oak tree. Apparently he had a belligerent personality, or else was familiar with helicopters, because he didn't make any attempt to fly. He simply sat there and fixed us with a cold, baleful eye, apparently speculating on whether we were too big to eat. For a moment his head and eye were in my field of vision, then he was gone and we were gliding on up the slope, riding the cushion of air thrust up by the wind.

Almost before I realized it we had flown over the outskirts of San Diego, had left the city behind and were crossing the border. A short time later we came down at the Tijuana airport.

Here we had our first point of assembly. Francisco Munoz was waiting with his aeroplane to take Jean, my chief secretary, to the Hattie Hamilton Ranch, a hundred and twenty miles below Ensenada, and nearly two hundred miles south of the border.

We had found that we couldn't take drums of aviation spirit across the border without a special permit, so we had decided to buy it at Tijuana and load the pick-ups at that point. There were crossing formalities to delay us briefly and all in all it was well past mid-morning when we again entered the helicopter and started the engine.

Once more I had that feeling of the ground falling away beneath me and then we were headed south, slightly to the east of the main business district of Tijuana.

From that helicopter I began to realize for the first time the extent to which Tijuana had grown. It was not only bursting at the seams, but had spread all over the surrounding country with residential districts creeping up the sides of the hills, fanning out in every direction.

Then we had passed Tijuana and were gliding along over the ocean.

Between Tijuana and Ensenada there are some beautiful secluded beaches, and we found many caravans parked along them, and occasionally saw families in tents on holiday.

Once as we came to a high bluff and dropped down to within a few feet of the ocean, we came on a party of bathing beauties basking in the sunlight. They looked up in startled surprise, then collected their senses in time to wave cordially as we went sliding by.

That of course brought a question to my mind. I leaned over to Bob and said, "Bob, what shall we do if we come on girls sunbathing in the nude?"

Bob's answer was laconic and typical of a helicopter pilot.

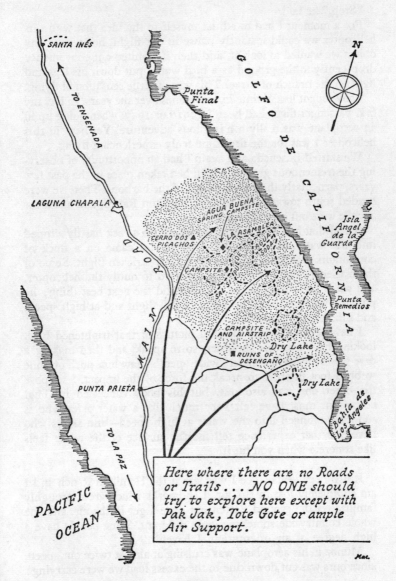

Here where there are no Roads or Trails ... NO ONE should try to explore here except with Pak Jak, Tote Gote or ample Air Support.

Mac.

"Stop," he said.

For a moment I had to adjust myself to the idea that with this helicopter we could instantly pause in our flight, hover over any object we wanted to look at, and then if it suited our convenience drop gently to the ground as a bird would put down his legs and light on the branch of a tree. This was the true sensation of flying.

I have spent lots of time in aeroplanes over the years. In fact my first passenger flight had been in 1916 or 1917, when going up in an aeroplane was really a hazardous adventure. Yet here in this helicopter I was for the first time truly experiencing flying.

We skirted Ensenada and again I had an opportunity of observing the tremendous growth which had taken place in the past few years, particularly the development of the harbour. Then we were headed south towards the Hattie Hamilton Ranch, and again for a while were out over the ocean.

A seal that had been sunning himself on a rock hastily slipped into the water. We rounded a point and came on a flock of cormorants that broke into sudden panic-stricken flight. Some of them tried to dodge. One of them tried to outfly the helicopter, and when he found that he couldn't did the next best thing: he plunged headlong into the water in full flight and at high speed, and submarined himself.

I have, etched in my mind, a picture of that frightened bird, looking back over his shoulder, so to speak, and then making a dive for the water, going in "wide open". I saw him push out one webbed foot in order to break the force of the impact. I suppose the other one was also out, but his body concealed it. That cormorant must have felt very much like a water skier who is suddenly plunged into the water at high speed—and skiers who have had that experience tell me the surface of the water feels like concrete when you hit it.

It had been years since I was last at the Hamilton Ranch and I am completely lost in the air. Landmarks which are thoroughly familiar on the ground flatten out once I get in the air, and the whole countryside somehow looks different. Some people have a high degree of air orientation. I haven't.

Munoz in his aeroplane was cruising at almost twice our speed, since ours was cut down due to the excess load we were carrying:

baggage racks on the side, extra petrol tanks and emergency supply kit of food and several gallons of water.

We were going into a country where one just doesn't take any unnecessary chances, and while all this equipment slowed us down, it gave us added comfort and an additional margin of safety.

Munoz, however, had to stop in Ensenada to get some official papers and so we both reached the Hamilton Ranch at about the same time.

Margo Cesena, who operates the Hattie Hamilton Ranch, is a remarkable character. Tall, vital, competent, freedom-loving and independent, she operates the ranch just as much by herself as is physically possible. She manages the ranch, supervises the comfort of the guests, does the cooking and the serving, cleans up and washes the dishes, and all the time carries on a running fire of conversation, keeping everyone cheerful, moving with the skilled efficiency of an artist who has learned to make every move count.

Margo is a colourful character and it is well worth a trip to the Hamilton Ranch simply to hear her cheerful laugh, her voice raised in song as she goes about her work, and to listen to her comments on the activities of the countryside, her latest trip to Ensenada and her thoughts about life generally.

There was to be a birthday party fiesta in the neighbourhood and not only was Margo going, but the hosts had been kind enough to invite our party to be present. So we all piled into a truck and Margo drove us through the darkness, jolting over the dirt roads, until finally I lost all sense of direction. After some thirty minutes we pulled up in front of a lighted house which was bursting with people, and went inside. There was the inevitable stringed orchestra supplemented by a cornet. There was laughter and motion and dancing, and there were some very beautiful women and some very courteous men.

A man who could have been cast for a typical Spanish Don hunted me up to shake my hand. "This is my house," he said. "I own it. It is yours," and then he gripped my hand again and took me into the dining room where quite a feast had been laid out buffet style.

"My turkey," he said, indicating the huge browned bird on the table, "will fly no more."

And he beamed with pride at the thought of being able to provide such hospitality for his guests.

This was an intimate party. The friends from the countryside had gathered to make a festive occasion and to do honour to the host and hostess. We were rank outsiders. These people knew each other, understood each other, understood each other's customs and had many things in common.

We were people of another race. Our language was somewhat strange to them and with the deference of persons who were self-conscious about making a mistake, they hesitated to talk except to make simple statements.

There were, moreover, many of the *vaqueros* there who knew no English at all. They had never seen us before, we were strangers and, if we wanted to be blunt about it, intruders on their festivities. We had been asked because we were the guests of Margo.

But we were treated as honoured guests. They went out of their way to show us their feelings of friendship. It was a warm, congenial gathering, and while under the circumstances I felt that common courtesy required that we return to the ranch and to bed at an early hour, there was the feeling that the country had opened its doors and its hearts to us.

Our party of helicopter adventurers stayed only a couple of hours or so and then Margo accompanied us back to the Hamilton Ranch. Margo returned and stayed until the party broke up, which was, I believe, at about three-thirty in the morning. She was, I understand, an active participant. Yet when I was up at six o'clock I heard the sound of the coffee-pot being put on the stove and a moment later Margo's voice raised in song as she started cooking breakfast.

20

A TRUE FLYING EXPERIENCE

WE had several objectives for our trip south. We wanted to visit the palm-lined canyons we had seen in the northern district as well as to explore La Asamblea and Sal Si Puede in greater detail. We also wanted to land where we could take a look at a wrecked aeroplane we had seen on our trip of exploration with Francisco Munoz. The aircraft had made a forced landing and had been abandoned far up in the high mesa country near the backbone of the peninsula. It had contained two people who had been able to "walk away" from the scene of the landing.

What happened after that was tragic. Since they were on the backbone of the peninsula, they had the choice of going in either of two directions, but the route to the east seemed the shorter; they could see the gulf from where they had landed and it was probably not more than twenty miles direct to the gulf, although the intervening country was exceedingly rough.

To the west however it was perhaps forty miles to the ocean in an air line. So, probably after some considerable discussion, the two men had started east, trying to intersect the road which stretched south from Puertecitos.

They never made it. Not only had they died of thirst, but when eventually their bodies were found they had become so completely dehydrated that the bodies had mummified and were found in that condition only a relatively short distance from the road they had been trying to reach.

The irony of the situation was that our exploration from the helicopter indicated that if they had headed to the west they needed only to have gone a mile and a half to have encountered a canyon with shade and good drinking water, and from there on they could have worked their way down to the road, having water all the way until they were within perhaps ten or twelve miles of reasonably level going.

Viewed from a high elevation it seemed that the light aeroplane might well be intact, and because there was a terrific downdraught over this part of the peninsula the abandoned aircraft was always viewed from several thousand feet. We decided to make an inspection of the aircraft one of the first of our objectives.

However, our planned schedule was interrupted by bad news. It seemed that when our trucks reached Ensenada the drivers learned Ensenada was having a "fiesta". The government offices were all closed and would probably be closed for another two or three days. As a result, the drivers of the pick-ups couldn't get the necessary clearance, tourist-card permits, etc. So instead of meeting us at Hattie Hamilton's as had been planned, the members of our party and all the reserve supplies were being held up in Ensenada and might be held there for another two or three days.

The trip had been so carefully planned and the time element was so important that this was in the nature of a major calamity, but Francisco Munoz, who "knew the ropes", felt certain that he could fly up to Ensenada and get things straightened out.

So at daylight, Tuesday, Francisco headed north to try to get the red tape untangled and Bob, Pete and I set out in the helicopter for the site of the wrecked aeroplane, intending to fly over some of the palm-studded canyons on the way. Munoz and Jean were to join us at noon at a little landing strip Munoz had found and explored not too far from the palm-lined canyons.

Munoz insisted he could land and take off from this strip, provided he was flying light with the least possible load. However, it was a short, rough airstrip and while at the time I hadn't any misgivings, later I had plenty of them.

So Bob, Pete and I left Hamilton Ranch and started flying on a compass course for our objective. We went over some wild, rough country and then much to my surprise came to a little house, a corral and even a little stretch of barbed wire fence out in the middle of hills where there was no road, and no well-defined trail; in short no evidences of civilization and no reason for a ranch to be there. We circled around looking the place over and I wish now we had landed. Apparently there was no one at home, so we kept on our way, and after a while came to the first of the palm trees.

The palm trees began in a rolling country where the canyons were not deep but were little more than valleys. Then gradually as we progressed south and east the valleys became canyons and the canyons became a little deeper and the walls more abrupt. Here the palm trees grew in greater abundance.

It was quite evident that there was water in these canyons and that there were many, many canyons. We saw trails going to the water holes in places, but whether these were trails made by game, by wild burros or cattle we had no means of knowing. We saw no living thing in the country, although there was unquestioned evidence that the country was full of wild life.

The sand in the washes was liberally dotted with coyote tracks, rabbit tracks, deer tracks, and there were well-defined trails which had undoubtedly been made by deer, but the sun was now well up and the animals were all under cover.

As we continued flying towards the mountains, the canyons became deeper and deeper. The canyon walls were more abrupt and there was more and more evidence of water and of palm trees.

Here is a section of Baja California which is in all probability absolutely unknown except to a few ranchers. It has also, perhaps, been visited by prospectors from time to time.

I feel reasonably certain that there are parts of this country my friend Goldbaum had explored and of which he had shown me photographs many years ago. But it is a country no writer has ever described to my knowledge and as far as the tourist is concerned, it is nonexistent.

Rough, rugged, palm-lined canyons with great water holes in the rock would open up into little valleys covered with palm, mesquite and various types of desert vegetation. The sandy washes were literally covered with game tracks and there was cool shade, an abundance of water and marvellous scenery. There were, however, no signs of human beings, no human habitations, apparently no means of communication with any of the roads.

We hopped around exploring the canyons briefly and then went on up to the high mesa country looking for the wrecked aeroplane. And we couldn't find it.

It was one of the most embarrassing experiences I have had in a long time. I had flown over that aircraft several times. I thought I knew the country as well as the proverbial palm of my hand, but after I got there the country all looked the same. I found dozens of places which looked exactly like the place where the aeroplane was, the only difficulty being that the aeroplane wasn't there.

So eventually, as it was approaching the hour when we were to meet Jean and Munoz at the landing strip, we started back, taking time to explore some of the canyons that we had previously flown over with Munoz.

A most challenging circular mark we had seen in the bottom of one of the canyons, and which had variously been interpreted as a corral, a cavern, or a natural depression, turned out to be a little of all three. A cap of hard granite rock had crossed over the water-course, causing a waterfall which in turn had resulted in a big circular depression, running back well under the hard granite.

Here there were evidences of civilization because someone had put a fence across the lower part of this depression to make a species of corral, but there was no clue as to who had done it or why it had been done, or how long ago.

Occasionally we ran on to a few cattle that looked as though they belonged to someone, and up in some of the wilder country we encountered cattle that undoubtedly had reverted to a wild state. They were completely "bronco" living in virtually inaccessible terrain where it would have been a sheer impossibility to have put on anything like a profitable cattle drive. But some of the "tame" cattle in the lower reaches of the canyons and this rude corral, which had been made out of the cavern beneath the cap stone, indicated that there were *vaqueros* who worked the lower and more accessible parts of the canyon country. Beyond that in the palm-lined canyons we found no indication of human beings.

So we hopped over a couple of ranges of mountains and descended to the little ranch with its landing strip where we were to meet Jean and Munoz. They were already on the ground and had brought a good lunch which with cool water was very welcome indeed.

The rough strip on which Munoz had landed was pretty well

covered with vegetation which seemed insignificant from the air, but on the ground presented formidable obstacles. Some of the vegetation had great wicked thorns fully capable of puncturing the tyres of an aircraft. So all of us pitched in with machetes and a short-handled shovel to try to make the landing strip a little safer for the take-off.

When we had finished, Jean and Pete stayed at the corral with the aeroplane while Francisco Munoz climbed into the helicopter with us to guide us back to where we could find the wrecked aircraft.

Once more we went over a whole network of palm canyons with great pools filled with water carved into the granite, but since we now had a definite object in mind we kept fairly well up in the air until we located the aeroplane. Then we came down, circled round it and finally landed.

Some Mexicans with burros had managed to get to the wreck. It had been quite thoroughly dismantled so far as anything of value was concerned, and sheets of aluminium had even been taken from the wings. Although in rather isolated country, knowing the country to the west as we did from our helicopter explorations we were not too surprised to find that someone had been in there with a pack string and probably secured enough from the wreckage to build a little cabin somewhere, the walls lined with sheet aluminium.

After looking round we started back for our landing strip and this time dropped down to inspect the canyons along the way, finally deciding to land in a particularly attractive canyon to see if we could find signs of human occupancy. We lowered the helicopter until we were only a few feet off the canyon floor, glided along between the abrupt walls until we came to where we wanted to land by a big water hole, put the helicopter down on the sheer granite and shut off the engine.

We scouted round for some time and finding nothing to indicate any human being had ever been in that canyon, got back in the helicopter, flew on a few miles and again came down to explore the tracks in the sand.

As we had surmised from the air, there were numerous deer tracks, some cat tracks, coyote tracks, rabbit tracks, the tracks of quail and of dove. Here again we found no link with civilization, so we returned to the landing strip. Munoz and Jean got into the aeroplane, and Pete, Bob and I climbed back into the helicopter.

I watched with my heart in my mouth as Munoz took off from that landing strip. From our vantage point in the helicopter, poised a couple of hundred feet above the landing strip, we could see the whole procedure, and as Munoz started lifting the craft into the air I felt certain he wasn't going to make it.

As Munoz explained to me later, on a short landing strip it is always advisable to take advantage of all the landing strip there is. Some people, he explained, get nervous and try to use only half or three-quarters of the strip. Munoz takes it all.

However, Munoz got safely in the air, and we set out towards the Hamilton Ranch looking for the pick-ups since Munoz had managed after his early-morning flight to Ensenada to get the necessary procedures "expedited".

Munoz flew on ahead, keeping in touch with us by radio. Eventually he found the pick-ups far to the north of where our schedule called for. It turned out they had had more delays after they got on the road, and what with having to fight their way over rutty, bumpy, wash-boarded and dusty roads, they were in no mood to be argued with by someone who came drifting down from a helicopter insisting: "The roads are good. We've been looking at them from the air."

However, that's one of the penalties a person pays for not keeping up to schedule and so it gave me a great deal of pleasure to point out to them scornfully that we had flown over all the roads they had traversed and there was nothing on earth to keep them from being at least three hours ahead of where they were.

The others controlled their homicidal impulses with an effort, and went on to make camp while Munoz, Jean, Pete, Bob and I went back to the Hamilton Ranch to spend the night.

The next day we tried to make it up to the fellows who had been slogging their way down the road. I landed from the helicopter and took over one of the pick-ups. Pete took over one of the other pick-ups and the others took turns in the helicopter, exploring the canyons they had seen from the air when flying with Munoz on those first trips of aerial reconnaissance. They gently descended into the canyons, landing by deep water holes where Emery even went so far as to take a swim.

That night we were to make camp up in the granite country. Munoz took off late in the afternoon to get Jean back to the ranch, to pick up some mail for me and to bring one of the other secretaries down to join the party.

21

WE TACKLE THE CANYONS AGAIN

THE next day we started our caravan south with Pete Rivas taking over the job of driving one of the pick-ups. Sam, Bob and I got into the helicopter to start exploring in earnest.

We first flew down to the old mission of Santa Maria, a mission which as yet has no road to it. An interesting and enterprising rancher at Cataviña is slowly and laboriously building a jeep road to it, but since he is working under considerable difficulties and without the aid of machinery, it is a pretty rough job. At this time the road was still some three miles from the mission itself. The plans for this road are most ambitious. The rancher wants to follow the old trail from the mission all the way down to the Bay of Gonzaga.

We wanted to see just what the new road was like, survey the old trail and take a look at some canyons behind the old mission. So we started out with cameras, films and high ambition. We had a full day planned.

We reached Santa Maria Mission without difficulty and Bob put the helicopter down in front of the ruins. We took some photographs, and then took off again gaining elevation so that we could determine just where we wanted to go next.

Sam thought there were interesting canyons to the south of the mission; I thought there were interesting canyons to the north; and for the purpose of clarifying the issue Bob put the helicopter pretty well up.

It was this that saved us.

Suddenly and without the slightest warning a wall of wind that attained a speed, as we afterwards learned, of ninety miles an hour, hit us.

Our helicopter was heavily loaded for a day of exploration, with a full supply of petrol in the main tank and two auxiliary tanks, which could be attached to the aircraft, also loaded to the brim. In addition to that we had our survival kit, some repair tools in case we had to use them and had the side racks attached to the runners. Taken by and large our top air speed was cut down by at least twenty-five miles an hour.

This wind picked us up as though it had been a giant hand, shook us as a terrier shakes a rat and then started hurling us down to the south and out towards the gulf.

Bob saw that it was useless trying to buck that wind at the higher elevations so went down lower to see what could be done. Down low we had no difficulty in measuring the velocity of the wind. We found how fast it was moving by the simple expedient of turning the helicopter into the wind just above the ground and watching the air-speed indicator. At a time when the air-speed indicator was showing fifty-five miles an hour, the helicopter was standing perfectly still.

So we "hit the deck" and started looking for one of the passes which led through the mountains and up to the country of Dry Lake Chapala (Laguna Seca Chapala).

As we got into the rough terrain at the point where the road entered the pass, we encountered turbulence of such a degree that it would have frightened anyone.

At times the helicopter would be hit by a wall of wind and sent spinning up in the air, only to have a gust swirling round the mountain catch it like an avalanche of snow coming off a steep mountainside and beat it down towards the ground. We made two efforts to get through passes and couldn't make it because of the terrific turbulence.

Then we came to the last pass between the really high mountains and the lake. I don't know what would have happened if we hadn't made this pass. I was afraid to ask at the time and I haven't cared to ask since, because we made it. But Bob confided to us afterwards that he was giving the helicopter 100 per cent power as we entered the pass—something which is almost never done with this particular model. In fact it is possible to take a heavy load and rise straight up from the ground like a shot when using only sixty per cent power. But here Bob was using every bit of power he had. There just wasn't any more.

I have never ceased to marvel at the manoeuvrability of that machine or at Bob's skill as a pilot. While we could feel the turbulent air currents pushing and pulling, lifting and descending, Bob managed to keep the helicopter at a fairly uniform distance off the ground and away from the canyon walls. It was, however, an experience I wouldn't care to repeat.

Looking back on the experiences of that day, I begin to realize why the helicopter companies hesitated when I suggested they charter a helicopter to explore Baja California.

When we finally got well into this pass we were not more than fifty or sixty feet from the wall of the mountain on the one hand, not over thirty or forty feet above the ground on the other. Moreover, Bob was giving the helicopter everything it had, and I felt like an egg yolk in a cake-mixing machine.

But we got through the worst of it, came to a point where Bob had some reserve power, and soon found ourselves on the other side of the high mountain range where the wind was still strong but the turbulence had subsided somewhat. From this point we were able to get to Arturo Grosso's house on Lake Chapala, where we made a landing, shook hands with the genial Arturo, and went inside the house to have coffee and tortillas while we waited for our caravan to catch up.

They arrived about one o'clock and were mightily relieved to see us there. They had been experiencing terrific winds and the roads had given Pete all the Baja California driving that he ever wanted. So after a brief conference it was decided that we'd take the helicopter on down to the Bahia de Los Angeles without doing any more exploring, and the caravan would try to make it in there that night.

Back in the helicopter with the wind behind us we went down the road at a hundred and fifty miles an hour and in such a short time that it seemed hardly possible, found ourselves coming into Bahia de Los Angeles. There we found the bay glistening in the sunlight, the air completely calm and not even the sign of a whitecap.

We landed, saluted Antero Diaz and then a surprised Juanito. Ynes, it turned out, was making a truck trip into Ensenada but was due back within twenty-four to forty-eight hours.

So we got in our cabins and made reservations for the rest of our party, knowing that they were going to be thoroughly tired when they arrived. Thinking of the punishment they were taking, I know that I felt somewhat guilty as I stretched out for a siesta—but slept soundly nevertheless.

The others arrived a little later than had been expected and were bone-weary from fighting the road. We had some liquid refreshment which was well calculated to change their entire outlook on life and after they had experienced a couple of jolts of that and a good dinner, they regarded the situation much more philosophically.

The next morning we started the caravan out for the dry lake country, a journey of some forty-odd miles most of it in four-wheel drive. It would take them nearly all day to make it. They were not only going to make a base camp on the dry lake but were going to find a hard, smooth place and mark out a landing strip on which Munoz could land.

Munoz was due in that night with Peggy, one of my secretaries who was bringing the inevitable high-priority television scripts from the office. She would be accompanied by Dr Westphal and his wife Lilie.

Those of you who have read *Neighborhood Frontiers* will remember Dr Westphal as the devoted friend and family physician who had made a 750-mile drive to get Jean through an acute attack of influenza when we were making our trip into Mexico's barrancas. At that time Lilie was one of my secretaries who lived at my ranch and who went along on that trip, taking dictation on the manuscript of the book as we travelled.

Westphal, then a widower, had subsequently taken an interest in my personal health, which I found most flattering. I rang up Westphal one night (it's about thirty miles from his office in Elsinore to my ranch) and said, "Look, Doctor, I've got a little tickling sensation in my throat which usually means I'm starting a cold, and a cold would raise the deuce with me at this time because I'm going to have to do a lot of dictation tonight and tomorrow.

"It's about five o'clock now and if you'll telephone a prescription over to the drug store, I'll have Sam get it before the store closes."

Westphal said, "Erle, I'll be down there within thirty minutes."

I said: "For heaven's sake, Doctor, it's not *that* important. Just give me something for my throat and——"

"You look here, Erle Gardner," he interrupted, "I don't tell you how to write mystery stories and you're not going to tell me how to practise medicine. I'll be down there within thirty minutes."

And within thirty minutes there he was. He gave me medicine for my throat. He gave me medicine for my sinuses. He gave me antibiotics. He took my blood pressure. He looked at my throat. He went up to the main house and had dinner and stayed there during the evening, coming down about every hour and a half to see how I was getting along.

I was up to my ears in an emergency matter which required pouring words into the dictating machine and it wasn't until midnight that I decided to roll in and take a much-needed rest.

Dr Westphal was still there looking after me.

It wasn't until some months later when he had married Lilie that I began to entertain a deep-seated suspicion.

I wanted to make a test.

"Look here," I said to Jean, "ring up Dr Westphal. Tell him that I've just been bucked off a horse and hit my head on a rock; and that blood is oozing out of one ear; that I'm seeing double; and that I'm coughing up a little blood.

"I'll bet you twenty dollars that he says, 'Tell him to take two aspirins and go to bed and if he isn't better in the morning have Sam bring him into the office'."

Jean wouldn't make the call. She said it was ridiculous. That Westphal would burn up the roads getting there. She didn't even think the idea was funny. Perhaps it wasn't, but I thought so at the time and since it was good for a laugh in a world where laughs are all too few, the idea served its purpose.

Because Westphal is one doctor who can't regard his patients impersonally but who considers each and every one as a member of his family, suffers when they suffer and when they are faced with some incurable disease gets all broken up himself, the guy is continually overworked and weighted down with responsibilities.

He had seen some of my coloured pictures of the palm-lined canyons and I knew that he would give a great deal for a Mexican adventure, but under the circumstances the time element made it virtually impossible for him to get away.

The thought that I could give Dr Westphal an opportunity to see these canyons at first hand was intriguing. I knew that his commitments were such that he couldn't possibly make the trip except over a week-end in an aeroplane, and when it turned out our schedule would enable us to fly down over a week-end, I was as the expression goes "tickled pink".

So while we were planning this helicopter trip I invited Dr Westphal to come down and suggested to him that in view of the fact that I was going to have Munoz flying back and forth bringing mail and television scripts, if he could arrange to get a Friday and Saturday off he could make the trip down with Munoz, come into camp in one of the palm-lined canyons in the helicopter and then return on Sunday with Munoz so that he could be in his office on Monday morning. Westphal's eyes lit up. His voice had a note of enthusiasm I hadn't heard since he had told me over the phone he would be at my ranch within thirty minutes to take care of my sore throat.

While we were waiting for the machines to get in place in the dry lake and a base camp to be established, and since Munoz, Peggy, Westphal and Lilie weren't due to arrive until the afternoon, Bob and I decided it might be a good plan to explore some of the very rugged mountains to the south of Bahia de Los Angeles and see if we couldn't perhaps get a look at some of the bighorn mountain sheep which are supposed to be rather plentiful in the area.

So we left Pete there at Bahia de Los Angeles, got Antero Diaz in the helicopter to guide us and took off on a trip of exploration.

I had also been asking Bob Boughton if it would be practicable to take a helicopter up into a section of mountain territory where it was impossible for any human being to travel (except with the aid of ropes and regular mountain-climbing equipment), to land on some inaccessible ledge, and then go out and walk round on whatever ground was available for walking, returning to the helicopter and on to some other ridge.

Bob assured me that it was perfectly feasible and promised a demonstration.

So with a crowd watching us at Bahia de Los Angeles we shot straight up in the helicopter, poised for a moment over the camp and then took off for the high mountains to the south and east.

Looking these mountains over I could well believe that no one had ever been among them—except perhaps some prospector who *might* have followed some of the more accessible ridges; but up in the higher places the mountains consisted of loose rock, of perpendicular ridges, of smooth material like sandstone, of tumbled boulders, and all in all a terrain that was exceptionally forbidding.

In exploring country of this sort it is hard to realize the difference that exists between flying in an aeroplane at low elevation, on the one hand, and in getting down into the canyons with a helicopter so that one is moving along within a few feet of the sheer cliffs on the other. It becomes possible in the latter instance to explore canyons where the walls come down on each side a seeming scant fifty feet from the sides of the helicopter.

We rounded a rough promontory and came on two mountain sheep who had been alerted by the sound of the engine and were looking about with startled curiosity.

As soon as they saw the helicopter they took off, running round the side of the mountain, and Bob immediately swung the helicopter off to one side and out over the canyon so as not to alarm them further.

The better class of helicopter pilots are very careful about chasing deer or similar game in rough country, fearing that the animals may become so panic-stricken when they realize they are being pursued that they will hurt themselves. It would be a horrible thing to leave an animal lying with a broken leg on the side of a mountain.

However, I did get a quick picture of the animals running away from the helicopter along the steep slope.

We then went up another canyon and finally came to a narrow ridge perhaps fifty feet wide but with an almost straight drop on both sides and an imposing view of the country.

Bob landed here to show how easy it would be to go out sheep hunting in a helicopter, land in some remotely inaccessible place and start hunting operations from there.

I got out of the helicopter and walked the narrow ridge as far as I could go, trying to get a picture that would show the terrain, but there wasn't room enough for me to get into a position of vantage. I took a couple of pictures, but with a two-dimensional camera it's quite difficult to look at these pictures and have any idea of the nature of the country either to the right or to the left.

We took off again and went back in the general direction of the place where we had seen the sheep and suddenly came on two more sheep—or perhaps they were the same ones. I couldn't ask them their names.

These sheep showed no evidence of fear, only curiosity, and stood looking at the helicopter as we hovered over them. I was sitting there in plain sight and trying to talk to them, hoping that the sound of my voice, as I assured them we only wanted to take their pictures, would hold them steady.

The larger of the two sheep looked at us with speculative appraisal. The smaller one tried to hide behind a little bush, and it was surprising how quickly he blended with the scenery as soon as there were just a few branches to break the view. We remained there within a few feet of the sheep. I could even see the eyelids of the animals as they regarded us. From the look of curiosity on the face of the large sheep and the manner in which he acted, I feel certain he had never seen a human being before.

We photographed them for a while, then dropped down the steep slope, turned and twisted with the windings of the canyon until at length we came down to sea level and turned off in the grasses to see if we could jump a coyote.

We were successful within the first few seconds. The coyote took off at high speed in a straight line. We followed along taking pictures of him until it became apparent he was getting exhausted; his mouth was wide open, his flanks heaving with laboured breathing. But during all this time he kept running at top speed and in a straight line, doubtless feeling that he was being pursued by a super-eagle.

We left him so that he wouldn't become too exhausted and went back looking for another adventure, and within a couple of minutes located another coyote in marsh grass along the edge of the ocean.

This coyote acted entirely differently from the other. It ran only a few feet, looking back at the pursuing helicopter, then dodged and doubled back, moving so rapidly that it was all but impossible to get a picture.

The coyote was evidently thinking every minute of the time.

We next flew low along the beach, returning to the Bahia de Los Angeles, flying over a school of fish which was being "worked" by a flock of birds, watching what happened as some of the birds dived under the water and swam frantically beneath the surface. Feeling we had perhaps saved the lives of countless anchovies, we kept on flying towards Bahia de Los Angeles and then came in to hover over the camp.

Antero Diaz was one very pleased individual. He picked up the microphone of the public-address system on the helicopter and, as we hovered over the camp, told everyone of his exciting experiences, of the sheep he had seen, of the coyotes he had chased and of the places he had been to.

It was just too much.

In the minds of the people we hadn't been gone long enough to go anywhere, and as Antero Diaz related our adventures I fancied I could see a look of scepticism on some of the faces that were staring up at us.

We landed and had lunch, and then Munoz came in with Peggy, Lilie and Dr Westphal.

We flew out to the dry lakes and inspected the camp which the fellows had located and which they were putting up as a permanent camp even as we landed. They had worked out a landing strip for Munoz's aeroplane and everything was all fixed for an assault on the canyons.

That night we flew back to sleep at Bahia de Los Angeles while the others got things shipshape in camp and arranged for the material to be transported to the Sal Si Puede Canyon. I had a feeling of great satisfaction. Tomorrow, I assured myself, there would be many adventures. Those canyons had been a continuing challenge from the time I had first seen them from the air, and I know Emery had spent many a waking hour at night wondering how a person could use ingenuity, the inventions of a modern age and persistence in order to plumb their mysteries.

And now it looked as though we were going to master their secrets.

We were out at the dry lake early the next morning. The helicopter picked up a load of camp equipment, took off over the rocky ridges for Sal Si Puede Canyon and a little exploration to locate a camp site. It was back within thirty minutes, having located a camp where there was water, shade and firewood. It was necessary to dig down a few inches for the water and it had a peculiar taste, but it was certainly all right for washing purposes and we could carry enough drinking water for our camp needs.

So the helicopter picked up another load of material, I climbed in, we rose from the ground and within a few minutes were drifting over the rough, boulder-encrusted mountain barrier. Almost before I realized it, we were over the coveted canyon, and were settling for a landing at the place where they were making camp.

We now had Juanito and Ynes with us and things took shape very rapidly. A "spike" camp was established there in the canyon and the helicopter shuttled back and forth bringing in men and supplies.

We didn't as yet have the Pak-Jaks over there, but I couldn't wait, nor as it turned out could the others. We all started out on foot exploring the canyon, leaving Juanito and Ynes to get the camp set up while Sam and J. W. Black supervised getting the Pak-Jaks transported "over the hump", into the canyon and then tuned up for operation.

I hadn't gone very far before I realized why those canyons were unexplored. Here it was the middle of February with much of the United States covered with snow and ice, while we were in a semi-tropical climate surrounded by palm trees and walking up country which had perhaps never known a human foot within the memory of any living man—and it was hot!

The sunlight was so intense and so highly actinic that the needle on the exposure meter for my camera instantly shot up to the highest reading. The sun came pouring down from overhead and then was reflected back from the canyon walls as well as from the sandy floor of the canyon in a blinding glare.

Because the air was dry the shadows seemed coal black, contrasting with the dazzling highlights. Between sunlight and shadow there was that sharp line of demarcation which I have seen so frequently on the desert and which is caused by the fact that the atmosphere is so free of moisture there is no diffusion of the sunlight.

I was, of course, tremendously excited. It was impossible to be otherwise. Here were animal tracks all over the floor of the canyon. Some of the tracks I could classify and some I couldn't. For instance, I came on a place where water had been standing until it had recently evaporated leaving a dry, silty deposit, and in this silty deposit some huge animal with great claws had been trying to catch something and had left the tracks of claws raked across the silt, or had been perhaps trying to catch some animal in the water before the water had evaporated.

I found numerous bird tracks, cat tracks, fox tracks, mountain-sheep tracks, deer tracks, and then a little fox ran out ahead of me, took one look and decided he didn't want any part of me, and drifted across the floor of the canyon with his tail all fluffed out. This was an instinctive reaction. There was no chance whatever that the fox had even seen a human being before.

Then Leo Roripaugh and I came on a covey of quail. Here again were wild things that knew nothing of human beings. Quite evidently we puzzled those quail. They circled together in a compact group, each one voicing his opinion in the liquid gutturals of quail language.

After a while the big cock quail that had assumed a position of leadership decided that the flock had better clear off, so they flew briefly some twenty or thirty yards.

I thought it would be interesting to see how quickly the quail reacted to being pursued—it is pretty generally conceded that what makes animals wild is not so much being shot at as being pursued by hunters.

So Leo and I started following them to see how close we could get to them for the second time and a third time. After about the second encounter, those quail were just as wild as any quail I have ever seen in the United States. They simply didn't want anything to do with us and took flight and disappeared. We searched that darn canyon and every clump of brush in it up one side and down the other and we couldn't find a trace of them.

So we went back and resumed our explorations. I personally had had so much excitement in one day that I was emotionally weary. Just as the man whose legs have had all the walking he can take in the course of a day hates the idea of getting up and climbing a flight of stairs, so when my eyes fixed on something interesting I just didn't want it to pan out. I didn't want any more excitement that day.

Pink mountains at the mouths of the canyons

Munoz and Jean take off from a dangerous air-strip

Possibly part of the Lost Mission of Santa Ysabel

The author leaving the helicopter

I finally sat down in the shade of a palm tree and it came to me that it was a long, long way to walk back. I realized that I was feeling the heat, that although the air was so dry there was no sense of perspiration, my body had been perspiring profusely but the moisture had evaporated just as soon as the air touched it.

I was just tired out—bushed, all in, hot and dehydrated.

And then I heard a welcome sound: the helicopter was coming up the canyon looking for us. Bob hovered overhead and then came to a landing within fifty feet of where I was standing. He opened the door of the plastic bubble and said casually, "Get in and I'll take you back to camp."

Oh welcome words!

I got in the helicopter and a second later was hovering over the tops of the palm trees, then gliding down the canyon, and within a few minutes was back in the welcome shade of camp, a camp which had now become pretty well fixed up, with a little fireplace flanked by boxes containing pots, pans and provisions. Our sleeping bags had been deposited in a pile, and, using one of these sleeping bags as a backrest, I settled in the shade and was almost immediately dozing, half conscious of my surroundings, half wrapped in refreshing slumber.

Sam and J. W. got the Pak-Jaks running and after a while we did some motorized exploration down the canyon.

It soon became apparent that despite the fact that we had managed to get into the canyon and establish a base camp, we hadn't conquered the canyon by any means. In fact it was inevitable that the canyon was going to conquer us because there was simply too much canyon to be explored within anything like the time we could give to exploration.

Every cave we found that was big enough for human habitation had the unmistakable marks of prehistoric fires. Every so often there were interesting side canyons a little too rocky to pay us to ride the Pak-Jaks up them, but studded with palms and potentially even more interesting than the main canyon. And we knew that it would be up these side canyons that we would be more likely to find the remains of prehistoric Indian settlements.

The country was interlaced with veins of lighter coloured material running through the granite and in places there were quartz veins in plain sight, some of them too far up the almost perpendicular walls to be reached without the aid of ropes and professional mountain-climbing equipment, but some of them were where it was possible to climb up and get samples.

And it is interesting that we came out of that canyon without a single mineral sample. We were simply too busy doing other things to waste time prospecting.

By nightfall we were all weary. We tumbled into our sleeping bags and I doubt very much if anyone was bothered by insomnia. I felt as if I had been drugged.

The next morning I tackled a television script which Munoz had brought with him, and using my portable dictating machine made a whole series of comments concerning our explorations of the canyons and the wild life we had seen. Then I tackled some of the important correspondence Peggy had brought and shortly before noon had pretty well caught up with emergency matters.

Quite a wind was blowing at this time and it began to look as if we might have a problem with turbulence later in the day.

Munoz was going to fly the Westphals and Peggy back to Tijuana that day and I could see that he was looking at the weather with just a bit of concern, so it was finally decided they would start a little earlier than intended.

Bob Boughton ferried them across the hump in two loads and then shortly after his second return we heard the roar of the engine of Munoz's aeroplane, and he flew over the canyon headed for Tijuana, bucking a headwind which, as we afterwards learned, attained velocities of eighty-five to ninety miles an hour.

Back in camp we settled down for a little rest and waited for the wind to go down.

Sam, J. W. Black and Leo Roripaugh, restless individuals filled with energy and enthusiasm, were off on Pak-Jaks exploring the country.

Emery and I sat watching the palm fronds whipped by the wind and trying to reassure each other that it would go down within an hour or two. However, I think we both remembered our previous experience with the wind on the ocean when we had sat there trying to wait out the storm.

Sometime early in the afternoon Bob Boughton announced that while the wind didn't seem to be going down he didn't think it was getting any worse and if he didn't have too heavy a load of extras he thought we could have a fairly comfortable trip of exploration.

So Emery and I jumped in the helicopter and we took off, exploring the canyons. It was windy all right, and there was considerable turbulence; but we explored those canyons from the height of the palm trees up one side and down the other.

With the helicopter not over forty or fifty feet above the fronds of the palms we followed the Sal Si Puede up to the mountains, then hopped over to La Asamblea and went down it to the ocean.

At that level there was quite a bit of turbulence and I didn't take very many pictures—an oversight for which I have been kicking myself ever since. I had the cameras and the films, but I kept thinking that we would have smoother flights later on and at the time I just didn't realize how extensive those canyons were.

After we had explored the canyons to the point where they came into the big wash some five miles above the beach, we flew on down to the beach, then took some time exploring the interesting highly coloured cliffs by the wash. And so finally flew up the canyon and back to camp.

Black, Sam and Leo had by this time come to the conclusion there was a lot more canyon country than they had at first realized, and they wanted to ride the Pak-Jaks down Sal Si Puede to reach the point where we had turned back on our last trip. They thought it was a matter of only three or four miles. When Emery and I had surveyed it from the air we also felt that it couldn't be much more than that. Actually, it turned out to be about eight miles of winding, twisting, sandy wash.

However, we started out on Pak-Jaks and rode down some three or four miles until we came to a large cave which stretched back some distance into the mountain and gave unmistakable signs of human occupancy.

Emery wanted to dig in that cave; Sam, J. W. and Leo wanted to go on down to the point where we had turned back on our previous expedition; and I decided that I would start walking back the three or four miles to camp just looking the country over.

I had a wonderful afternoon. I again encountered quail and this time made up my mind I would see what happened when they disappeared. I used infinite patience and then made the discovery that they didn't fly away at all. They simply started walking up the tumbled rocks of the mountain, moving slowly but steadily up out of the canyon.

Why quail should do this is more than I know. But that was their ace in the hole. It was their secret of protection. They walked quietly but steadily, covering quite a bit of ground and simply taking themselves up out of the canyon until finally they got so far up I could no longer see them distinctly.

Evidently they were from time to time pursued in that canyon by something that made this type of defensive tactics the only practicable means of escape.

It could hardly have been any four-legged animal because then they could have resorted to flight. It must have been something in the nature of a hawk or an eagle which delighted to feed on quail, and by keeping on the ground and up in the jagged, tumbled rocks they had a semi-subterranean line of escape which baffled whatever it was that was pursuing them.

I finally arrived in camp tired out and after a while the others got in. We had dinner and then again the subject of the burning palm trees came up.

Just how dry and explosive were those palm trees anyway? There was a dead palm a couple of hundred yards down the canyon which had lost its top and all semblance of life, but still clung to the skirts, or rather the skirts still clung to the palm. It was a stunted, dwarfed palm, not over some twenty feet high, but at least it would give us an opportunity to see just how combustible these palm skirts were.

We touched a match to the skirt and almost instantly the tree was enveloped in smoke which swirled up through the skirt just as though the dried palm leaves had formed a circular chimney— which was just about what they did.

A split second later the smoke was followed by flame and then almost before one could realize what was happening the palm tree was wrapped in flames, the wind giving the sheet of fire a circular motion so that the palm tree became a vortex of roaring fire, the flames shooting high into the air, many times the height of the tree.

As I said before, the palm leaves, when they get hot, emit some highly combustible gas, and not only did the flames shoot up in the air several times the height of the palm itself but, suddenly, high above the flames a pocket of gas exploded into flame.

It was one of the most spectacular fires I have ever seen, and the fact that the entire camp watched with breathless, astounded silence is perhaps the best way in which I can describe the effect. We were simply speechless. We had never expected any such spectacle.

The swirling flames continued for many minutes; it must have been perhaps ten or fifteen minutes in all, and then embers wrapped the dead trunk of the palm tree and the base of the tree for more than an hour.

Having started something like that it was hard to stop. We had fired our first palm tree in the interests of scientific research. Promptly the others suggested that we would wait until it got dark and then do a little more "scientific research" to see what would happen.

What happened in the dark with the second palm tree was so breathtakingly spectacular that there were those in the party who wanted to carry on the "scientific research" to see what would happen if we burned a really big palm tree—those that we had been burning were not more than a quarter the size of some of the larger ones.

However, after more sober thought we put our official stamp of disapproval on any more "scientific investigation" conducted with matches.

It is, however, plain to be seen why many of the Mexican prospectors must have treated themselves to an evening of fiery entertainment and this undoubtedly accounts for many of the burnt palms in the more accessible areas.

Later on that night I made the mistake of bringing out the pocket calendar I had with me.

22

PROBLEMS OF FURTHER EXPLORATION

A CALENDAR is a remarkable instrument. We are inclined to take it for granted. Each December various firms issue complimentary calendars adorned with pictures of horses, nude women, beautiful scenery, all reproduced in vivid colours bearing advertising slogans and twelve detachable tags which mark the days of the coming year. Probably no one stops to think what that calendar really means.

The Book of Nature is one of the most deceptive books ever printed. It is as if the Deity wanted to convince us that the evidence of our senses has no real validity. When man tries to measure infinity by the yardstick of his infinite mind he invariably comes to grief. His eyes assure him that the world is flat. He knows that the sun rises in the east and sets in the west because he can see it do so every day. He knows that the stars revolve round the world because he can see them doing so, and when man wants to make a calendar he has nature's own pendulum, the phases of the moon, to guide him.

How many times primitive man must have wondered what was wrong when his wisest men tried to determine the passage of time and the length of the year. Man needed to know the length of the year because he needed to plant crops. He needed to take advantage of the seasons, but there was no way of getting an accurate measurement of the year. There was no way he could predict the arrival of the seasons. The problem was so cunningly designed to baffle mankind that it wasn't even possible to get a fixed number of days in the year. There was an inevitable fraction.

The Mayan civilization was founded in large part upon the fact that its wise men did determine the length of the year. They knew when crops had to be planted. They knew when the rains were due. They knew when the year began and they knew when the year ended. And Mexico is enormously proud of its calendar stone which was the first accurate determination of the length of the year reached and perpetually recorded on stone. The calendar stone gives positive proof that one cannot understand the intricacies of nature and the problem of existence unless one first discards the evidence of one's senses and disciplines one's mind to accept the dictates of reason—and perhaps of pure faith.

But on a trip such as we were making the calendar could be one of the most diabolical of all inventions. When we had left home I had thought that two weeks with a helicopter would give us ample leisure to do everything we wanted. We could explore the canyons. We could look for old ruins. We could visit the site of wrecked aeroplanes and perhaps still make some interesting discoveries. We could prospect interesting outcroppings. But I reckoned without the inexorable facts of life as disclosed by the calendar. Actually it turned out we could do no such thing.

The helicopter was invaluable when it came to transporting provisions and material over the hump. It was a wonderful invention to use in exploration and in making a map of the canyons so that we could find out what were the main canyons and what were the tributaries and how far they went. It had proved to be the key to a number of most interesting adventures.

On the other hand, the helicopter could carry only enough petrol for limited cruising. It couldn't carry all our personnel and camping equipment over long distances. It was dependent upon pick-ups, and our existence, in turn, depended upon the things that could be carried in the pick-ups: petrol, drinking water, provisions, tents, sleeping bags, cameras, films and all the various and diverse things that are needed while living in the open.

The transportation of those things in four-wheel-drive trucks was very much of a problem. It was possible to make perhaps a hundred miles a day over the rough main roads of Baja California, but when it came to the side roads and establishing camps within a reasonable distance of where we wanted to make our headquarters we were faced with an entirely different problem.

We wanted to go again to the old mission of Santa Maria. We wanted to camp at the end of the road and explore that trail which we had seen from the air, a trail which had evidently been used to supply the mission from the Bay of Gonzaga on the gulf side, a distance of perhaps twenty miles or so in a straight line.

From the air this trail was a most interesting sight. It had been carefully laid out and all the rocks along it had been pushed to the side of the trail, to form a boundary on each side (an interesting marker of all the old trails in Baja California).

Not only were the rocks taken from the trail but the boundaries they formed provided such sharp contrast with the beaten path that even on starlit but moonless nights it would have been possible to follow the trail.

Heaven knows whether this was the reason for combing the rocks from the trail and accurately delineating each side of the trail. It must have been for some similar purpose. In any event it was done. The rocks were moved and placed at regular distances outlining the trail.

We wanted to use our Pak-Jaks to explore that trail from the mission all the way down to the Bay of Gonzaga. This trail had seen an enormous amount of use. A couple of hundred years ago, hundreds of thousands of steps by bare feet had worn that trail down through the solid rock, across the drifting sand from the mountains, to the bay where small boats could find a sheltered anchorage. But within the last hundred years it was quite possible that a person could count on the fingers of one hand the explorers who had actually traversed the trail—in fact so far as we could ascertain no one had travelled it.

Moreover, we wanted to explore some country to the west of Puertecitos where Francisco Munoz had from time to time and from a high elevation shown us what seemed to be the roofs of two huge buildings: arched roofs, with very definite indications that there was water in the vicinity. And people would laugh when anyone mentioned the possibility of water being in these dry, barren hills.

There were also palm-lined canyons in the vicinity of the Santa Maria Mission which no one knew anything about.

In addition to all of this we had some private objectives of our own.

Years ago Juanito and a companion, prospecting in a wash below Puertecitos where they were trying to find gold, had decided to sink a shaft at a place where they thought an ancient well might have been excavated. In fact there was the possibility that this was the scene of some old and very rich mine or perhaps a burial place for pirate treasure.

Juanito and his partner had come upon the bones of a man who had evidently been slain there by having his head cut open with some heavy, sharp instrument, perhaps a sabre, perhaps the edge of a shovel.

In any event they had started excavating where they thought the well might have been located and had soon dug into a circular hole which had been lined with cut stone. They excavated this to a distance of thirty feet where they encountered good drinking water and were never able to continue their excavations below the water line.

Juanito said he could guide us to this place and we wanted to explore it.

Now it was one thing to get the helicopter into these places, but quite another thing to get the helicopter *and* the supplies into them.

Moreover, I personally had had my fill of trying to fight my way through the turbulent canyons of Baja California during periods of high wind—and we had to face the fact that at this season of the year it was quite possible we would encounter high winds which would be almost certain to last for three successive days and might well last longer.

A look at the map of Baja California, an estimation of distances, an examination of the problems of logistics so far as petrol was concerned, and the problem of getting our four-wheel trucks spotted where we wanted them, was something which caused the days of the calendar to dissolve like a lump of sugar dropped into a cup of hot coffee.

I simply couldn't believe the facts as we started marshalling them and by the simple process of addition and subtraction arriving at certain mathematically accurate but unwelcome answers.

It now became apparent that a person could take three to four weeks exploring these canyons with Pak-Jaks and still have only a rudimentary idea of all the various things that were in them.

Emery had done a little excavation in the Indian cave and had brought back some very interesting objects that had been buried some four feet below the surface of the ground among ashes and wind-blown dust which had constituted the floor of the cave some 200 years ago. Because of the dry air these things were in a state of perfect preservation.

He had a fraction of a fishing net cunningly constructed from palm fronds, and he had a small line which in all probability had been used as a fish line. It was made from fibres of plants, perhaps from the roots of palms. It had been so skilfully braided that it was thin but strong and there had been a knot worked into one end of it so that the loop in the knot was a complete part of the cord, somewhat in the way the expert archer of today makes a loop in his bowstring.

We had seen more caves we wanted to explore, outcroppings of quartz we would like to look at, side canyons that were clamouring for exploration. We had seen a ledge with partially obliterated Indian writings and, of course, we had the urge to look about where Emery had found that old prospector's pick, because by this time we had heard the story of the dead prospector, the rattlesnake, the sack of rich ore, and knew that somewhere within a relatively short distance of the place where Emery had found that prospector's pick there must be an outcropping very rich in gold; perhaps a vein that had enough value to make what is known as "jewellery rock".

But to break up our spike camp, get things transferred to the dry lakes, then get them loaded in the pick-ups, then get the pick-ups back to Bahia de Los Angeles so that we could replenish the supplies of petrol, then get the pick-ups up the long road through Lake Chapala and down to Cataviña, then over the hand-constructed road towards the mission, another camp established and then to start explorations with the helicopter, all ate into the remaining days on the calendar.

It now became apparent that the delay in Ensenada while the trucks had been held up by the fiesta waiting to get the necessary clearance papers for personnel, and the delay incident to that terrific windstorm we had encountered the day we first landed at Santa Maria Mission had cut into our schedule more than we had realized. In fact we simply hadn't worked out an intelligent schedule. We had thought in terms of getting into those canyons, establishing a spike camp and traversing the canyons with Pak-Jaks, and our other thinking had been hazy. Exploring by helicopter would be easy. Two weeks with a helicopter? We'd cover hundreds of miles.

That much of our thinking had been all right, but the problem of transporting personnel, supplies and pick-ups over rough, four-wheel-drive roads was the real determining factor.

Sam, J. W. and Leo had now closed the missing link. They had ridden the Pak-Jaks down the eight miles or so of canyon to a point where they had picked up the familiar landmarks indicating our point of greatest exploration on the prior trip. Emery and I had been in the helicopter when Bob piloted it up the Sal Si Puede Canyon to the very end over the divide to La Asamblea and down the entire length of La Asamblea to the mouth of the wash at the ocean and then back up the wash to Sal Si Puede Canyon, and up Sal Si Puede Canyon to camp.

So we started chalking off the days of the calendar, allotting activities for exploration and praying that we wouldn't run into any really bad head winds because no matter how we handled things we had to have the helicopter loaded so heavily with personnel, auxiliary petrol tanks and some emergency supplies and tools that we couldn't hope to get a speed of more than eighty or ninety miles an hour, if that, in calm weather; and of course if we encountered a few more ninety-mile-an-hour head winds we would be using up all our power standing still, even if we could keep out of the canyons where there was the terrific turbulence.

Even as we were making our plans the wind was howling overhead with such velocity that as we subsequently learned it had taken Munoz an extra hour and a half to get to Tijuana.

So we reluctantly decided that if the wind hadn't gone down by the next day we were going to have to break camp.

I went to sleep that night with mingled feelings. There was satisfaction that we had to some extent conquered the problems of the canyon, but there was also the suspicion that the combined forces of the canyon and the calendar had conquered me.

The next day the wind was blowing again so we decided we had better move camp, get packed up and get started. And we knew it would represent an enormous amount of effort to accomplish all that and get the outfit back to Bahia de Los Angeles during daylight.

So again we started the long chore of getting all our material and all the various personnel back to the dry lake—and the wind started blowing with ever-increasing velocity.

By the time I got to the dry lake I found that dust and sand were blowing; the tent which had been put up to house our material that had been left behind was just on the point of blowing away; the wind had whipped the canvas until many of the stakes had been pulled out of the sand so many times that replacing them did no good.

At about this time Munoz returned from Tijuana with another of my secretaries, Ruth ("Honey")[1] Moore, and her husband Walter and the inevitable television scripts and important mail.

So I took my portable dictating machine, moved off into the shelter of one of the pick-ups and again started the endless chore of dictating while the others got everything loaded into the pick-ups, and then I let the Moores ride into Bahia de Los Angeles in the helicopter so that they could have the experience of a helicopter ride, while I got in with Munoz and we again made rendezvous at Bahia de Los Angeles.

By working like Trojans the others managed to get the trucks in there that evening shortly after dark, and then the next morning they started loading up with petrol and making plans to start up the road for camp at the end of the hand-made road by the Santa Maria Mission.

A great deal depended upon what they found there in the way of conditions on the ground. If it was going to be exceedingly difficult to get the Pak-Jaks down over the rock-strewn mountains to the trail we were going to have to give up exploring the trail as a part of the helicopter expedition, although the others would have time to make a hurried survey.

Leo Roripaugh had received some news which made it necessary for him to return to his ranch near Temecula and Sam Hicks had to be present for the wedding of his eldest daughter.

We had of course tried to make the entire trip at an earlier date but difficulties of getting everyone together, getting the helicopter on the job and arranging the charter appointments of Francisco Munoz so that we could count on him made it neces-

[1] Everyone has called her Honey from the time she was knee-high to a grasshopper so it has really become her name.

sary to fix dates in accordance with what we could do rather than what we wanted to do.

So it was apparent that Pete, Bob and I would have a day or two at Bahia de Los Angeles while we were waiting for camp to get established at the end of the hand-constructed road three miles more or less from Santa Maria Mission.

We decided to accept this delay philosophically and since Walter Moore decided he wanted to go north with the pick-ups and let his wife go on with the aeroplane when it was ready to leave, we got Antero Diaz to take Honey, Bob Boughton, Pete Rivas and me on a fishing expedition and a pelican egg hunt.

The pelican is a huge bird and the eggs are about the size of turkey eggs. The quota is three per pelican and the nests are made in sheltered canyons where the sun can perform most of the job of incubation; little canyons which are sheltered from the wind but so situated that the sun will give maximum service.

The manner of gathering pelican eggs is simple in the extreme: you simply carry along a container filled with fresh water. You pick the eggs out of the nest and drop them into the container. If the egg sinks, it is edible. If it floats, be very careful not to break it. Put it back on the nest, because you are handling an embryo pelican encased by a very thin and fragile shell. That was an interesting adventure and I would have enjoyed it even more if it hadn't been for the realization that time was clicking remorselessly away.

When it became necessary for Munoz to fly north in order to take Mrs Moore back and get Sam home in time for the wedding and Leo back to his ranch, we realized that we had some further problems that required communication with the campers.

Since we were a restless lot and intensely impatient, we instantly accepted Munoz's suggestion that he fly up to locate the pick-ups and drop a note containing a revised schedule in accordance with things I had learned over the ship-to-shore telephone in calling the office from Bahia de Los Angeles; and Honey, Bob Boughton and I decided to fly up, look the situation over and deliver the note.

I wish now that we had had some two-way radio communication with the pick-ups. It would have been relatively simple, if I had thought of it in time, to have arranged for a portable radio in the pick-ups which could have picked up the wavelengths of the radio on Munoz's plane, but that was simply another thing we hadn't thought of.

Never again will I criticize the army for overlooking things in the problem of logistics. The human mind (meaning my cranium) simply isn't capable of looking ahead and anticipating all the problems which are going to arise in connection with a somewhat complicated expedition where it becomes necessary to synchronize the activities of a helicopter, an aeroplane, four four-wheel-drive trucks and the delivery of supplies, particularly when one throws in a family wedding, a weekly television show, an impatient book publisher, an overdue serial at *The Saturday Evening Post* and the urgencies and emergencies which are the result of each day's incoming mail.

Flying north, Munoz took us over one of the highest peaks in Baja California and circled close to the side of the peak to show us where a DC-3 had come to grief several years before.

This twin-engined aircraft had been flying a cargo of live lobsters and some freight to the north. In addition there were nine passengers. It was heavy weather and the machine had come to grief on the very summit of the peak.

If the pilot had been fifty feet higher or if he had been a couple of hundred feet to one side he would have missed the crash. Such is fate.

Munoz managed to fly quite close to the wreckage strewn along the side of the mountain, but since we intended to go back there by helicopter, land and make a closer inspection, Munoz, after a couple of passes, was on his way taking us over the Dry Lake Chapala and the ranch of Arturo Grosso, then on to Cataviña to the start of the hand-made road that the rest of the party was going to take. This road had now been completed for some eleven miles and we found that our party with the pick-ups had just arrived at the end of the road when we came flying over.

Since we had a note to drop I prepared to launch it on its way.

Dropping a note from an aeroplane requires a little doing, particularly if those who are to receive the note are in rough country. It is necessary to have some sort of a streamer on the container which will make the falling object readily visible and at the same time slow down its flight somewhat, and it is of course necessary to drop the note with due allowance for speed, wind resistance and distance so that it will come reasonably close to those for whom it is intended. In rough country a distance of a few hundred yards might well land the note in some inaccessible ravine or permit it to become concealed behind some massive boulder.

We had the note in a small cloth sack weighted with a rock. We had then tied a streamer of cloth to the sack.

In getting rid of the note it was necessary to throw it down with a hard motion so that the streamer wouldn't get entangled in the tail assembly of the plane.

I held the door of the aircraft partially open, bracing against the wind resistance while Munoz made a couple of passes over the pick-ups, then suddenly yelled, "Now!"

I threw the container down fast and hard, then released my pressure on the door and the wind resistance promptly slammed it shut.

The country was quite rough. There was some turbulence and Munoz was busily engaged in piloting the craft for the next few seconds so that we couldn't any of us make sure the others had received the note, but as we made another circle over the cars we saw the men clustered together as though reading a note. They gave us a go-ahead signal, so we took off, satisfied that our message had been received. Later there was some doubt, particularly on my part, because I had been so concerned the fluttering streamer might become entangled in the tail assembly that I had rolled it up pretty tight.

Since the note called for a rather complicated series of manœuvres and meetings, it would have been quite embarrassing if it hadn't been found. For instance, the air strip at Cataviña where Munoz had been planning to pick up Sam and Leo Roripaugh had proved on a survey from the air to be too short for safety, so we had instructed Sam and Leo to go on over to the field at El Marmol where Munoz would pick them up on the following day.

It was true we had received a go-ahead signal from the men on the ground but did it mean "Go ahead and tell us what you want us to know", "Go ahead and drop the note", or did it mean "Okay, we have the note"?

239

We kept on going north because Munoz wanted to show Bob the object he had sighted from high in the air which he thought might be the ruins of a big adobe building.

So we flew over the ghost city of El Marmol, site of the big onyx mine which had been operated for so many years by the Brown family. It was from this mine that virtually all our ornamental onyx desk sets had originated.

While there are huge deposits of onyx here and it has for many years been quarried in huge slabs, shipped out for cutting and polishing into ash trays, pen and desk sets, etc., it finally became necessary to close the mine despite the fact that slabs of onyx are piled up awaiting shipment.

It is here that they built a schoolhouse of pure gem stone of the highest grade onyx. It is a beautiful structure, although the affluent atmosphere of gem rock contributes nothing to the ease with which pupils learn the three R's.

To the north and east of El Marmol the country becomes very tumbled and seemingly very barren, a succession of confused mountain ranges, long sandy washes, with only occasional patches of level ground. It is a country which is avoided by aviators wherever possible and when not possible it is flown over at considerable height.

Flying at some ten or eleven thousand feet Munoz had frequently looked down on what seemed to him to be the ruins of large buildings. On at least one occasion he had caught the unmistakable glint of the sky being reflected from water. Since there was not supposed to be any water in this country Munoz felt that his discovery indicated some artificial reservoir and had been eager to investigate and find out just what was below, but he was too cautious an aviator to lose altitude while flying unescorted over such terrain.

I had been with him on a couple of these trips when we had spent some time trying to puzzle out what was beneath. So now that we had the helicopter with us I was very anxious to get a close look.

On this present scouting trip, however, Munoz was flying at only about half the elevation that he maintained on his through flights and from this elevation as we came over the objects in question it looked as though they *might* simply be odd-shaped rocks which had been worn by water in such a way that the top of the largest rock looked like the arched roof of an adobe building.

Bob Boughton marked the place in his memory, and agreed that we would investigate it with helicopter, then Munoz turned the plane and we flew back to Bahia de Los Angeles, arriving just as the sun was setting and the islands were turned to golden nuggets in a sea of deep blue.

23

LOST MISSION OF SANTA YSABEL

WHEN we started out again with the helicopter we were intending to land on the peak at the site of the wreck of the DC-3. Munoz, with his greater speed, was going to fly his aeroplane on ahead but would keep in constant touch with us by radio.

It soon became apparent that there was going to be quite a bit of wind and some turbulence. Munoz, flying very high in order to avoid the turbulence, became as solicitous about our welfare as a mother hen looking after her sole chick at a time when a hawk is circling overhead.

Bob Boughton's wife had flown down to join him at Bahia de Los Angeles and was with us in the helicopter, while Pete Rivas was flying with Munoz and was in charge of keeping in radio contact with us.

As the turbulence increased Bob reluctantly decided it might be unwise to land on the mountain by the wreckage of the DC-3 but we could hover over it and get a pretty good view as well as some pictures.

So Bob relayed the information to Pete Rivas in Munoz's aircraft and told him to tell Francisco that we wouldn't try to land but would hover over the wreckage, then come through the pass and be over Lake Chapala at an estimated time.

Shortly after that message had been transmitted I looked down and saw a very well-defined trail which was of the sort that had been made to supply the old missions; so I asked Bob, after following the trail for two or three miles, if we couldn't go down to a lower elevation and take a look.

Bob obligingly put the helicopter down closer to the ground and in doing so lost radio communication with Munoz.

Following the trail for several miles we suddenly came upon some ruins, and as we hovered over those ruins taking a look at them it became apparent that they were rather important ruins.

This was not simply some old ranch house which had been abandoned. The construction had been elaborate and carefully executed. There was a graveyard with one very large white tomb and some smaller tombs. The structure had been built in at least two parts and, in part, on ground that had been levelled after first erecting a rock retaining wall and then laboriously filling the ground.

These were things which would hardly have been done in building an ordinary ranch house. Moreover, one could see no reason for the location of a ranch house in this particular locality. We all knew, of course, of the famous Lost Mission of Santa Ysabel. The stories of that mission are somewhat varied to suit the individual, but generally the legend is that when the King of Spain ordered the evacuation of the territory by the Jesuits who had been in charge of the string of missions up and down the peninsula, the head of the Jesuits passed word that the priests were to surrender their missions peaceably and not to try to resist the order in any way; but that the missions were all the priests were to surrender, they weren't to turn over their treasure.

According to legend the word went out that a new, hidden mission was to be constructed in an inaccessible place, and this was to be the storehouse of all the treasure that had been collected by the Jesuits. And, again according to rumour, this mission was constructed and was known as the Mission of Santa Ysabel. The location was kept secret, but it housed all the wealth which had been accumulated by the Jesuit fathers.

When the time came for the Jesuits to evacuate, they were not exactly put under arrest but they were so closely supervised in their evacuation that they were able to carry nothing with them except the bare necessities of their personal wardrobe.

And so the legend of the Lost Mission of Santa Ysabel has gained strength over the years and the secret mission has been the object of much search.

The early mission fathers lived a life that was Spartan in its simplicity. There is considerable reason to doubt that they ever amassed any wealth, or whether they ever wanted any wealth. They were interested in building the missions, educating the Indians and in saving souls. They were not primarily interested in treasure hunting.

However, that was during a period when various Spanish military expeditions were diligently searching for gold. There were rumours of great treasure, so it is not surprising that the military authorities, having made certain that the Jesuits did not remove any treasure with them, would have expected that much gold had been left behind somewhere in a secret storehouse.

Regardless of historical rumour and the probabilities that the Jesuit priests had no treasure to hide, the fact remains that it is distinctly possible the lost mission does exist, and there are stories which have come down from the old Indians indicating more or less definite locations.

It was, therefore, only natural that as we hovered over these ruins and saw the extent of the ground that had been levelled and realized the magnitude of the buildings, we should become excited.

Under the circumstances there was only one thing to do and that was to land. As Bob Boughton pointed out, however, he was out of radio communication with Francisco and had been for some time. Our last message had been to the effect that we would be coming through the pass in the mountains about twenty minutes behind Munoz.

Nevertheless we simply couldn't miss this opportunity, so we put the helicopter down but realized that in fairness to Francisco and Pete we must make our stay exceedingly brief.

I would have given much to have had a full day to explore those ruins. Someone had been living there rather recently. In fact it was quite possible that two people had been living there. Lean-tos had been constructed against the walls of the old ruins and it was evident that some prospector or explorer had spent some time there. It was also evident that this construction had taken place since the wreck of the DC-3, because aluminium which had been brought down from the wrecked aeroplane had been used in constructing the lean-tos.

It was also apparent that the main adobe building had been used as a ranch house for a good many years. Before the roof had caved in, some family or families had been living there. But that didn't answer the question of *when* the buildings were constructed and *why* they were constructed. We found evidence which was quite persuasive that the buildings had been constructed prior to the time they had been used as a ranch house and the construction had been part of a rather elaborate plan and carried out under the supervision of people who had considerable executive ability.

In short, during our brief stay we found nothing which indicated this could *not* be the Lost Mission of Santa Ysabel, but we found some things which indicated the strong possibility that it *might* be the ruins of the lost mission.

In the meantime, as it turned out, Francisco was tremendously concerned about us. As the time passed with no word from us, Munoz insisted on turning back, and as it became apparent we had never come through the mountain pass his concern mounted to such a point that Pete Rivas, who had unlimited confidence in the helicopter's ability to take care of itself under any conditions and over any terrain, started faking radio conversations and telling Munoz that he was in communication with us.

This reassured Munoz only briefly, as he soon detected suspicious flaws in Pete's improvisations and started a frantic search close to the ground looking for our wreckage. This in turn caused Pete considerable alarm, because neither the weather nor the terrain was conducive to low flying on the part of a fixed-wing aeroplane.

We cut our stay short, grabbed a few hurried pictures, climbed into the helicopter and shot straight up above the ruins, then started climbing up the mountains and finally got to a point where our radio signals reached Francisco's plane and Pete was able to let Francisco hear for himself that we were all right.

This caused tremendous relief on the part of Francisco. He knew that country, knew something of the turbulence and had become pretty well convinced we had encountered some major emergency.

So we both turned north again and flew on to the place where the pick-ups were camped. Munoz went on to make a landing at the strip in Cataviña, which he could do since he was now travelling light, and we put the helicopter down at the place where camp had been made.

It soon evolved that while Sam and Leo had received our message that they were to go to the landing strip at El Marmol, they had decided to leave my Land Rover there instead of having one of the men come along to drive it back to camp. David Hurtado, who was spending some time at my ranch, was an expert driver and I had assumed he would take Sam and Leo to the air strip and return with the car so that it would be available when camp was broken.

However, the car was now at the landing strip at El Marmol, there were only the pick-ups in camp and, as it turned out, the personnel was widely scattered. Some of them had gone to explore the trail, J. W. Black had taken a Pak-Jak and gone down to the mission, the others had been walking trying to reach one of the well-watered, palm-lined canyons we had seen from the air near the location of the mission.

According to the new and revised schedule we had been forced to adopt, we weren't going to have any more time to examine the country around the mission by helicopter. Emergency matters had necessitated my arrival at the ranch and the helicopter people had wired that Pete Rivas had to be in the Argentine within the next few days.

So Bob Boughton had to start rounding up the various people while the others started breaking camp. It was quite a job.

Bob had to fly low over the trails until he spotted one of the men, then drop to a landing, pick the man up, bring him back to camp, then start off after another.

He came in with J. W. on one side of the helicopter and J. W.'s Pak-Jak strapped to the other side as balancing ballast. He found Ynes, David and Emery and gradually got the camp together. We left. The men were working like ants while we got in the helicopter and again started north to join Francisco and Pete, faced with the realization that there would be another inevitable delay while we were waiting for the pick-ups to catch up.

We made rendezvous with Peter and Francisco and then Bob and I took off to explore the country to the north and east, and particularly to see if we could get a close look at what Munoz had felt might well be the ruins of old buildings, including the ruin of one very large building.

It was interesting to note the precautions that were taken so that we could be located in case we had any trouble. Bob Boughton gave Pete and Francisco a series of bearings they could follow on the map in case we were not back by a certain time.

The trip that afternoon was one of the most interesting and eventful of all the trips I made on the entire expedition.

We flew high until we came to the place where Munoz had seen what he thought were buildings, and how Bob located the spot was a mystery to me.

It was a rugged, rough, scrambled terrain with ridges running in every conceivable direction. One section of the country, so far as I was concerned, looked just like any other section of the country. There was nothing I could see which could be used as a landmark, but Bob unerringly picked out the particular place we wanted and flew in low enough so that we could see unmistakably that these were simply rocks which had been shaped by erosion so that the sides were straight up and down and the top of the largest rock had a dome-shaped appearance.

He hovered round and finally landed right on them.

I still can't understand the action of the erosion which had formed the rocks in this manner. Apparently there had been a stream which had followed a channel for many, many years and then for some reason had changed its channel and left some of the older channel high and dry. Then the more recent flow of water had cut across the old channel and carved the bedrock in perpendicular walls of perhaps some thirty feet in height. Evidently there had been periods of storm when the stream ran with considerable force and carried a great volume of water.

I started exploring the watercourse and then came on something which was tremendously exciting: a place where the old channel of the stream had deposited some five or six feet of alluvial gravel on top of the old hardpan, then as the stream had changed its channel this hardpan had been cut down. The action must have gone on for thousands of years, because there were these perpendicular walls of hardpan some twenty or thirty feet in height and on top the deposit of ancient alluvial gravel.

Since this "hardpan" was hard enough to furnish a bedrock for the old prehistoric stream and since this was a very rich gold-bearing country, it was certain that this old channel would have very considerable value. Perhaps fabulous value.

It was also apparent that with these perpendicular walls to be scaled and the alluvial gravel through which one must dig to come to the bedrock where the gold would be, the time element would not permit any exploration except with camera. I took some interesting pictures and subsequently when I showed the pictures to placer miners got quite a kick out of watching their tremendous excitement.

Apparently this is the type of discovery a placer miner dreams about. Here was an old prehistoric channel with the bedrock exposed and sections of alluvial gravel lying on top of the bedrock which had been undisturbed for the thousands of years it had taken the new stream bed to cut through the bedrock for a distance of some thirty feet.

This was, moreover, in a gold-bearing country of fabulous richness but the trouble had always been finding a place where bedrock was sufficiently shallow and level so that values could be recovered.

Juanito's story had been of finding a canyon in this country where the values were so fabulous that when he was still some forty feet above bedrock and had tunnelled down below the surface to the depth of forty-two feet, he had simply by the use of bucket and windlass got more than a pound of gold within six weeks.

When one realizes that much of his time was consumed in digging through profitless overburden, in going some twelve miles for water and many more miles for provisions, that the pay dirt had to be hoisted out with a windlass from a forty-foot shaft a bucket at a time and then put through a tedious dry-washing process, one can speculate that on the bedrock which Juanito estimated as being another forty to fifty feet deeper, the values would have been fabulous indeed.

However, we had very definitely promised that we would be back at the landing strip at El Marmol at a certain hour and we had no time to hunt for gold mines. We climbed back in the helicopter and Bob and I started out for one other objective we had marked out—what seemed to be an interesting canyon with palm trees which Bob wanted to explore.

We were flying along over this country barely skimming the tops of the ridges and seeing things which it was impossible to detect from higher elevations—and there was plenty to be seen.

We came on a surprising waterfall and a huge water hole lined with grass in the midst of a barren canyon where there was not supposed to be any water. We couldn't resist putting the helicopter down briefly on this little oasis.

The water was slightly mineralized as it had a taste of baking soda but the pool was broad and deep and lined with a natural grass which quite evidently gave feed for wild game, judging by the tracks and the trails leading to the water.

Here again we had no time for detailed exploration but had to content ourselves with a few hurried pictures and then start again for the landing strip at El Marmol.

Once more we came to a deep water hole in another canyon which looked so inviting we wanted to descend and explore but we had run out of time. We were then overdue at El Marmol and we realized the complications that could result if Munoz started a search party and we should miss each other.

So we kept the helicopter in the air after hovering briefly over this new water hole, then went on to arrive at El Marmol just as the others were really beginning to worry about us.

Since Munoz was taking off for Tijuana and since night-flying over that country in a single-engined aeroplane is somewhat in the classification of playing Russian roulette, we knew that every additional minute we were taking in exploration was imposing great additional risk on Munoz—but I do wish we had had just an extra sixty minutes for exploration in that country.

However, we picked up Pete at the landing strip at El Marmol, Munoz took off into the late afternoon shadows for Tijuana and Pete, Bob and I went down the road to pick up the trucks. We found them at almost exactly the spot we had anticipated and made our last camp together.

Early the next morning Bob, Pete, Bob's wife, Jill, and I took off for the Hamilton Ranch, then for Ensenada, Tijuana, San Diego and home, a trip which was made without incident other than fighting a terrific head wind part of the time, turbulence part of the time and working under such a split-second schedule that we arrived at my ranch just about dark.

The next morning as Bob, Jill and Pete were taking off I suddenly realized that I had never fully ascertained what would have happened if we had had an engine failure over some of the rough country over which we had been flying.

I asked Bob about it and Bob said he could bring the helicopter down to a dead-stick landing without any trouble, although others had given me dire warnings of what would happen if the engine went dead.

So, deciding that I wanted to find out for myself exactly what would happen, I asked Bob to take me up some seven hundred feet over the ranch and shut off the engine.

We did this not only once but twice. I found that, with this particular type of helicopter at least, it is just as easy to come down with a dead engine as it is with the engine running. At least I couldn't tell any difference.

So, our test completed, we again landed at the ranch. Bob, Jill and Pete got into the helicopter and for the last time we saw the whirlybird shoot straight up into the air, hover for an instant and then take off like a homing pigeon for the north.

24

HOW DEEP THE CANYONS

I HAD expected that after a helicopter exploration of Baja California I would know all there was to know about it, I would have explored all the inaccessible canyons and would be satisfied. I now realize that I have only scratched the surface.

I know that Baja California, at least the northern part of it, in place of being the barren, waterless desert it is supposed to be, is interspersed with numerous palm-lined, well-watered canyons. I know that there are undiscovered water holes, that there are places where the possibility of making a rich gold strike is very great. I know that we have uncovered ruins which could well date back to the period when the Santa Ysabel Mission was supposed to have been constructed.

I know that two weeks by helicopter is utterly insufficient to explore the terrain satisfactorily and I know that so far as I am concerned Baja California is an even greater mystery than ever it was.

I have seen things no other writer has ever seen. I have seen things perhaps no human being has ever seen within modern times. But I know that there is much more that I haven't seen and that under the blue, cloudless skies and the beating sunlight there are canyons where one could probably live in luxury if one had a weapon and ammunition, but where one would probably die of thirst if one tried to reach these canyons from any of the roads which have as yet been opened up.

Instead of knowing Baja California intimately as I expected I would after this helicopter trip, I now realize that I hardly know it at all.

When we had first discovered the palm-lined canyons of La Asamblea and Sal Si Puede I had regarded them as a challenge. I wanted to get among them and explore. It was a conquer-Baja-California-or-bust sort of feeling.

When we had finally managed to get into the canyons by Pak-Jak there had been a lot of conversation about "conquering" the canyons. We were brash and impudent and filled with a desire for adventure. The canyons had become an "objective" and we couldn't see anything except the canyons and "conquering the canyons".

Looking back on it now I realize that there is no such thing as "conquering" those canyons. They were there long before we were born and they will be there long after we are dead. They remain silent, majestic, mysterious, flooded with sunlight, laced with streamers of gold ore, and deadly dangerous to the explorer who cannot keep up his lines of communication.

With a proper weapon and sufficient ammunition, with a relatively small amount of supplies, a resourceful man might well live in them for a considerable time. But he could never hope to get out alive once his line of communications had been severed.

As has been pointed out, establishing a line of communications in the first place is exceedingly difficult and maintaining it without the aid of equipment which is so expensive as to be out of all reason is a virtual impossibility.

Then a couple of nights after Bob, Jill and Pete had taken off in the helicopter, after some of my pictures had been developed, and "the gang" had gathered to look at coloured photographs on the screen, I suddenly realized that while we hadn't "conquered" the canyons and could never expect to do so, the real advantage of the expedition had been something I had never thought about when I was concentrating on getting into the canyons and hovering over Baja California in a helicopter.

Over a period of many months while we had been planning how to get into the country, we had come to know each other better, to have the thrill of a friendship built on the co-operation necessary to achieve a group objective.

We had spent many nights around camp fires. We had faced dangers together. We had planned and dreamed and had shared unusual experiences.

I had come to know Juanito with his unwavering loyalty to his ideals, his uncomplaining acceptance of conditions which would have driven most men to the depths of despondency. I had learned to appreciate Ynes, his keen eye, his indomitable energy, his remarkable outdoor ability.

And Francisco Munoz had turned out to be a companion, a pilot, and a friend. He had won such a place in my thoughts that as I look back on the trip I can realize many things I didn't understand at the time. Francisco knew that country and knew its dangers. He cheerfully handicapped his charter flying in order to be with us. During conditions of extreme turbulence he had worried about us even more than we had worried about ourselves.

And on that first trip when we had entered the canyons when we knew that we were flirting with danger, when any unforeseen accident could have resulted in death, we could from time to time look up as we heard the drone of the engine of an aircraft, and there would be "Faithful Francisco" making a circle high overhead, studying the canyons and not returning to the course of his interrupted flight either north or south, as the case might have been, until he had satisfied himself we were all right.

Antero Diaz and his wife we had known before, but while we were exploring the canyons we had come to know them much better. We had come to be virtually a part of the family, and Bahia de Los Angeles was no longer a place we visited as tourists. We had become a part of the community.

In short, my life had become much richer because of my association with these people.

The canyons lie there, bathed in sunlight during the daytime, silvered with moonlight at night. The various people who were actors in the drama of trying to explore them go about their separate ways. At this writing Bob Boughton and Pete Rivas are in South America. Jill Boughton is working at her job in Palo Alto.

Murl Emery is back in the desert prospecting for a new mine, since his last mining deal blew up and "a million dollars went down the drain". (Everything had been there to make Emery a millionaire except that the material failed in one important test —a colour test.)

But Emery is quite philosophical about it all. He didn't want money anyway, except that he *would* now like to buy a helicopter.

The Pak-Jak has attracted lots of attention. J. W. Black is working until late at night trying to keep up production. Lee Sine is in a spot where he has to think more of rationing deliveries than promoting sales.

Leo Roripaugh is running his ranch, coping with the problems of a dry year. Dr Westphal is once more deep in the problems of practising medicine in a good-sized rural community—confinement cases, car accidents, emergency operations, an office overflowing with patients, night calls and all the rest of it.

My secretaries are running themselves ragged, filing mail, answering phones, transcribing records from my dictating machine.

But those long, mysterious, palm-lined canyons in Baja California have somehow intertwined our lives, strengthened our friendships and given us memories which have filled the storehouse of our thoughts with the treasures of life.

No matter how we may be separated in the future, those who were on the Baja California explorations forged bonds of friendships in the flickering light of the camp fires, in the adventures and the dangers we shared.

Those canyons have enriched our lives. None of us now thinks about "conquering" the canyons. They have introduced us to unforgettable experiences, have given us a new insight.

How deep are those canyons?

They are as deep as human experience, as human thought, as human companionship. They are as inscrutable as the desert itself, and as cruel. One mistake and a man could die in them.

But they also have their benign side. They have exerted an influence on every one of us who looked on the waving palm fronds, heard the mysterious whisper of drifting sand on the wings of the night wind.

These are the things of which life is made: adventures, dangers, memories and friendships.

ERLE STANLEY GARDNER

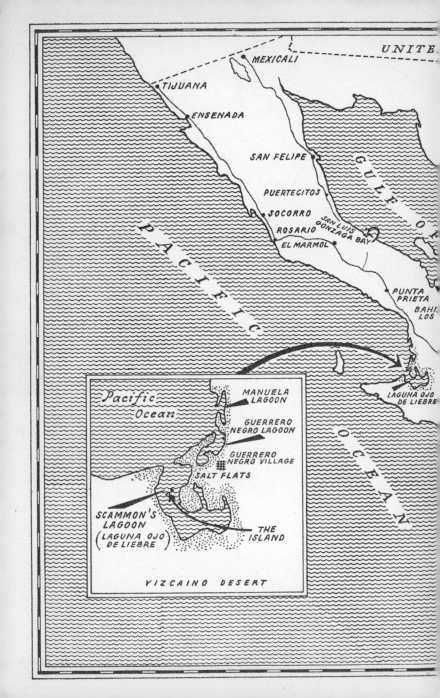